WESTWARD WHOA

- - - - - - - - -

*In the Wake
of
Lewis
and
Clark*

W. Hodding Carter

Simon & Schuster

New York   London Toronto Sydney Tokyo Singapore

SIMON & SCHUSTER
Rockefeller Center
1230 Avenue of the Americas
New York, New York 10020

Designed by PAULETTE ORLANDO

Manufactured in the United States of America

1 3 5 7 9 10 8 6 4 2

Library of Congress Cataloging-in-Publication Data
Carter, Hodding.
Westward whoa: in the wake of Lewis and Clark / W. Hodding
Carter.
p.   cm.
1. Lewis and Clark Expedition (1804–1806). 2. Lewis and Clark National Historic Trail. 3. West (U.S.)—Description and travel.
4. Carter, Hodding—Journeys—West (U.S.). I. Title.
F592.7.C37 1994
917.804'2—dc20   94-6525
CIP

ISBN: 0-671-79891-X

To Preston and Lisa

Acknowledgments

— — — — — — — — — —

If not for the following people, I never would have slept beside a foulmouthed, bad-breathed space hog for nearly three months in search of Lewis and Clark and lived to write about it. Many heartfelt thanks to: Sally Wofford Girand, Gary Luke, Hilary Evans, Clay Felker, Michael Cody, Larkin Warren, Lisa Grunwald, Jill Herzig, and Anita Leclerc. And more thanks to all of my family.

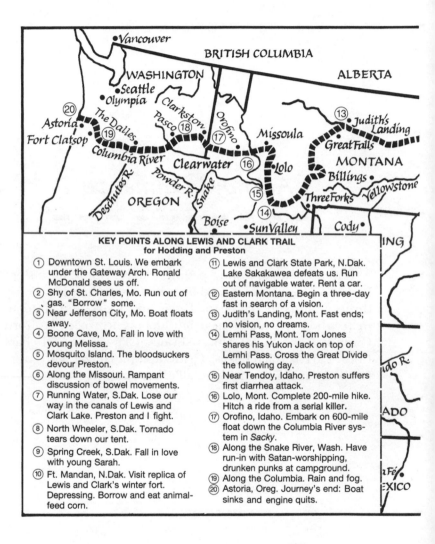

KEY POINTS ALONG LEWIS AND CLARK TRAIL
for Hodding and Preston

1. Downtown St. Louis. We embark under the Gateway Arch. Ronald McDonald sees us off.
2. Shy of St. Charles, Mo. Run out of gas. "Borrow" some.
3. Near Jefferson City, Mo. Boat floats away.
4. Boone Cave, Mo. Fall in love with young Melissa.
5. Mosquito Island. The bloodsuckers devour Preston.
6. Along the Missouri. Rampant discussion of bowel movements.
7. Running Water, S.Dak. Lose our way in the canals of Lewis and Clark Lake. Preston and I fight.
8. North Wheeler, S.Dak. Tornado tears down our tent.
9. Spring Creek, S.Dak. Fall in love with young Sarah.
10. Ft. Mandan, N.Dak. Visit replica of Lewis and Clark's winter fort. Depressing. Borrow and eat animal-feed corn.
11. Lewis and Clark State Park, N.Dak. Lake Sakakawea defeats us. Run out of navigable water. Rent a car.
12. Eastern Montana. Begin a three-day fast in search of a vision.
13. Judith's Landing, Mont. Fast ends; no vision, no dreams.
14. Lemhi Pass, Mont. Tom Jones shares his Yukon Jack on top of Lemhi Pass. Cross the Great Divide the following day.
15. Near Tendoy, Idaho. Preston suffers first diarrhea attack.
16. Lolo, Mont. Complete 200-mile hike. Hitch a ride from a serial killer.
17. Orofino, Idaho. Embark on 600-mile float down the Columbia River system in *Sacky*.
18. Along the Snake River, Wash. Have run-in with Satan-worshipping, drunken punks at campground.
19. Along the Columbia. Rain and fog.
20. Astoria, Oreg. Journey's end: Boat sinks and engine quits.

SASKATCHEWAN

MANITOBA

ONTARIO

⑫ ⑪ NORTH DAKOTA

Lake Superior

Ft. Mandan
Bismarck •

⑩

MINNESOTA

WISCONSIN

SOUTH DAKOTA

Minneapolis •

• St. Paul

Milwaukee

•Pierre

Lake Michigan

⑨ ⑧

Mississippi

Des Moines

⑦

Missouri River

Sioux City

NEBRASKA

Chicago •

Cheyenne

Platte River

Omaha •

Lincoln •

IOWA

• Des Moines

ILLINOIS

•Denver
COLORADO

⑥ ⑤ St. Charles

KANSAS

④

Topeka •

② •St. Louis

③ ①

Arkansas River

Jefferson City •

MISSOURI

OKLAHOMA

Oklahoma City

Contents

— — — — — —

PART 1

- - - - - -

CONQUERING THE WEST IN A RUBBER RAFT

ONE

- - - - - - -

Boils and Sores

The Asian tiger mosquito was out there waiting for us. Mosquitoes, in general, are an unwelcome lot. They zero in on heat and carbon-dioxide-emitting elements (us) from hundreds of yards away. Then they land, brace their spindly legs, thrust their damned neck muscles, pierce delicate skin with their proboscises—grabbing ahold with their maxillae—drive their labrum into a blood pool, deposit their anticoagulating saliva, and finally suck up some blood.

Their saliva scared me the most. It causes all the swelling and itching. It also transmits the mosquitoes' diseases.

Now here was this tiger mosquito. Tired of the same old blood or simply hungry for new scenery, the painful pest immigrated to the United States in 1985—traveled as a stowaway on a freighter filled with used tires from Japan.

It took her a while to settle in, but by August of 1992 she was well established, sucking on every warm-blooded creature she could find.

Why be afraid of a little mosquito? What grown-up is afraid of a few mosquito bites?

I was, and for two major reasons. First of all, the Lewis and Clark journals were full of mosquito torture accounts. "Musquiters are verry troublesome," was one of Clark's main complaints. They couldn't go anywhere on the Missouri River without being bitten crazy by them. Since Preston Maybank and I were about to retrace their trail in an open raft at the height of the mosquito season, I had a feeling we were in for trouble.

Secondly, the very nature of the tiger mosquito bothered me. It was said to be well equipped to carry eastern equine encephalitis—a rare but sometimes fatal brain affliction. Rare, the summer newspaper accounts led me to believe, until the tiger mosquito showed up. The tiger is large, aggressive, and overzealous about sucking blood— much more so than the relatively docile swamp mosquitoes that had carried equine encephalitis in the past. Also, the tiger had moved into twenty-three states in less than eight years. It would be waiting for us at every turn.

Only a few of these tiger mosquitoes were shown to be carrying the equine encephalitis, but those few had me worried. Half of the people who recover from it "have destroyed brains," a biologist was quoted saying. "Of all the kinds of encephalitis, this is by far the worst."

I'd had California encephalitis in college. My brain swelled, and if I moved my head the tiniest fraction, the sharpest pain imaginable cut through my skull. I remember tears flowing uncontrollably down my face. And that was one of the mildest encephalitides known.

Besides the tiger mosquito, there were other good reasons to fret. It was extremely late in the year, considering the trip would take three months to complete. Two other fellows, backed by corporate sponsors, had just covered the trail in a jet boat. And the longest Preston and I had previously spent alone together was a rock-climbing trip in Joshua Tree National Monument in Southern California for three days; we had argued much of that time.

So why go?

I could only blame it on Landmark Books. In the summer between fifth and sixth grades, Landmark Books entered my life. They were a series of rose-colored young-adult history books that were a little fuzzy on politics and accuracy but strong on guts and glory. *The Vikings* led me on ocean voyages and feats of strength. *Ben Franklin and Old Philadelphia* taught me about America's liveliest revolutionary. *Pocahontas and Captain John Smith* revealed love and hope. But it was *The Lewis and Clark Expedition* that captured my heart and imagination. Two brave army captains, Meriwether Lewis and William Clark, led a few dozen men four thousand miles across the Louisiana Territory and into unknown western land, all for the sake of exploration and honor. They were, according to *The Lewis and Clark Expedition*, looking for the Northwest Passage—the golden waterway that would forever open the Orient to Western trade. They were the first Americans ever to cross the continent, but they and their men couldn't do it alone. A young Indian woman, Sacagawea, helped them find their way.

That captured my heart.

"The men had to tumble overboard and wade through water, dragging the boats with ropes tied around their waists. Every few minutes someone was swept off-balance and drenched from head to toe in the cold river. Boils and sores began to appear on the skin of the explorers. Clark had a large swollen carbuncle on his ankle which he could not bear to touch. Moccasins came apart in the rushing water and feet bled from the sharp stones. . . . To add to their discomfort, the rocks were alive with rattlesnakes. No one could put down his foot beyond the edge of the water without examining the ground closely." Tumbling overboard, boils, sores, carbuncles, bleeding feet, and rattlesnakes— these words captured my imagination.

I spent much of that summer slashing through the brambles and bushes in the park behind my house searching for my own Northwest Passage. When Barthell Joseph, one of my best friends, got a pair of Clarkes leather shoes (nothing at all to do with William Clark or Meriwether Lewis, but I was ignorant), I had to have a pair, too. But, my mother said, my feet were too malformed; the shoes wouldn't give enough support to my arches. Still, I could imagine myself climbing over rocks and fording streams dressed in buckskin clothing with a bowie hunting knife clenched between my teeth—wearing my own pair of Clarkes.

As time passed, other fantasies and dreams competed with Lewis, Clark, and Sacagawea. Soon afterward, I read my first science fiction novel, *Have Spacesuit Will Travel*, by Robert A. Heinlein. I turned to the stars. I wrote NASA that I wanted to be an astronaut. They sent me back some photographs of jets and a couple of the Apollo crafts and suggested studying math and science—my worst subjects. Instead, I sat in my backyard staring at the moon with my telescope, waiting for an errant spaceship to come pick me up. It never happened, and I never had a chance to save Earth from an alien race that wanted to make earthlings their number one food source and a galactic police force that wanted to eliminate our species because we were too violent and upredictable.

Within a short time, though, dreams of naked girls tying me to various trees arrived. Visions of breasts, luscious lips, tangled bodies, and heavy breathing dominated my fantasy world. Now and then, I'd go tromping off into the woods or read another Heinlein book, but for the most part my imagination stayed focused on sex. Days of snakes, raging rivers, space suits, and intergalactic travel seemed less and less important.

Until a few years back. Home on a short vacation, I was helping my mom decide which books to keep and which to send to the local library when I happened upon my old Lewis and Clark book. I reread it that afternoon, and soon enough all those dreams of bleeding sores and perilous mountain hikes came flooding back. In the years between my first and second reading of *The Lewis and Clark Expedition*, I'd become more accustomed to sex, and there was now room in my head for more than a highly unlikely sexual encounter with a young, voluptuous baby-sitter or a domineering nurse. I was back in the woods with Lewis and Clark.

TWO

- - - - - - - - - - -

"You're Lewis, I'm Clark"

"Look, I'm gonna say this for the last time," I said, sitting behind a two-foot-high stack of Lipton noodles-and-sauce and rice-and-sauce freeze-dried dinners. Preston and I were sorting our provisions and equipment in a downtown St. Louis hotel room the night before setting off. "You're Lewis . . . and I'm Clark. And I don't want any more joking about it."

"Sure thing, Lewis," he quipped, "anything you say."

"Up yours."

Neither of us wanted to be Lewis because he committed suicide three years after the expedition was completed. Rankled by accusations of embezzling government funds, Lewis determined to clear his name before Congress in the fall of 1809. Traveling from St. Louis, where he served as governor of the Louisiana Territory, by boat and then horseback, Lewis stopped at an inn along the Natchez Trace in Tennessee.

By most accounts, he arrived delirious and sick. The innkeeper's wife was the only person home, but she agreed to let him stay in an adjoining cabin. During the night she heard him pacing and talking to himself. Around three in the morning, she heard a gunshot and then Lewis uttering, "Oh, Lord." Then there was a second shot. Later she heard him make his way to her door and beg for water. She was too afraid to open it, though, and waited until dawn to send for his servants, who were sleeping in the barn.

They found him in his cabin, wounded in the head and side. Lewis begged his servants to kill him. His last words were, "I am no coward, but I am so strong, it is so hard to die."

While there are those who believe he was murdered, suicide is the most commonly accepted conclusion. Both Thomas Jefferson and Clark believed that Lewis had taken his life, putting an end to his inner torment. Clark wrote, upon hearing the news, "I fear the weight of his mind has overcome him."

So I'd settled this many months before. As great as Lewis was, I didn't want to play him in our re-creation and therefore be compelled to kill myself a few years later. I would be Clark and Preston would be Lewis. Never mind that Lewis and I were closer in age and Preston and Clark were closer in age as well; that Lewis was anal and of the two of us I was more anal than Preston; and that Preston, like Clark, was more outgoing with strangers.

Preston walked past me to stuff something in a sack. He stunk. He was stripped to his shorts and sweating all too much considering the room's air conditioner was on high and the room was quite cool. I was stinky and sweaty, too, but that was different. I was used to myself. His scent was a completely different thing.

"I just want you to know how happy I am you asked me to go along," he said, turning to me as we continued to pack the dry sacks (rubber, waterproof packs). "This is going to be great."

We went to bed soon afterward. As I lay there, surveying all our goods, I wondered for the first time if all our equipment would fit in our twelve-and-a-half-foot rubber raft. The problem was that the boat really wasn't twelve and a half feet long on the inside. That wasn't a point the Zodiac Boat people had stressed when they sold it to me. The pontoons, when filled with air, had to expand somewhere, and inconveniently enough, they expanded inward. I guess, though, that if the pontoons expanded outward, then the overall length of the boat would be sixteen feet or so and some owners would be just as pissed about that. As it was, the actual size on the inside was only six feet three inches by two feet nine inches—smaller than a coffin. But I had told so many people that the boat was twelve and a half feet that I'd pushed the size of the usable space out of my mind. Anyway, who's going to take seriously a guy who only has a six-foot rubber raft ("inflatable boat" to the Zodiac people).

So there I was, the night before our departure (actually the morning of, as I'd fretted well past midnight), finally considering logistical problems. We had two large dry sacks—4 feet by 2 feet by 2 feet—weighing at least a hundred pounds each; a small dry sack—3 feet by 1 ½ feet by 1 ½ feet—weighing forty pounds or so. Two grocery bags of potatoes and rice that hadn't fit in the dry sacks. Three full backpacks. A six-gallon gas tank. A five-and-a-half-gallon plastic gas can. Two cases of sixteen-ounce motor-oil cans. Five gallons of water. A first-aid kit. A repair kit. And numerous loose articles, including life preservers, auxiliary paddles, binoculars, books, a camera, etc. Could it all fit? Would Preston and I really be able to sit on the side pontoons for twenty-eight straight days (that's how long I figured we'd be on the Missouri)? Why hadn't I thought of any of this before?

We woke at six-thirty the next morning—August 24, Departure Day—and drove our gear over to the concrete-covered levee that stands below the St. Louis Gateway Arch. The arch commemorates the westward expansion of the United States, and since Lewis and Clark opened up the West for the United States, it was only fitting that we began our journey in the arch's shadow.

We unloaded everything only a few yards from the shore. A hundred feet north of us, a large, plastic Ronald McDonald stood guard before the floating McDonald's barge/restaurant that waited to feed the expansion-hungry tourists.

I'd planned on our departing within an hour. At nine-thirty, we'd barely begun inflating the boat. Never mind, I thought, that'd only take a few minutes and then I'd return the rental car, grab a few last-minute items, and head back to the levee. I was in charge of reading the instructions and directing our efforts. At first it appeared that the pressure gauge for the pontoons wasn't working.

"Oh, God, what are we going to do?" I pleaded. "I can't believe I didn't pump up the boat in New York for a trial run. What a damn idiot. Jesus, I've got to go call the Zodiac company. We won't be able to leave until tomorrow."

"Wait, let me try something," Preston said.

"No, no, it's broken. Just leave it alone."

"Maybe we haven't pumped it up enough. The gauge doesn't begin until two sixty. Let's just give it a try," he suggested. Yeah, right, I thought. We'll burst the pontoon and then we'll have to postpone our departure even longer, but I let him try anyway.

He was right.

After that, we couldn't fit the floorboards in the bottom. We struggled with them for more than hour. It was already eighty-five degrees out and humid. Our hands kept slipping and we both cut ourselves with the screwdriver we were using to wedge the boards into place. Finally, I let Preston see the directions. He saw that I had us attempting to assemble the floor out of sequence. A few minutes later the floorboards were in place. We finished pumping her up. It was eleven o'clock.

While Preston guarded our stuff, I went for the last-minute articles: a knife, toothbrush, rat traps ("I need those for hunting," Preston said. "You can catch all kinds of birds with them"), pencils, notebook, pancake mix, pens, extra cotter pins (something for the engine that Preston said we needed), beef jerky, pepperoni, and a new water bag because our collapsible one had burst during the night.

The errands took two and a half hours, and I was unable to find the cotter pins, pepperoni, rat traps, or even a cheap enough knife. When I returned at two, Preston was burned bright red. It was ninety-two degrees and the humidity was nearly as high. But he was undaunted. We were more than six hours behind.

"Hod, I think we need a final meal," he said, nodding to the McD's. "My treat." We gorged ourselves. Big Macs, large fries, fish fillets, extralarge iced teas. There was, I hypothesized as the Special Sauce slipped down my throat, no better salute to Lewis and Clark than the open arms of Ronald McDonald. He was America's modern-day adventurer. Also, this would be our last meal that wasn't cooked by either of us for quite a while.

We returned to the boat and loaded her with all of our equipment, packing the craft from bow to stern. I had worried for good reason. Would it still float? We pushed and lifted it into the water, scraping the rubber bottom along the rough concrete. It floated. We picked up a cup of iced tea that we'd carried over from McD's.

"With this tea, we christen thee *Sacagawea*. May our trip be successful," I said, and together we bashed the cup against her bow. We shoved off at 3:25 P.M.—seven and a half hours behind schedule. *Sacagawea* kept us afloat, and we even started the engine with only a couple of pulls on the cord. Preston seemed touched that I let him drive the boat first, which meant that I must really have been a controlling ogre ever since his arrival the night before. I'd have to improve.

A plump man and his two sons waved from the railing of the McD's barge as we motored by. "That's Joe," Preston explained. "I met him while you were gone. He thinks we're crazy." Joe and the kids yelled to us, but we couldn't hear them. Preston idled the engine.

"Good luck, Lewis and Clark," they screamed. It was nice

to have an audience, although it was somewhat less noble than L&C's departure and less dramatic than the chiropractor and the teacher's departure.

The chiropractor and the teacher were two men who had retraced the Lewis and Clark Trail earlier in the summer. I had originally learned about them from a past president of the Lewis and Clark Trail Heritage Foundation. My intention—before I had to postpone our departure—had been to leave at the same time and playfully antagonize them along the way. Although we didn't know these men, we considered them rivals. They had traveled in a jet boat.

Before heading out, Tom Warren, the chiropractor, and John Hilton, the teacher, spoke to the press. *USA Today*, UPI, *The Washington Post*, and various other news agencies were on hand.

"People often think of the environment as something outside their house," Warren said. "I want them to realize that it's something inside their hearts."

"Lewis and Clark saw what was there," Hilton added, "and we're going to find out what's left." Not only did Warren and Hilton speak more nobly than Preston and I, but they were also better equipped. Their twenty-one-foot jet boat was powered by a 270-horsepower engine. They had two mountain bikes, two canoes, a cellular telephone, a global positioning system that used satellites, packaged meals provided by Nutri Systems, and a "support" van driven by John Hilton Jr., who met up with them at the end of each day's journey. They nicknamed John Junior "York" after Clark's slave, who was a member of the original expedition. All of their gear rode in the van with Johnnie. They were well prepared and had sponsors up the wazoo. They began their trip back at the beginning of June and finished a few days before we began ours.

We'd seen pictures in *People* magazine of them standing behind their boat's windshield. Both of them wore safari-type hats. They stared purposefully ahead.

"The proctologist and his buddy were shit," Preston said. He'd changed Warren's profession. "This is the way to travel. They sped right by all of this." He gestured to the thick-leafed trees that hung over the river's bank and also to the various smokestacks that stood along the shore. We'd quit counting the factories after half a dozen. Most of them were burning either clear or white, but one had been yellow and brown—a bad polluter. A spokesman for American Rivers, the conservation group that helped organize Warren's crusade, told me that the lower Missouri and Mississippi were akin to toxic waste dumps. Pollution threatened the rivers from every direction: agricultural chemicals, industrial waste, road and highway runoff (oil and gas), mines that spewed out heavy metals and mercury, and cattle grazing (erosion of entire soil levels). We passed some large drainage pipes that were gushing with yellow, frothy liquid, which we hoped was only sewer water.

It began raining—a hard, heavy summer downpour. The water bit into our skin and we were soaked. Would it do this every day? I couldn't handle day after day of rain. But twenty minutes later, the storm clouds had traveled on. The river was flat from the rain and the deep, strong current. Now and again an unruly whirlpool would appear and give our little boat a good shaking, but we were able to keep heading north on the mighty Mississippi. Six miles above St. Louis we'd head west into the mouth of the Missouri, but for now we were on Old Man River.

Around 5 P.M. we came upon what appeared to be a four-to-five-foot-high wall of water stretching the entire width of the river. I figured we needed to acquaint ourselves with breaching rough water sooner or later, so I headed *Sacagawea* right into the heart of the fall. Our speed decreased even as I revved the engine higher. By the time we neared its base, we were at a standstill. I kept pushing her. The flood forced us sideways. Preston was almost flung from the boat. Water poured in over his side.

We allowed the current to carry us back.

"Should we try it again?" I asked.

"Yeah," he answered. We tried a different spot. Same results. We crossed back and forth the width of the fall, looking for an easier ascent. The west bank appeared weaker; the water looked lower and less powerful.

We made it higher than before, slowly inching our way through the waterfall. The motor was at full throttle. Suddenly, the boat and the motor were shaken. The engine popped out of the water and painfully whined at a trillion rpm as the prop cut through the air.

As we drifted back once again, we lifted the propeller completely out of the water. It was pretty banged up. Those had been rocks shaking the boat. So it was either flip the boat underneath the cataract or mangle the propeller on the rocks. We put the propeller back in the water and started the engine. It could still propel us forward.

A few hundred yards offshore, two men and a boy were fishing, anchored against the current. We motored over to them.

"Excuse me," I yelled, trying to hide my desperation, "do you know how we can get over this thing? We've been trying for the last hour."

"I know," one answered. A small smile crept across his face. "We've been watching. It's impossible."

"Maybe you could do it in the spring at high water, but even then it's tough," the man standing at their boat's wheel said. "There's only a ten-foot gap that lets you through, and you have to hit it just right. Some people who've been on this river their whole lives can't find it. If you try it now, you're taking your life into your own hands." They suggested we attempt the weak side again.

We decided to walk it over the rocks near the shore. I pulled on the bow line and Preston pushed from behind. The water was anywhere from two to four feet high, depending on the rocks. If I fell, I kept thinking, the boat would knock into Preston, drag him underwater, and probably pull him, tangled in a rope, a mile downstream. Or if none of that happened, it would at least knock him out. I walked very carefully.

Painfully, I recalled sitting at home, feet propped up on my desk, chuckling at all the times the Lewis and Clark men had had to pull their boats through the water. It had seemed so amusing and fun. "We'd never have to do that," I'd thought.

"We're going to be changed men after this," Preston announced as we stood in the water, physically holding the boat steady against the rushing current. After thirty minutes we made it past the rocks. We high-fived each other—a queer gesture but heartfelt. We'd made, at the most, five miles since leaving St. Louis.

A blue heron lifted off from the western shore a little later. Preston identified it. The bird slowly and awkwardly flapped its way skyward, then glided more smoothly between the trees. It seemed so prehistoric with its neck all bent on top of itself. The heron reminded me of Preston and me—ungraceful at first but able to get the job done. And a little later the soft light of the descending sun settled on an entire family of great blue heron wading in the shadows. They all stood in an upright, head-down position searching for food.

We began looking for a secluded place to camp. At seven-thirty—two hours later than I'd planned—we gave up and pulled *Sacagawea* up onto a sandy beach. It appeared to be the worst-possible spot. There were no rocks or trees to tie the boat to, a problem I'd never considered. I always imagined there would be a convenient tree for mooring the boat along with some convenient rocks to climb onto and unload our equipment.

We jumped into the water with our new hiking boots on (why were we wearing hiking boots in the boat? I don't know. It had seemed like the right, explorer type of thing to do) and pretty soon had the boat completely out of the river and water on the inside of our boots—where they weren't waterproof. "What if it rains upstream tonight, and the water comes flooding down here, sweeping sweet *Sacagawea* back down to St. Louis?" I asked Preston.

So we unloaded the boat completely—she was too heavy to drag on the sand—carrying all of the bags one hundred yards up the beach to our campsite.

"Maybe we should anchor it," Preston suggested. Counting on convenient trees and rocks, I hadn't brought an anchor.

We hauled the large yellow dry sack back down to the

boat and tied the bow line to it. It held most of the sixty days' worth of food and weighed more than one hundred pounds.

We might still have the same trouble Lewis and Clark encountered on the river. "At half past one o'clock this morning the Sand bar on which we camped began to under mind and give way," Clark recorded on September 21, 1804. " . . . I ordered all hands on as quick as possible & pushed off, we had pushed off but a few minutes before the bank under which the Boat & perogus lay gave way . . . by the time we made the opsd. [opposite] Shore our Camp fell in."

Things weren't looking good.

Considering the distance we'd traveled and the amount of gas used (half a tank), I began to reconsider how long the trip would really take. On our first day we'd covered at the most five miles and it took four hours. We'd have to make many more stops for gas than I'd originally anticipated, and we'd only get gas if we could find it. We'd been told there weren't very many marinas along the lower Missouri. It would probably take us two extra months, I guessed.

At that moment, as we stood along the Mississippi, watching a swarm of tugboats across the river, I wanted to quit. This wasn't fun. We weren't prepared. The propeller was already busted. I could hear my adventurous stepbrother's warning echoing in my head: "The two things you've got to do, weasel-breath, are get a gun and an extra propeller. You've done that, right?" Was he going to be right about the gun also? Just how humiliating would it be if we quit right now? I wondered. I'd be in debt, yes, but I wouldn't be stuck attempting a hopeless cause.

Our first day had been only slightly similar to Clark's— Lewis was attending to some last-minute business in St. Louis. "I set out at 4 oClock P.M., in the presence of many of the neighbouring inhabitents," Clark recorded for May 14, 1804, "and proceeded on under a jentle brease up the Missourie to the upper Point of the island 4 miles and camped on the Island which is Situated Close on the right

Side, and opposit the mouth of a Small Creek called Cold water, a heavy rain this after-noon."

Yes, we'd both had rains, but enough points were different. Many "neighbouring inhabitents" saw them off. In other words, their voyage meant something to other people.

They'd reached the Missouri and we hadn't even made it off the Mississippi.

They had a gentle breeze, pushing their keelboat upstream. That alone made me want to quit. Here we were with a gasoline engine, finding the going almost impossible. Lewis and Clark had two canoes and one fifty-five-foot keelboat with sails and forty-odd men to row and pull the boats when the wind died down. They were expecting hardships.

Most of all, though, they knew what they were doing. Lewis and Clark were experienced outdoorsmen and soldiers. Working with nature was their life. Preston and I, well . . .

I began figuring how much money I'd be able to sell the equipment for. Would it be enough to pay my debts and send Preston and me home?

No. We'd have to go on until I could figure out a way to end this mistake.

"Preston, you know that itinerary I worked up for us? Well, I believe it'll be off by a few months," I said. "I don't think we'll be finishing this thing until January—the middle of the winter. Is that all right? You can think about it some, you know what I mean?" Please, please, back out, I thought.

"In for a dime, in for a dollar," he said, not missing a beat, and headed up toward camp to begin dinner.

After a miserable meal of boiled potatoes and onions that he cooked (I promised myself that I'd be the chef from then on) and a few slices of melting summer sausage, we sat around our gas lantern taking notes and listening to the night. The light attracted a lot of bugs, as well as a small green frog. It looked to be a southern leopard—the most common frog in the East—but it was difficult to tell in that light. I pointed it out to Preston.

"I wish I had my slingshot," he said. His weapon was packed away in the blue dry sack. I'd pressed the point about him being the hunter on the expedition a little too hard.

The frog leaped within three feet of the lantern. Was he excited about the light or all of the kamikaze bugs dying on the surrounding sand? He moved closer to the light and continued to stare at it. A few seconds later he turned, took a short hop, and shot out his tongue, nabbing some gnats. He was ideally situated for bug eating, well hidden in a valley between two three-inch-tall mountains of sand. His gullet continually quivered but everything else stayed absolutely still. His tongue shot out again.

"You know what we can do when we're up there on those lakes?" Preston said. He was referring to the lakes that the Army Corps of Engineers had created in South Dakota, North Dakota, and Montana. Huge dams blocked the flow of the Missouri to provide a constant supply of water for the farmers and cattle ranchers. "We can hitch a ride with some old fishermen or even some pleasure boats. There ought to be plenty of both around. We'll make up a lot of time that way."

The frog crouched down even lower behind one of the mountains, waiting for his turn at more bugs. It was eleven o'clock. Whipped by the long day, I barely noticed that the stars were magnificent, covering the sky in one huge Milky Way.

THREE

"Get Down on Your Belly!"

Lewis and Clark's journals aren't particularly revealing; neither wrote about anything too personal. No hint of anger, jealousy, or lust. Not once did Lewis write that he wanted to bash Clark's head in for contradicting him in front of the men. Never did Clark comment on Lewis's apparent moodiness.

They also mostly dispensed with any embarrassing accounts, except for a few here and there, which were scant on details. Those two guys were out there for two and a half years (including the return trip to St. Louis), and the best they could do was: "Capt. Lewis near falling from the Pinecles of rocks 300 feet, he caught at 20 foot." He slipped, slid, and tumbled twenty feet in view of his forty-man crew and that's all we get?

Most likely, the enlisted men would have had a little more to say. Patrick Gass, a soldier who completed the expedition, wrote an entire book on his experiences. He must have wanted to include many embarrassing episodes because Lewis fought desperately to suppress its publication. A letter to Lewis from Gass's publisher is quite telling: "I must pass over the unhappy affair with the Indians on the plains of Maria's river [when two Blackfeet Indians were killed because of Lewis's impatience and fear], also that very affecting one of your own posteriors, and conclude with congratulating you that Mr. Gass's journal did not fall into the hands of some wag, who might have insinuated that your wound [gunshot wound on his butt] was not accidental, but that it was the consequence of design—that the *young hero* might not return without some scars (if not honorable, near the place of honour) to excite the curiosity and compassion of some favorite widow. . . . In what a ludicrous situation he might have placed the young hero with his point of honour just past the point of a rock, with Crusatte [the man who "accidentally" shot Lewis's butt] taking aim!"

If only that publisher had been along, then I'd have something to compare our constant mistakes to.

Our second day was similar to the first—fraught with troubles. We rose late—after 8 A.M. Our most sound sleep had come in the last few hours, as we were finally exhausted from shifting and turning all night long.

We skipped breakfast, in a hurry to make up for the first day's failures, but it took more than half an hour to load the boat since we'd taken every single bag out the night before. Preston had a particular packing method he wanted to try to give us more room, and so I wasn't much help in speeding things along. The inside of the bow had a two-foot tarp that would protect anything underneath from spray; he stuffed the backpacks under there and then piled everything else behind them. There was now a little floor space in the stern for us to put our feet down. We shoved off at nine-thirty.

Within ten minutes we came to the mouth of the Missouri. It was choppy and turbulent where the two rivers met, but *Sacagawea* (now called *Sacky* for short) held her own. "You know, the whole river going down from here ought to be called the Missouri and not the Mississippi," Preston commented. "They say that when two rivers meet like this—the confluence, that is—the one with more water keeps its name. The Missouri, I read, has more water than any other American river."

I didn't say anything. One, because I didn't know what he was talking about, but also, he was maligning the Mississippi. That was my river. I had grown up with it in the state of Mississippi, running a tiny fishing boat in it against my parents' orders. I felt as if it were the blood of my state or some such romantic notion. And here he was, saying it should rightfully be called the Missouri. Hah.

We shot up to the northern end of the mouth because it seemed to be less turbulent. All of a sudden, it became clear that Preston was onto something. Above the confluence, the Mississippi was clear—well, not clear-clear but clearer and cleaner than the water below the confluence. This was the Mississippi as I'd never seen it. When we finally turned into the mouth of the Missouri, we were back in the milk-coffee river that I'd always thought was the color of the Mississippi. So it was the Missouri and not the Mississippi that was so muddy. (Most geographical books in fact now label the Missouri the longest river in the U.S., annexing the water south of the confluence to the Missouri, calling it the Missouri-Mississippi. I don't think they'll be too happy about this in Mississippi when they find out.)

A dark bird flew overhead and circled just above us, easily keeping abreast. *Sacky* wasn't moving too swiftly, maybe 8 mph tops. The damage to the propeller was slowing her down.

The bird appeared to be a hawk, but before we could positively identify it, we hit some more rocks. We were near the middle of the river. The current didn't look any different from where there were no rocks. How were we supposed to tell if there were rocks or not if it didn't look any different?

"Maybe we should use those river charts you got, Hod," Preston suggested without any sarcasm. I pulled out the chart book that covered St. Louis to Kansas City. It showed the river channel that had been made for the barges. There were channel markers along the banks that corresponded to the markers in the book. All of the rocks were marked in the book, including the ones we'd hit.

About two miles short of St. Charles, Missouri—our halfway mark for the first day—we ran out of gas. We could see the town as the current started to sweep us backward— back to St. Louis, I guess.

"Just angle it to the side," I screamed out. "We can let the current carry us over." We kept the bow facing up-stream and control-drifted to a lone houseboat on the north bank. This was the same side as St. Charles, so if there was a road, one of us could hike into town with a gas can. "Okay, paddle right, uh, I mean starboard," I contin-ued. I was in the stern and felt it was my job to steer. "Good, good. Hold it there."

To get to the houseboat, we had to paddle into an inlet created by a man-made jetty. The current—displaced by the rocks—was stronger here. The boat was going past the inlet. We weren't going to make it. The bank downstream of the houseboat appeared impregnable. We had to make it to the houseboat.

"Paddle on the other side," I ordered.

"I am."

"Look, you've got to paddle on the left for us to get there."

"I've done this plenty of times before, Hod. I know that if I paddle on this side, we'll go the opposite way. And if I paddle on that side, we'll go this way," he snapped. "So just don't fucking constantly tell me what to do."

"Well," I persisted, "if you know what side to paddle on, then why don't you do it?" We were now safely through the inlet and out of the current, but I was still angry. Why couldn't he just see I was right?

"I was," he said.

It was then that I fell overboard. The elastic grips hold-ing the oar that my butt was leaning against popped out of place. I fell flat on my back. It stopped me from saying one more smart remark, and by the time I pulled myself back I was laughing. Preston began to chuckle as well.

"I guess I was right," he said.

The abandoned houseboat was littered with cans and leaves. After we tied up the boat, I stayed behind to watch our things while Preston walked down an overgrown dirt road to find a road to town. A few yards down the dirt road sat a rusted-out trailer home, a houseboat, and a fishing boat. The fishing boat was filled with beer cans. As a matter of fact, there were faded beer cans everywhere.

The clicking of the grasshoppers became louder and louder. I expected some skinny coot with a double-barrel to saunter through the woods at any moment.

"What you doing here, city boy?" he'd say.

"Mister, I'm from Greenville, Mississippi. I've just been staying in New York City these past few years, not living there." I'd tremble. "And gee, we're following the Lewis and Clark Trail—in our rubber raft!—'cause I read about it when I was a little kid!"

"Get down on your belly!"

It wasn't a comforting vision. I opened the blade of my Swiss army knife.

Preston was gone about twenty minutes, much longer than needed. "There's another road out there, but it's a three-mile walk to the gas station," he reported. "This place is great! You should have seen this old guy sitting in a chair near the road. Just taking in the day with a colostomy bag propped on his lap. A colostomy bag!" Preston started laughing. Maybe the "proctologist" had stopped here as well.

"Well, should we walk to the station?" I asked. It had to be "we." I wasn't about to stay with the boat by myself or walk down that long road alone.

"I don't know. He might come take some of our stuff," Preston said.

"The colostomy guy?"

We snooped around the houseboat and the fishing boat tied up next to it. There was a gas tank with about a gallon and a half of premixed gas and oil—the kind we needed for our engine—in the fishing boat.

"We can leave him a dollar," Preston said. We were trespassing and now we were going to steal this guy's gas. Preston was in charge of the law. We poured it into our tank.

Preston ran back up the bank next to the trailer home. "Let's take this," he called, holding up a mud-splattered plastic gas can. "We need another one."

"I think we'll be pushing our luck if we take that, too," I said. Preston agreed. Afraid that I had been too wimpy, though, I stopped Preston from leaving a dollar for the gas.

We only stayed in St. Charles long enough to gas up and buy a new propeller. A wino lying on a park bench directed us to the gas station.

St. Charles was the oldest town in Missouri and the place where Lewis met up with Clark and the men to begin the voyage. Its "historic" district—a mile strip in the old downtown—was depressing as hell. It looked like Faneuil Hall, Bourbon Street, Beale Street, the South Street Seaport—take your choice. And the people were the same: big hairdos, bloated candy-and-ice-cream eaters, tight T-shirts that didn't quite make it to belly buttons.

Carrying the gas cans just the six blocks back down to our boat was much more difficult than I'd imagined. Oh, sure, I'd thought, we'll stop every other day and carry the cans a mile or so to and from a nearby gas station. Easy.

We had to stop every two blocks to rest. It was ninety degrees out again. And we stunk.

While Preston went to a boat store for the prop, I mailed back fifteen pounds of books and threw away one of his backpacks. It was old and full of holes. I thought lightening the load would help our speed.

It only took Preston twenty minutes or so to put on the new prop. He'd actually bought a repair book and read the instructions.

The boat ran much faster that afternoon, with the new prop and the lighter load. We were able to gauge our speed by the mile markers along the banks. If we crouched down low, we could go as fast as 15 mph, against a 6-mph current.

We reached Tavern Cave a little after six. This was where Lewis tumbled twenty feet and no one made fun of him. Clark recorded, "Many different images are Painted on the Rock at this place the Inds. & French pay omage. Many names are wrote on the rock." The river had moved by itself and been moved by the Army Corps of Engineers so that it no longer went directly by the cave. The cave was somewhere a couple hundred feet up the bank. A book on the L&C trail explained how to arrive there by car, but left out us boaters. And we were supposed to have permission to visit the cave from the railroad company that now owned it and the surrounding land. We started climbing through a tangle of willows and dense growth. The vines grabbed at our legs.

"Hod, this is impossible," Preston said. "And I'm worried this stuff is some kind of poison ivy." We only had on shorts and tennis shoes. He was right. It was poison ivy. I pretended for just a moment that I wanted to keep on going— be the true explorer—but not long enough to get him going again. We climbed back down to the boat and contented ourselves with remarking on the beauty of the bluffs. So that it wasn't a total loss, we looked up some tiny animal prints that were near the boat. They looked to be raccoon, but since there weren't very many prints, we weren't positive. There was no scat to inspect, but that didn't matter as much. "Raccoon scats are by no means as readily identified as the tracks ... ," explains Olaus J. Murie in *Animal Tracks*. "In color they range from black to reddish, sometimes bleached to white. Many samples are irregular in shape. On the whole they may be confused with those of the larger skunks or opossum." So even if we'd found the shit, we still wouldn't have a certain identification. This tracking would be tough. Even identifying the animals we did see was difficult. That hawklike bird had circled above us earlier, and we still didn't know what it was.

We beached the boat on a sandy bank across the river from the hidden cave. Having learned one lesson, we didn't pull her all the way up but simply used one of the dry sacks as an anchor.

We swam and bathed close to the shore. Preston washed his clothes using biodegradable soap. (Afterward, his clothes smelled like the river, a little fishy but with a slight scent of mint from the soap.) Since we'd seen two cottonmouths earlier in the day, snakes were on our mind. I'd had enough run-ins with them as a boy to be slightly concerned.

"Well," Preston said, his shriveled penis waving in the water like an inviting young perch, "it's a good thing that water moccasins don't bite when they're in the water 'cause this is prime snake country." The water smelled of dead fish, and the descending sun made it seem like ripe time for biting and eating.

"Where did you hear that one?" I asked.

"I don't know."

"No one ever told me that, and I grew up around water moccasins. As a matter of fact, I know it isn't true. One time when I was fishing in my grandparents' pond, trailing a strung-up catfish alongside the boat, two of those suckers popped up right alongside of me and a friend. One of 'em had his mouth wide open like he was dying to sink it in something. The other one had his mouth open, too, but it was filled with a small flopping fish that looked a lot like your dick, only bigger.

"We tried paddling away real easy like," I continued, "but they kept following us. The one without anything in its mouth came closer and closer. So we started whacking at the water with our paddles, but the damned thing still wouldn't go away. So we paddled toward it and kept on whacking at the water. That finally drove it down. But we kept on twisting our heads around three hundred and sixty degrees, making sure that thing didn't slither up the boat." Preston didn't look too happy.

"So I figure they can bite just about anywhere they please," I finished.

"Can't they kill you?"

"Naw. I think you just have to go to the hospital or something. You get all swelled up and stuff." The closest hospital was a full day's boat ride down or up the river. "Don't worry, though, I've got a snake-bite kit with me. I'll be glad to cut into you and bleed all the poison out."

The mosquitoes were bad, diving in for the kill just as we emerged from the water. We slopped on a lot of Skin-So-Soft, but I already had a dozen bites.

As Preston made camp—set up the tent and unrolled our pads and sleeping bags—I cooked dinner. It was a dish I cook at home. Pasta with anchovy paste, four garlic cloves, two medium onions, and olive oil. After sautéing the onions and garlic in the olive oil, I squeezed in half a tube of anchovy paste. After that simmered for three to five minutes, I poured in a cup of water and cooked it down for another five minutes. I then set that aside (although we both brought stoves, it was too much of a bother to use them both) and cooked a pound of pasta. Poured the sauce over that once it was done, and we were instantly happy. Preston said he would cook the dish for his wife, Marina, when he got home.

As we sprawled outside the tent, watching the sky fill with stars and listening to the katydids and grasshoppers, I hardly noticed that my bowels were two days behind, my hands were raw, my lower back was aching, and that my right shin looked as if it had a goiter from being banged against the engine and oars. I barely worried that we were only at mile 51.9: sixty-eight miles, or one full day, behind on the second day.

We were far away from everyone we knew, and the only boat that had passed us all evening was a tugboat we'd gone by earlier. Preston blew some blues on his harmonica.

FOUR

Mosquito Buffet

"I think we ought to go as far and as hard as we can today," Preston announced as I squatted next to a simmering pot of instant grits. After another night of tossing and turning, this wasn't what I wanted to hear.

Then, he slightly touched his cup of coffee to mine. "Happy thirtieth," he said. It was my birthday.

We shoved off by 8 A.M. and kept going until six that evening.

The morning went fairly well. Once, while we were pulled over onto a beach to refill the gas tank, *Sacky* floated away. Preston had noticed it because he looked up to wonder where a bandanna was so he could wipe up the oil we'd spilled. It was hard to pour the oil into the tank without a funnel.

"Huh?" He sounded startled. I looked up and there was the boat—about fifty yards away—in the current. It wasn't too hard to get her back, though. All we had to do was get ourselves caught in the current, too, and then swim toward her.

A little later we reached Washington, Missouri. Its marina was a fifteen-by-ten-foot tin shack set on a raft with an old rusty red pump beside it. No one was there and it didn't look like anyone had been for years. Figuring this would be typical of our luck from then on, we walked into town and bought two more five-gallon, plastic gas cans. We filled them plus the reserve can we already had. The filling station owner drove us back to our boat. "No one should have to walk all that way with all that gas," he said. We could now go 115 miles without stopping because we had twenty-three gallons of gas and made five miles per gallon.

This was the kind of thing that had begun consuming my mind: logistics. It had been the furthest thing from my mind before the trip began, and now it was nearly all I could think of. I'd look at the map, figure the distance, judge how big the town was to guess if it had gas, plot out a camping area, estimate our time of arrival, etc. I didn't even notice Washington, and the same for Jefferson City when we stopped there for more gas.

It began raining around noon and continued for about five hours. My rain suit—an imitation-Gore-Tex outfit (cheaper)—leaked around the pockets. We kept forging our way upriver, against the rain, current, and wind. We didn't talk except to tell each other where to go on the river. The one not holding the engine was the navigator, holding the map under a tarp that we'd spread across all of our equipment. I was concerned about keeping the map dry since we'd need it for at least another week. Every time Preston didn't hold it exactly under the tarp, I drew his attention to it.

During a short break in the rain, we saw two more of those hawks we'd been seeing each day, except they were no longer hawks. "I was looking in my book last night and I'm sure those aren't hawks," Preston said. Their huge black wings were spread out for gliding, and they circled again and again without a single flap. "They're turkey vultures and they stay up there so long because they use thermals. That gives 'em a chance to look for food. They'll eat any dead animal from an elephant on down to a tadpole."

A little later, Preston decided he had to do some real hunting for us. We'd seen migrating Canada geese all day in flocks of hundreds. As our boat came puttering along, they would take to the air; their heavy honking could easily be heard above our engine. Preston would vainly shoot at them with his Wrist-Rocket slingshot, and the ammunition would land harmlessly in the sand.

Around one bend sat a huge flock that didn't take off at our approach. I steered the boat past them and then cut the engine. We floated back to their sandbar. Preston silently climbed out of the boat; one hand held the slingshot, and the other held its pouch and the ball bearing. With neither tree nor boulder to hide behind, he crept toward them in a crouched, SWAT-team style. He paused, slid to his left. Every single goose turned to stare at him. He bent lower and crept forward a few more feet. He crept to his right. There arose a dark, undulating cloud as every single bird fled at once. Blowing his cover, Preston ran wildly through their scat and prints, pulling back on his weapon with all his might. He let it loose and the bullet soared.

A few seconds later it plinked into the water behind the sandbar.

We covered more than one hundred miles by the end of the day and were only twenty miles behind schedule. After tying the boat to a jetty built by the Corps, neither of us had the energy to explore or do anything except eat. About ten pairs of mating dragonflies did catch my attention, though. Since there are more than 450 species of dragonflies and damselflies in North America, I'm not positive what they were, but they looked to be blue damselflies. They were all on one log, and each pair was doing the same thing. One insect gripped the back of the other insect's head with the end of its abdomen (what one might call the tail). And there they stayed for as long as I could watch— more than five minutes. They seemed to be pulsating. Now and then the one underneath would bend its abdomen so it connected with the others. What were they doing?

"The male first lands on the female's back, then takes the tip of his abdomen and fastens it just behind her head," explains *A Guide to Observing Insect Lives* by Donald Stokes. "He then pulls the tip of his abdomen up so that it touches his abdomen's second segment. The male's penis is actually on the second segment of his abdomen, but his sperm is produced at the tip of his abdomen. So what he has just done is transfer sperm to his penis. After this, the female bends the tip of her abdomen until it engages with the male's penis and she is fertilized. Copulation lasts about two minutes." This explanation left one thing unanswered. Why does he latch onto the back of her head like that in the first place? And my damselflies certainly were taking longer than two minutes. Hell, all these males were yanking on the back of their women's heads for two minutes alone.

The mosquitoes paid us a visit again that evening. We figured out—by the number of bites we were receiving—that the Skin-So-Soft worked much better as a skin moisturizer than as a mosquito repellent. If one were able to sit or stand perfectly still so as not to sweat a single drop, then I'm sure the Skin-So-Soft would work for more than the twenty minutes it performed for us. But even on a warm, humid night—as that one was—staying still would have done no good. Sweat and Skin-So-Soft trickled down our dirty, smelly bodies, and the mosquitoes swarmed in to feed. I killed a few of them. Not simply to stop them from biting us, but to see what species they were. It wasn't so much that I was worried about contracting malaria, dengue, yellow fever, or encephalitis. I knew that was going to happen. I just wanted to be able to identify exactly which disease we were going to get, and I knew I could do that if I knew what species was eating us alive. I was particularly worried that it might be that dreaded tiger mosquito. I figured that since I'd only read about it that summer, not very many doctors would know that it had bitten us and would therefore not know how to treat Eastern equine encephalitis.

The mosquitoes eating us were either the dreaded tiger or the salt-marsh mosquito. They both have white bands on their abdomens and legs. The only problem was that the salt-marsh mosquito was only supposed to be in coastal regions of the United States.

I slopped on more Skin-So-Soft, wishing I had a nice big can of DDT. And I looked closely at Preston's head to see if there were any visible signs of encephalomyelitis or maybe even dengue. I was sort of hoping for dengue or "breakbone fever," as it is commonly called. He'd get a rash, fever, and terrifically aching joints. I, having appointed myself expedition doctor, would have to bleed him.

Lewis and Clark bled their sick men regularly, to the point of passing out. They each packed lancets for this sole purpose, as bloodletting was the most modern medical technique of the day. If someone had a dislocated shoulder, they bled him. Fever, pleurisy (Clark often diagnosed this condition), almost anything received bleeding as a treatment. I'd packed sterile razors for whenever Preston needed the treatment.

We fell asleep by ten and didn't rise until seven the next morning. The sky had cleared during the night. It took us nearly two hours to depart, but that was because after each movement we would both stretch and rest a moment. Also, having had such a long day the day before, we decided to spend a little less time in the boat. I suggested we sightsee if we could, still feeling guilty about not making it to the Tavern Cave.

Around noon we came upon a sign on the starboard bank that read BOONE CAVE. Hundred-foot-high sandstone bluffs lined the shore, and we hadn't seen any power lines, roads, or buildings the whole day. We pulled the boat over to inspect.

The shore was overgrown like at Tavern Cave, but this time we changed into long pants and our boots. We hacked our way through to a dirt path and followed it away from the river. It turned onto a road, and within a few hundred yards we reached Boone Cave. Well, we were at the Boone Cave office. It would cost us $6, the sign said, to enter the cave.

"I don't know if I want to pay six bucks to see a cave," I said.

"Maybe we can sneak in," Preston said, grinning, but we went inside the office anyway. And there we found Melissa of the light brown hair.

We both started smiling like baboons and babbling about every detail of the last four days. Here was a woman (probably seventeen) who was live and listening. She was actually laughing at our stories. We pushed on, taking turns to win her affection, slyly trying to put the other down.

"He's Lewis! He's Lewis," Preston nearly shouted. "You see, Lewis killed himself and Hod here fits the bill best. Ha, ha, ha."

"Don't get too close to him," I warned her. "He's all soggy, humid, and stinks like a skunk."

Oh, we were witty. After we told her we were going all the way to the Pacific Ocean, we really won her heart.

"I admire what you two are doing so much," she said, looking into my eyes. Preston thought she was looking into his. I think one of us asked her to go along.

"Jack and I are going spelunking in a couple of weeks," she said. Who's Jack? A few minutes later Jack appeared. He was her age and a good-looking fellow. They were planning a seven-mile spelunking trip into an offshoot of Boone Cave. Our mood sobered somewhat.

"Should we check out the cave?" I asked. "Or the Lewis and Clark one down the road?" We'd read a brochure about Boone since entering the office that explained, "We are very pleased that a large bat colony shares Boone Cave with our visitors. Most every visitor to the cave has an opportunity to see at least one of the six species that reside here."

"Well," Melissa said, fetching as ever, "the Lewis and Clark cave is famous for its Indian pictograph [a bow with a dot], but I wouldn't bother. Last year some geologists did a test on it and it turned out to be spray paint." Jack joined in the conversation about then. He told us that the barking we'd heard the night before was definitely from a coyote.

Preston bought a book about the stars (I'd sent his big star book back when I mailed off the books in St. Charles) and took pictures of Melissa and Jack. As we were leaving, Melissa gave us each a lapel pin to remember them by. Mine said BOONE CAVE and Preston's KATY TRAIL, an old railroad line that had been turned into a nature trail.

"They sure were great," Preston said when we were back on the river. "All rosy cheeked and happy."

"Yep."

"Too bad she's not with us."

"Yep."

The soldiers of the Lewis and Clark expedition evidently had sex with Native American women during the voyage. Soon after reaching the Pacific Ocean, Clark recorded, "An old woman & Wife to a Chief of the Chunnooks came and made a camp near ours. She brought with her 6 young Squars I believe for the purpose of Gratifying the passions of the men of our party and receving for those indulgeiences Such Small [presents] as She thought proper to accept." Neither Clark nor Lewis ever mentioned their own sexual adventures, but it is hard to imagine they never took advantage of such opportunities. They were out there for twenty-eight months, after all.

We traveled two more hours after leaving Melissa and Jack and camped in a grove of willows and cottonwoods two miles south of Glasgow, Missouri. The water was fairly polluted. Straws, cans, bottles, rags, and bits of plastic drifted by *Sacky*, who was tied up to another Corps jetty. The Army Corps of Engineers is a branch of the Army. They built these jetties (or dikes, as they called them) and dredged the river to keep the Missouri running controlled and deep. Their work made it possible for huge barges to travel the river and increase commercial trade, but their work had also made the river into a highway. They had, under our orders, stolen the river's mystery.

The land at our campsite was beautiful, though. The trees and vegetation were so thick that it felt as if we'd stepped back in time. A little after five, a large hawk with a white belly soared above. As he started to circle, a tiny bird shot out into view as well.

"There he is, he's being chased by a sparrow. Those little guys'll fly above a hawk and peck at him," Preston said, and then he started clawing at the air as if he were a fearless sparrow on the attack.

"The sparrows?" There was no way he could be right about this. I could imagine blue jays doing it, but never sparrows.

"Yes, sparrows," he answered. "They're ferocious. Just before coming here I saw a mockingbird kicking the shit out of a cat." Mockingbird? Cat? What did they have to do with sparrows and hawks?

"I don't know, Preston." He ignored me.

I sat on the jetty soaking up the sun. I felt relaxed. The sun was glittering on the water, changing colors with each ripple. It had been cloudy most of the day and cooler, probably only in the low seventies. "We're gonna have to get out our cold-weather clothes pretty soon," Preston had said earlier, but it didn't seem very likely yet. A few fish jumped to the surface. Having been told about all the pollution in the lower Missouri, though, I wasn't about to cast a line out there.

I thought about something that I'd been keeping from Preston all day. Earlier in the morning I'd realized that when mapping out our trip, I had us going too few miles a day. The Missouri from head to mouth was 2,700 miles. Using a small piece of twine one afternoon, I came up with 2,340 miles and had us at the head on September 30. We would have to make up 360 miles, which meant we'd have to do a few more 100-mile days. I'd really messed this one up. Should I tell Preston? (Later, it turned out that I hadn't been wrong. The measurement of 2,700 miles goes all the way to the beginning trickle of the Missouri and not to where the name, Missouri River, begins.)

I sidled over to him and mumbled my new findings. I expected him to get really angry or at the very least really depressed. He didn't do either. He accepted it as our fate and didn't even rib me about it.

The sun began to set. "I'm really glad you asked me to do this, Hod," he called, staring out at the water. It was being painted by the sun, dancing with orange and red. "Isn't this the most beautiful time of day?"

Preston gathered wood and built a fire while I prepared dinner. We ate reconstituted freeze-dried pasta for dinner, with some fried onions and garlic thrown in for fresh flavor. I had figured on our eating only two pasta or rice packets a night and had bought 120 of them. But Preston had to have more. "It's the Maybank family motto," Preston explained, "that we eat anything that doesn't eat us first." So we ate three at a time, enough for twelve servings according to the directions on the back.

Preston suggested we sleep outside the tent. I acted calm, but this was scary. What would get us first—the flooding river or the lonesome coyotes we'd been hearing off in the woods? They were crying back and forth to each other. It was eerie—as if we were finally cut off from the world we knew. The coyotes, though, were not coming any closer. So I figured it would be the river that got us.

We were only five feet from the water's edge, but it was straight down a steep bank. Everything appeared peaceful and still: the sky, the air, and even the Missouri. The river kept running of course, but it seemed calmed by the night. As I sat by the fire, Preston walked a few feet away holding his new star book. He alternately turned his headlamp on to look at his book and off to look at the stars.

"Okay, there she is . . . uh-huh. . . . Now where is Cassiopeia? . . . Ah, yes. . . . I can't find the Great Square." He went on and on. I tried to ignore him. "Hod, I want to show you something. Come on, come on." I stood up. "There's Draco—the dragon." I looked in the wrong part of the sky. "No, there between the Big and Little Dippers, and then it curves around the Little Dipper. See?" I actually did. I didn't let him know, but I was pretty excited. I now knew a constellation.

My mood was going up and down, vacillating between fear and joy. Preston, unwittingly, kept pulling me toward joy. My overactive imagination kept pushing me toward fear. As Preston continued to point out more and more constellations, my mind wandered toward more earthly matters. (I had stubbornly decided to learn only one constellation at a time from him.) I switched on my headlamp and picked up my copy of the *Simon & Schuster Pocket Guide to Wilderness Medicine* by Paul G. Gill Jr. Regrettably, unlike many wilderness guides, it was a highly readable book. As my legs were itching and I had been scratching the dozens of bites on them, I turned to the chapter "Insect, Spider, and Scorpion Bites and Stings."

The chapter does not begin very innocently. Gill quotes from Elwyn Brooks White at the top of the page: "When I get sick of what men do, I have only to walk a few steps in another direction to see what spiders do." It doesn't get any prettier. "No matter what your feelings about these creatures, you should know that there are about fifty species of poisonous spiders in the United States. The two most dangerous spiders found in the United States, the black widow and the brown recluse, hang out under stones, logs, and bark, in clumps of vegetation, in fields, vineyards, woods." We were surrounded by every single one of those. "Up to 2 million may live in an acre of grassland, 265,000 in an acre of woodland . . .," he continues. "Spiders are meat eaters. . . . Most spiders are harmless to humans, but about a dozen of the thousands of species that make their home in the United States can cause at least mild illness. The bites of some can be fatal."

Preston had been going on and on about brown recluses since before our trip began. Some cousin had shown him one (or what was purported to be one) over the summer. I looked up the brown recluse. "*Loxosceles* spiders, the brown recluse and its cousins, are much more of a threat to outdoorsmen than black widows. There are more of them, both sexes bite, and their bites can cause 'necrotic aracnidism': gangrenous ulcers, systemic poisoning, and even death." It got worse. "True to its name, it remains secluded during the day, venturing out at night to hunt beetles, flies, and other spiders. During these nightly forays, it sometimes finds its way into bedding or clothing, thus setting the scene for a spider-man encounter of the worst kind."

I didn't really want to read on from there, but I had to learn the treatment. I was the team doctor. "Brown spider bites can't be effectively treated in the wild. The best thing to do is to apply cold packs, elevate and immobilize the bitten extremity, and head for a hospital." Hah.

Somehow I fell asleep soon after reading Dr. Gill's warnings but woke up a few hours later to the approach of a large UFO bearing down on us. It was lit up and rumbling like an earthquake. It kept coming. I hit Preston so he wouldn't die in his sleep. But then it turned, following the bend in the river. It was a tugboat.

I didn't wake again until the following morning. I had a tiny, painful bite on my chin. The dreaded brown recluse, I thought. But with the light of day, my spine had returned. I casually scratched it.

"I think I've been bitten by a brown recluse," I told Preston, waking him.

"I hope you die."

"Time to get up. Up, up, up. Ahhh!" I continued. I had taken on the responsibility of waking us in the morning.

A heavy fog blanketed the world around us; our sleeping bags were soaked. It would be tough going on the river. I pumped up the stove to fix breakfast.

Preston climbed out of his sleeping bag. "Where's the bung roll. I've got to go," he said, hopping around. I dug in my sack and tossed him some toilet paper. "Don't forget to bury it all," I yelled after him. I had brought a plastic trowel along just for shit burial and nothing else, but so far we'd been able to dig well enough with our hands. Burying it was highly important. In *How to Shit in the Woods*, Kathleen Meyer devotes an entire chapter to "The Hole." She also recounts a number of instances where outdoorsmen had forgotten proper shitting technique. "Edwin" was the best. "Coming upon a log beneath a spreading tree, Edwin propped up his rifle and quickly slipped off his poncho, sliding the suspenders from his shoulders. Whistling now, he sat and shat. But when he turned to bury it, not a thing was there. In total disbelief, poor Edwin peered over the log once more but still found nothing. It began to rain, and the pleasant vision of camp beckoned. Preparing to leave, he yanked up his poncho and hefted his gun. To warm his ears, he pulled up his hood. And there it was on top of his head, melting in the rain like so much ice cream."

Despite the fog it was a fairly warm morning. Preston was walking around in only a T-shirt. After a proper burial, he returned to camp and stood by the river, singing incoherently.

"Hey," he suddenly screamed out, pointing to the river, "there's a log floating upriver! I can't believe it." I stood up from the stove. I couldn't make out what he was seeing because it was still so dark. "Wait," he continued, "that's not a log. It's something." He couldn't run along the bank because we were on the rock jetty. I had on my shoes, though, and ran after the swimming log. A furry, triangular head rose above the water. It was swimming so fluidly against the stream, as if it were out for a morning stroll. I wanted to get in and swim beside him. I thought it was a river otter. I turned back to tell Preston and saw him hopping his way toward me with the lantern in hand.

The little creature stayed long enough for us to shine the lantern on him for a few seconds. "It's either a river otter or a beaver."

"We haven't seen any beaver dams," Preston said. "There's no place for them to build one here." We looked for tracks in the mud along the bank and found some that looked like river otter (after looking them up in Olaus J. Murie's *Animal Tracks*). There were only three or four prints, but the shape was certainly otter. They weren't large enough for beaver. I looked for a river-otter signpost, which would be twisted up tufts of grass where the otter could deposit scent from its anal gland. I didn't find one or any droppings, which, according to Murie, would be "irregular in form, sometimes merely a flattened mass of fishbones and other undigested matter."

While I was rooting around for these otter signs, I came across deer and raccoon tracks. Some of the deer tracks were deep in mud, maybe made by a large buck, and others barely made a dent in the surface. The foreprints of the raccoon looked like tiny human hands. "The raccoon's nimble fingers, almost as deft as a monkey's, can easily turn doorknobs and open refrigerators," explains the Audubon Society *Field Guide to North American Mammals.*

Seeing an animal's prints and droppings was as good as catching a glimpse of the actual animal. If I had only been looking for the animal, then I would've only known about the otter (and even then, without the prints, I wouldn't have been sure it was an otter). But this way, I knew there were deer and raccoon all around us.

We packed the boat and crept our way upstream in the thick fog. We could only see thirty feet or so in front of us. After an hour, we arrived at the Glasgow public landing. I jogged up the rampart (my legs felt like rubber) to see if a gas station was nearby. Although the fog was clearing then, I couldn't see any buildings. An old man drove up in a light blue pickup. I ran over to him.

"Howdy."

"Good morning. Do you know where there's a gas station?" I asked. He told me, but I didn't listen. "Do you think we can walk there? My buddy and I are traveling upriver in a rubber raft and have to fill our gas cans." I'd never used the words *my buddy* before, but I felt as if that's what cowboys always said when they came into town in westerns and wanted to show they were friendly.

He got the hint.

"Well," he said, wrinkling his brow. His faded overalls looked nearly as old as he did. His skin was weather-beaten and blotchy from years of working outdoors. "I go for my walk about once around the park. I could take you after that."

Preston arrived and introduced himself.

"My name's Geb Hart," the man continued, "and I've lived along this river my whole life except for the six years in the service. I signed up to see the world. And I did. I was at Pearl Harbor the day the Japanese bombed her."

We talked a little more and Geb drove us to the filling station before he took his walk.

Geb became excited about our trip and told us about the salmon running up the Columbia in Oregon—how we could see them using the ladders at the dams. Geb moved pretty slowly at the station and back at the landing when we returned. He'd had open-heart surgery recently and was walking in the park for his heart. He'd also had three back operations. "Good luck!" he called as we shoved off. "I wish I'd done your trip. And make sure you stop in Waverly for their peaches. They're the best."

Preston had been pretty funny in the truck. I caught him looking at himself and smoothing his hair in the side-view mirror. He went out of his way to do this, leaning down and sliding into view. Maybe he was as fixated on his looks as Lewis had been on his. In a letter to a friend, Lewis once complained of his tailor's handiwork: "Of all the damned pieces of work, my coat exceeds. It would take up three sheets of paper, written in shorthand, to point out its deficiencies or, I may even say, deformities. However, let it suffice that he has not lined the body at all; he had galoon [galloon; narrow band or braid used as trimming] furnished for that purpose. The lace is deficient . . ."

"I saw you fixing your hair in Geb's truck, Lewis," I said, laughing. "Squirming around just so you could get a look at your pretty face."

"What about you and all your hair-combing every morning," he shot back. "I haven't said anything about that."

"I'm only doing that because my hair will knot up otherwise." My hair was near the bottom of my neck and I felt completely justified. But if I weren't a little vain also, then why was I bothering to grow it long?

The cliffs gave way to lower flood plains. The land, which had been covered by woods and weeds, was now mostly farms. Corn and soybeans were the dominant crops. Preston suggested we pull over to steal some corn. The first time we tried, too many fences and hills separated us from the fields. The corn had looked much closer from the river.

We tried to borrow some again, a little later. I tromped through tiny willows in my bare feet to get to the field. I had no shoes on because I first had to wade through some mud that came up to my knees. I kept expecting a rattlesnake or at least a cottonmouth to strike.

The corn was no good. It was animal feed and drier than the stuff people hang on their doors at Thanksgiving. We were looking for the sweet, juicy kind and left the field dejected.

We steered the boat in one-hour shifts, and late in the afternoon while it was my shift, Preston began exercising. First he pumped one biceps, back and forth, exerting pressure on that biceps's arm with his other hand. He switched biceps after ten minutes. Then he pressed his palms together in front of his chest, tightening and relaxing on some interval for another twenty minutes. And lastly, he worked his triceps for about twenty minutes by pushing down on the side of the boat with each hand at his side.

I had originally suggested that we try to exercise each day to keep in shape for the hiking leg of the trip. I had even gone so far as to suggest we bring boxing gloves along—to stay in shape and release our aggressions. Preston had wisely talked me out of it.

Camp that evening was on a peninsula ten feet at its widest and narrowing down to less than a foot at its tip. On both sides, the bank consisted of crumbling sand. The island widened north of us, but dense undergrowth kept us pinned in. I figured we'd end up in the water by the middle of the night.

A light evening breeze arrived around eight. It brought the mosquitoes with it. They were in a mad frenzy. I'd put extra garlic in the pasta for three reasons: no one was there to smell our breaths; we liked garlic; and people have always told me garlic would keep mosquitoes away. The first two reasons held true, but the last failed miserably. We only had to endure this onslaught for about thirty minutes, though, because as soon as the sun had set, the breeze would die and the mosquitoes would disappear. It had been like that every night.

The mosquitoes were a little thicker than on previous evenings. Preston lit a fire to drive them away. "It's just great how this river is populated with old men who'll run us anyplace we want to go," Preston said, leaning back on his elbows once the fire was going. "That Geb was something. Poor old fucker."

Our skin was heading Geb's way. Both of us now had dark red faces. It didn't matter how much sunscreen we slopped on. We just kept getting redder and redder. The wind burned, too.

Ka-plop! A loud smack came from the river.

"What was that?"

"I don't know. Maybe it went away."

Ka-plop!

Preston peered over the bank with the lantern, but nothing was there.

"You know, that sounded a lot like a beaver," I said. "I really think that's what it was. They smack the water with their tail when they're angry."

"But we haven't seen any dams."

"I know, but what else could it be? I saw a beaver in the Adirondacks earlier in the summer, and that's exactly what it did." Even though I was pretty sure it was a beaver, I was still a little frightened. I didn't like things going *ka-plop!* in the night. During the day, ka-ploping was fine, but not at night. Mercifully, no coyotes started howling. We were too close to Kansas City.

Preston suggested we sleep outside the tent, so we laid the sleeping bags down in front of the fire. I had about two feet of sand and then the big drop-off into the river. I fell asleep to the sound of Preston reeling off the names of the constellations he could identify. He was standing with his back to the fire. "There you have Cassiopeia and then there's Cepheus. Together they had Andromeda." I was supposed to be paying attention. "That's how you find Andromeda. You see, if you know your Greek mythology . . ."

I woke a few minutes later to the sound of an approaching boat. It had a light and was coming straight for us. "Get the knife," I told Preston. "It's in the tent on the floor." He went for it and their light followed him. I sat up. Preston came back.

"Should we kill the lamp?" he asked.

"No," I whispered, but we should have. We stood out like fireflies in heat. The boat stopped beneath our tent. It was an old bass-fishing boat. Four huge guys were in it. I was shaking a little.

Preston walked toward the boat. I followed. We stood over them, not walking all the way down to the water. They seemed to be studying us.

"Um, excuse us. I . . . we were wondering . . ."

"We're lost."

"We're fishing. Y'all catch anything?"

They were drunk. Finally, one of them took charge.

"Do you know where Napoleon is? We're a little lost."

We'd passed Napoleon a few miles back, looking for a place to camp. We told them how far it was. I started to calm down. Before they took off, the guy driving the boat said, "I've had my vodka, and now I'm just seeing some of those shooting stars. This sure is a good night. Take it easy." They took off back into the night.

We both admitted we'd been scared. Preston's hunting knife hadn't seemed like much protection. "They were looking for trouble," Preston said. "It's a good thing you look like such a redneck with that long, greasy hair of yours."

I put out the lantern. It was a Friday night. The river was probably full of drunken men like that. Preston and I slipped into our bags, but the mosquitoes had returned. I started slapping my face to drive them away. Preston did the same. We put on the Skin-So-Soft. They kept coming. I put my bag over my head, but I could still hear them buzzing, there were so many. It was also too hot to sleep with the bag over me. I tossed around to scare them off—nothing doing.

"I've had it," I announced after half an hour. "I'm going into the tent. You coming?"

"Nah, it's too nice of a night." Slap, slap.

As I scurried to the tent, I batted at the air, but they kept biting. It was unbelievable.

We'd left the tent flaps unzipped, and the tent was alive with them. I didn't bother to check what species. I zipped it up and began killing. For forty minutes (I checked my watch) I sat there, catching them in my right hand and smashing them against my thigh—a method I'd perfected while a Peace Corps volunteer in Kenya. I was averaging about one and a half per minute. Once I had them in my tracker beam (my headlamp light), they were mine. The difficult ones were in the corners, but I waited them out. Sooner or later, they had to come after me. Blood and mosquito guts were crusting on my hand and leg. The only thing that kept me going was hearing Preston slap his face and tussle in his sleeping bag every few minutes. When the last one was dead, I crumpled onto my bag, an exhausted warrior.

I woke a little before six the next morning, and for the first time Preston was up before me. I heard him lighting the stove.

I was exhausted. We'd been visited by another boat around 1 A.M. This one didn't stop at our site but shined us with a high-powered beam that must've been used for poaching. It was a fan boat that sounded as loud as an airplane. Also, that mad beaver continued to slap his tail on the water throughout the night. And every once in a while I was awakened by Preston slapping his head.

"Take a look at Mosquito Buffet," someone said as I crawled out of the tent.

I looked around, but Preston was nowhere in sight. I was sure it had been his voice. A strange man stood before me. Those fan-boat boys had stopped after all. I felt sorry for this guy because he was in great pain. His face was swollen and purplish red. He appeared to be crying and had evidently been in a boxing match the night before against a far superior opponent. I guessed six rounds before he'd been knocked out. His lips and his eyes had taken most of the beating, obviously. The odd thing was that there were no cuts: just this swollen, mushy face. Poor fellow, and we had no ice. Maybe the Skin-So-Soft would make him feel better.

I was about to ask him where Preston was when I noticed a familiar red bandanna tied around his neck. It was Preston's bandanna. I looked more closely, shining my headlamp on his face. Hey, it was Preston!

He good-naturedly stood there as I took about five different pictures of him. Otherwise, no one would believe this transmogrification.

"I name this site Mosquito Island," Preston announced. "And I have christened it with my blood." So be it. The mosquitoes were still biting, and so breakfast was a hurried affair.

We shoved off before seven—to escape the mosquitoes and also to ensure we made it well past Kansas City. The only feasible place to camp near the city was next to the garbage dump, and Preston had nixed that idea long ago.

The river and the shoreline grew noticeably dirtier. Bottles, cans, and plastic debris floated past us. By the time we reached Kansas City, we were dodging flotsam and jetsam—right and left. We pulled the engine—now named Pompy in honor of the son the real Sacagawea birthed while on the expedition—out of the water half a dozen times to remove pieces of wood caught around its propeller.

"This place looks horrible," Preston said. I agreed. "Let's not stop here." We had three full gas cans, so there was no reason to pull over. We passed the Kansas River on our port side. I'd been worried that we might travel up it by mistake, but with the aid of our channel maps it was easy navigating. The Kansas looked as muddy and polluted as the Missouri. Clark had observed of the Kansas, "The waters of the Kansas is verry disigreeably tasted to me." I suggested to Preston that he taste it for the record, but he declined.

Maybe that's where all the trash and dirty water are coming from, I thought. But as we steered north of the confluence, the water was the same. If anything, it was worse. A couple of huge whole tree trunks barreled toward us, but *Sacky* escaped being hit. Just one of them would have punctured her irreparably.

While Preston was steering, I daydreamed about court-martialing him for disobeying orders. The Lewis and Clark expedition had a trial at the mouth of the Kansas, and it only seemed fitting that we hold one also. And if I were Lewis, as Preston still claimed, then I was actually in charge of our expedition. (Lewis had tried to have Clark made a captain before setting out, but Congress only granted him the level of second lieutenant. Lewis kindly fooled the men into believing Clark was a captain, so he was actually called captain by the men. But he was lower in rank to Lewis. Preston, as Clark, was thus my subordinate.)

Preston had disobeyed my order to taste the Kansas. On June 29, 1804, John Collins was charged with "getting drunk on his post this Morning out of whiskey put under his charge as a Sentinel, and for Suffering Hugh Hall to draw whiskey out of the Said Barrel intended for the party." Collins pleaded not guilty and received "one hundred Lashes on his bear Back." Essentially, Collins had been lashed one hundred times because he had disobeyed an order. It only seemed fitting, in an attempt to keep our recreation an authentic venture, that Preston also receive one hundred lashes. We needed discipline just as much as they had.

I pointed out the logic and necessity of his being punished or maybe even hanged, but no matter how hard I pressed, Preston disagreed.

The trash in the river increased. I counted nineteen floating bottles in one hour. Oddly, though, the birdlife also increased. We passed great blue herons again and again. The great blue had become our mascot. Some days we saw more than two dozen. During the hottest part of the day, around two-thirty or so, eight turkey vultures circled above us, blatantly vying for our affection. They resembled a living tornado, swirling in a constantly fluctuating funnel. As one of our guidebooks pointed out, we could tell they were turkey vultures, rather than black vultures, by the silvery lining beneath their wings. We could make out some of their red heads, as well. It really did appear as if we were being followed by them, even though we weren't quite carrion.

Since it was still the weekend, we started looking for a campsite early on. We wanted a more protected and hidden place than the night before. We also wanted a swim. A little after mile 420, Preston pointed to a tree-lined cove. "There. Let's camp there for the night. It's Mosquito Cove," he joked. Despite its new name, I steered the boat into it. The cove had been created by two Corps of Engineers jetties and was well protected.

"Let's swim across to the other side of the river," I suggested. This was insane. The boat had been buffeted around all day by the whirlpools and swift current. When I was a boy, however, a man had swum down the Mississippi, passing through my hometown, Greenville, on his way. He'd said that whenever one of those whirlpools took him down, he simply didn't struggle. He held his breath and waited to be ejected farther downstream. Supposedly, he would sometimes pop up a hundred yards downriver. I explained this technique to Preston and then we set out.

Immediately, the current carried me downstream. I turned straight into it but still couldn't hold my own. To get back to shore somewhere near our campsite, I had to swim nearly head-on, but with the slightest angle toward shore.

Back on land, I looked toward the water and there was Preston, farther downstream. He'd done the same thing as I but was still having to angle in. He eventually made it ashore before being pushed into the rocks that protected our cove. Anyone else would have given up, but he had kept swimming, determined not to have to walk back. We gave up on the idea of swimming across.

We went for another swim, to the side of the jetty. I figured that way, if one of us tired, he could always swim behind the rocks and out of the current. The jetty created harmless whirlpools that made the water go in a big circle in the cove. Whatever got caught in the jetty whirlpools would circle again and again within the cove, making it (maybe a body in this case) easier to catch.

Preston slipped into the jetty whirlpools. "Hey, Hod!" he called, treading water. "Look at me. I'm in the whirlpool!" He was extremely excited. Circling right alongside him were logs, dirty Styrofoam, bubbly river scum, bottles, and plastic. I wondered how long it would take for the toxins to affect him.

After swimming, Preston tromped into the woods armed with his slingshot to kill dinner.

"Is this poison sumac?" he asked, pointing to some innocent ivy. He was dressed in shorts and a T-shirt, poised on the edge of the woods. After receiving my okay, he plunged in.

A strong wind was blowing in a front, and the wind in the trees suddenly rolled in a wave of melancholia. It felt like a Sunday afternoon, but one in which I was stranded on a desert island. I began to long for something. Luckily, Preston returned within a short while, cursing the mosquitoes.

Maybe Preston had sensed my mood even before I recognized it because he was incessantly funny all afternoon— playing in the filthy whirlpool and cursing the mosquitoes. While he set up the tent, he released a constant barrage against them.

"Get outta here, you twerps," he yelled, jiggling his body up and down. He looked mad. I hadn't heard the word *twerp* in a long time. I started laughing.

Although it wasn't even six, we ate dinner. Preston sat cross-legged. "This is amazing," he began. I knew he wasn't talking about the dinner because it was just noodles-and-sauce with some hot sauce tossed in for flavor. He paused to slap at the mosquitoes. We'd splashed on a little deet (I'd found some in my medical kit), but that obviously wasn't working either. "I've been eaten constantly for twenty-four hours. I'm completely consumed. There isn't an unbitten spot on me . . . I'm exhausted. How many times do you think you have to be bitten for all the blood to be sucked out of you?"

Spurred on by my laughter, he continued. Preston, I was finding, loved an audience and also seemed to want to give me something. "Last night, as I suffered that constant attack, I had two running fantasies. One of them was that a crop duster loaded with deadly, toxic pesticides would make one, slow, blessed sweep over our island. Oh, I might cough and mutter some, but all around me would be dead and dying mosquitoes. The other was much simpler. I dreamed that we would have a freak, twenty-degree cold snap for five hours or so—just long enough to wipe out every single mosquito in Missouri."

Preston watched some bottles float by the dike. The whirlpools swept them into our cove, circling again and again until another current pulled them back out into the river. Many other things were floating in there as well.

"Grab the slingshots so we can shoot at the flotsam," he called. I handed him his and he quickly busted two bottles. He cackled with glee. "Do you think it's more P.C. or less to bust the bottles? . . . Look at us: nature boys!" I took a few shots and missed. We began to make an inventory of the flotsam in our cove. More and more debris swirled in as other junk worked its way out.

There was one plastic Aunt Jemima syrup container, shaped like Aunt Jemima. A quart-size Budweiser bottle. One jar of Miracle Whip. An empty pickle jar. Another jar of syrup—Log Cabin. An old tennis ball.

"Hodding, that beer's full!" He shot and the can exploded.

Tons of Styrofoam. A walking cane. A mule post for a banister. A large white, plastic orange-juice container.

"Here comes a large whiskey bottle." He picked up his slingshot. "Is it a whiskey bottle?" He shot at the bottle. "It is a whiskey bottle." He missed.

A newer tennis ball. A few more Styrofoam cups. A Wendy's coffee cup. A plastic plate. A large plastic Pennzoil container. A two-by-four. Some Zesty dip jar. (Preston chased it down. It was salsa-and-cheese flavor and it was half-full.) Another tennis ball.

More and more trash floated in, but the sun was setting and it became impossible to keep track of it all. We both regretted that we'd swum and bathed in the water. Preston was especially upset that he'd played in the whirlpools. He slept inside the tent that night.

We traveled another one hundred miles the next day. It took nine hours.

Numbed by the rattling engine and the vibrating boat, I spent much of the day speculating about extending our expedition. Thomas Jefferson had many reasons for sending Lewis and Clark up the Missouri. Some of them he stated publicly and some were only implied. On the surface, it was a "literary" pursuit—a mission to map the land and explore the flora and fauna. Jefferson also made it clear he wanted to extend commercial trade all the way to the Pacific Ocean. All of this was decided before the Louisiana Territory was purchased. After that acquisition, the expedition became a race to stake claim to the lands on the Pacific coast. The United States would then be able to trade directly with the Far East while owning the best fur-trapping land. To accomplish this, Lewis and Clark attempted to find the Northwest Passage—the mythical waterway that would end the perilous journey around Cape Horn.

At the end of the voyage, both Lewis and Clark believed they had found a Northwest Passage, of sorts, even though it took them two and a half years for the round-trip. "In obedience to your orders we have penitrated the Continent of North America to the Pacific Ocean," Lewis informed Jefferson on the expedition's safe return to St. Louis, "and sufficiently explored the interior of the country to affirm with confidence that we have discovered the most practicable rout which dose exist across the continent by means of the navigable branches of the Missouri and the Columbia Rivers." The world thought otherwise and eventually the Panama Canal was built. But as Preston and I motored along, I decided I would prove the Northwest Passage by extending our voyage to Japan. After resting in

Oregon for a few days, we would set out on the Pacific in our rubber raft towing a smaller vessel that was loaded down with fuel. If we could make the entire trip by rubber boat, foot, and horseback, then it was obviously a passage of some sort.

"I don't know about that," Preston responded to my new plans. He'd been timing himself over a one-mile stretch between the blue markers and wasn't paying much attention. "Ha! I did it in three-fifteen. That's the record. . . . I don't think we can tow enough fuel." Kindly, he didn't point out that we would surely die; that his wife, Marina, would never allow it; and that if we weren't killed by the ocean, we'd definitely kill each other.

When we arrived at camp that night—a glade of cottonwoods on the Nebraska side of the border—I walked far into the woods with my bug net.

Slightly afraid that at any moment some forgotten forest creature would drop down out of the trees and start clawing at my back, I crept within the thick of the woods, swooping my net through the tall grass. Dozens of tiny, winged insects flew out as I brought the net up to inspect my catch, but a single grasshopper remained. It was all light green and its wings extended well beyond its abdomen. I looked it up in one of my bug books. It was a fork-tailed bush katydid. I figured it was a female because it didn't chirp, but that could've been because of the giant that was staring at her.

We didn't talk much at dinner and we both fell asleep well before ten. The long days in the boat were taking their toll.

FIVE

To Befriend a Redneck

Nightmares consumed me. One was quite protracted. This woman told me she didn't want to be with me anymore. I'd already decided I wanted to break up with her, but she said it first. To show she meant it, she had sex with another guy in front of me. It was the longest drawn-out sex scene imaginable. I woke up in a sweat.

It was a little after six so I woke Preston, telling him my dream. He listened and then told me one he remembered as well. It was about an unusual McDonald's with a French chef and a beautiful waitress who wore sheer panties. The McDonald's was having a special on pork chops. In the dream, Preston was turned on by the waitress and the pork chops. He was in heaven. But he couldn't have either. The waitress flirted with him (taunted him really), but she wouldn't serve him the pork chops; they were a special order. Someone would be coming for them later. Instead, he was served a burnt burger.

It was our first cool morning, maybe in the high forties. I didn't know how cold it was exactly because our unbreakable sports thermometer had broken on the first day. I'd stepped on it. (The Lewis and Clark expedition had kept their last thermometer intact all the way to the Continental Divide—more than a year into their voyage. It was highly fragile and about one and a half feet tall.)

We stopped in Nebraska City around noon. It was one of those towns I didn't think existed anymore. Not only was there a downtown, but the stores weren't even boarded up. Walking down the main street after tying *Sacky* up to a rusty pylon was a stroll into the past. There were diners with people eating in them. An old brick Sears building still had a Sears in it. People said hello to us as we walked down the street.

We visited a sporting-goods store to buy another propeller for the boat and some mantles for the lantern. The owner didn't have our propeller so he called around to the different supply shops in the area. Although he failed to locate one, he tried for nearly twenty minutes.

A teenage boy with long, straggly hair walked into the store, which doubled as a pool hall. He had a "coon" in the back of his truck that he was going to let his dog practice with. The big coon competition was coming up in a week. He talked with us as if he'd known us all his life.

"Coon hunting," explains the Audubon *Field Guide to North American Mammals*, "is a popular sport in late autumn. . . . At night, dogs trail the Raccoon until it is treed; then hunters make their way to the tree and shoot the animal out. If the Raccoon is young or small, the hunters may spare it; for many, the sport lies in listening to their hounds and observing the skill of their performance." The boy explained that the raccoons don't get killed at the competition, and he invited us to come watch.

As we were walking back to the boat, Preston pointed to a run-down cafe called Johnny's. It looked like the kind of place that had flat, overcooked hamburgers and crispy, greasy french fries. One of my favorite meals. I'd insisted we eat our lunch—granola bars, dried fruit, and nuts—before coming to town so there wouldn't be any temptation to stop in just such a place. Preston made a face that asked, "How about it?"

I said, "Okay," pretending that I was only doing it for his sake.

The burger and fries were just as I thought they'd be— perfect—and we were given free refills on our iced teas. "You better not tell anybody about this," I warned him. Then we split a slice of banana-cream pie. People, supposedly friends, had already given me a hard time about using a motor to travel up the 6-mph current of the Missouri, saying it wasn't very authentic. No matter how often I pointed out that they had more than thirty men to pole and push their boats for them, I was still treated like a second-class explorer. I knew I could never live down these burgers and especially not the pie.

Preston looked completely satisfied as we made our way back to the boat. He was happy and so was I. Right then, I decided to make a policy change. We would eat in diners and cafés every now and then.

Back on the water, he played his harmonica while I steered *Sacky*. We were a team again. And corn was everywhere, it being Nebraska. "The only thing I know about Nebraska is that there's lots of corn," Preston said between songs. "And we need some." I headed for the western shore to tie *Sacky* up to convenient wooden pylons that lined the shore.

A foot from the bank, *Sacky*'s bottom caught on something and we suddenly stopped. We could feel the rubber being torn.

Some water leaked into the bottom, and we proceeded up the river a half hour or so until we came to a flat sand beach. Dark-green-leafed trees, mostly cottonwood and ash, lined the horizon. We emptied the boat, flipped her over on the sand, and sure enough, there were four holes. Luckily, they were all less than an inch in diameter and

were not on the inflatable part. We patched her with the repair kit, apologizing to her as if she were alive. Neither of
us knew what we were doing with the rubber patches or the
cement glue that came with the boat, so treating *Sacky* as if
she were a sentient being seemed a reasonable precaution.

While waiting for the patches to dry, we skinny-dipped—
so much for not swimming in the river anymore. It had
warmed up into the low eighties and we'd both been sweating a lot while trying to fix *Sacky*'s bottom.

We'd just put our clothes back on when we heard, "Hey!"
screamed from out on the water. A blond-headed guy was
desperately trying to maneuver his canoe toward our
beach. "Do you know where Nebraska City is?" he called
out.

We started to answer, but all his energies were directed
toward not capsizing. He madly paddled on both sides of
the canoe.

He was lying in the bottom of his canoe with his back
propped on a life preserver against the stern. A mountain
bike was tied down in the bow. His gunwale was, at the
most, four inches above the waterline.

Once he was safely beached, he started talking. His
name was Scott Failor, "just like *sailor* but with an *f*." He
wore dirty, faded blue jeans and a black T-shirt with the
sleeves torn off. It said DESERT STORM and there was a picture of a fighter jet in the middle.

"I need to get to Nebraska City for some provisions," he
said. He was busy tying something down. Preston mouthed,
"We should give him something," and started rummaging
through our stuff for him. We gave him coffee, grits, and
granola bars, and he gave us sweet corn, bell peppers, and
a large cucumber.

"Where'd you get this corn?" I asked. He said it was from
some other boaters. "We've been trying to borrow corn for
the past week, and every field we've come across has only
had feed corn. Doesn't anybody around here grow the
sweet kind?"

"Well," he said, laughing, "you've got to find the last four
rows. That's where they grow it. They keep it either near

their barn or work road. That way they can keep an eye on it. But I can usually find it alright."

Scott had been traveling for three days. He'd started on a Saturday after a big fight with his girlfriend. "I'd had enough of her and so I packed up these things and drove over to the river. I left my keys and the signed deed in the truck. I don't care who takes it. I'm heading down to Louisiana because of the hurricane. It tore up that area I've heard. I expect I'll get a job in construction and work there for two years. I always said I was going to do this someday, float down this old river. She'll be sorry."

I told him that was a good idea even though I wasn't too sure Hurricane Andrew hit Louisiana. I did tell him that unemployment was high there so it might be tough finding work. He didn't pay much attention to my warnings.

He asked us what we were doing on the river. Preston told him a little bit, but then Scott interrupted to show us his guns.

Alongside where he'd been sitting he pulled out a .38 that had to be primed before shooting. "It's an antique," he said, although it was only a replica. Then he showed his single-barrel twelve-gauge shotgun. It had an unspent shell in its chamber. Trying to fit in with Scott, I told him I had an old twenty-gauge that had been passed down from my great-grandfather to me. Scott said he came by his shotgun the same way.

"It's about all I got of my family's," he said, looking me straight in the eye. "My grandmother, mother, and sister all died in a car wreck a few months back. My dad didn't know how to handle it. I guess that's another reason why I've just taken off like this." Scott was at least six inches shorter than Preston or I, but he was much more comfortable with his body. He seemed to move with grace. His stringy hair, which was down to his neck, and whispy, brunet mustache recalled all the rednecks I'd been afraid of as a kid.

This reminded me of the dilemma Preston and I faced before setting out: Do we take a gun along to fight off rednecks? Having grown up in Mississippi, I shouldn't have had such a redneck hang-up. I was around them all the time. But the problem was, they, by definition, could beat the shit out of me, and therefore I'd always been afraid. So I was constantly asking friends if I should take a gun with me. Everyone who was from New York said, yes, take a gun. They'd all seen *Deliverance*. As a matter of fact, all the gun proponents suggested I watch *Deliverance* before setting out on my trip. All of my friends not from New York or who were living outside the city suggested I leave the guns behind. I was pretty confused. But then I asked a fellow Southerner, a friend who always gives me sage advice, if I should tote a gun.

"No, no," he responded. "Just take some beers along and toss those to them. That'll take care of them."

I was incredulous.

"It's usually easier to befriend a redneck than to shoot him," he explained. I thanked him profusely, but before hanging up he added, "Those are the kind of words a person lives to regret."

But I wasn't afraid of Scott. He just kept on talking.

He was twenty-eight but had lived all over—from Washington to California to Australia. He'd also lived off the land a lot. "I even lived in a cave in Yakima Valley for eight months when I ran out of money once. I just ate berries and wild plants. And I killed rabbits, squirrels, and even a bear to eat. I loved staying in that cave."

"That must've been amazing," I said. "How high up was it?"

"Oh, about twenty-eight thousand feet. Hell, one time I even had to scare off a bear from my personal berry patch. I didn't have my gun with me or nothing, so I just yelled and stomped aroun' and he tore outta there."

We started to prepare our stuff to go. "I thought you guys were going to stay here for the night. We could throw our stuff in together and eat a big meal," Scott said.

Preston gave me a look that suggested it might be best to continue on, but for some reason (odd only because I am more chicken than Preston) I told Scott it'd be fun to stay together for the night. "But watch out for Preston," I warned, "he's been having some really heavy dreams about a waitress with sheer panties. He might try to hop you."

"I've got just the thing for Preston," Scott said, and ran to his canoe. He came back with the August issue of *Playboy*. "I'm not going to give you the whole thing, but here's the centerfold."

"No, no thanks," Preston said, turning red. It was funny to see him blushing about a centerfold. "You keep it." Scott insisted, and when Preston continued to refuse, Scott put it on top of one of the dry sacks. I put it inside my pack once I saw Preston ignoring it. It might come in handy.

"I don't need this magazine all that much. I was staying at a state campsite last night and I had the best time. These two girls were camping next to me and pretty soon we got to talking. One of them seemed to have a thing for me. After a while, we started making out and she said, 'Hold on. I want to do something special for you.' So she drove back to her house and came back dressed in a beautiful dinner dress. And then she took it off. She had on a black teddy. . . . We made love all night.

"Now don't you try anything," Scott continued. "Remember, I have loaded guns. Ha, ha, ha. I don't travel much of anywhere without my toys. You never know when you'll need them or just when you might want to use them." Preston and I looked at each other in horror. About then, Scott pulled out his ax.

"I'd better go get some wood," he said.

Preston went with Scott while I set up our camp. Their wood-chopping echoed through the woods, and I thought how good it would be to have Scott along with us. There would always be conversation and he seemed pretty comfortable outdoors.

After they returned toting enough wood for two nights, Scott set up his fishing pole to catch a catfish. He swabbed some paste from a jar onto a tiny rag and stuck it on his hook. Three minutes after he cast out the line, a huge cat pulled at his line. Scott struggled with the big fish—his fishing rod had a terrific bend in it—and had it almost onto the bank when it shook itself free of the hook.

"That was fast," I said. "That bait is amazing. Where'd you get it?"

Scott paused for a few seconds, letting the question hang in the air. "Why, I made it," he finally answered. "They sell the stuff, but it's just not as good. I hook a fish every time I throw a line in with my stink bait."

"Can you give me the recipe?" I asked. Preston took out our fishing pole (we'd lost the other one overboard earlier in the day bouncing over some tugboat waves) and asked Scott for some of his bait.

"Well . . .," he said in response to my question. I begged a little more. "Okay, you need a licorice base, flour . . . baking soda, cooking oil, garlic salt . . . You cook it over a low flame for about an hour—hour and a half. Then, you know, add your cooking oil if it's too thick, and if it's too thin, add flour or starch, something like that."

"It smells like it has peanut butter in it also," I said. Preston cast his line out, crossing Scott's.

"Oh, yeah, yeah. It has peanut butter in it also. That ought to work." I couldn't understand why Scott hadn't said anything about the peanut butter or why he'd been so hesitant in giving the recipe out. Was he simply guarding his secret recipe? While Preston continued to fish, Scott scrambled back into the woods with his ax, saying we needed more firewood.

"You made a good call, staying here with Scott," Preston whispered to me. "This isn't New York City after all. Hell, we ought to bring him along with us."

For dinner I cooked freeze-dried chili from a camping store but added fresh kielbasa and some green peppers of Scott's. Preston and Scott built a huge fire. Then we sat down to talking. In truth, Preston and I mostly listened as Scott drove home each subject that we brought up. When we talked about hunting, he explained everything:

"Every animal has enough brains to tan his own hide with. You just boil up his brains and use that for your tan-ning. It's easy. I figure I'm going to drop a deer and make a pair of buckskins pretty soon. Maybe I'll even do it here." He looked around as if to survey the hunting grounds. Preston asked if he could go along.

Ka-plop! It was the same smacking against the water we'd heard the other night.

"Is that a beaver?" I asked.

"Yep. Sure is," Scott answered. "That was right out front. We're probably messing with his territory. Those suckers have sharp teeth. You don't want to get one of them mad at you. You kill beaver by drowning them. I've done it plenty of times. You place the trap in their crawl space and one of their feet gets caught in it. They get stuck under the water and die. But the pelt stays fine."

An owl called from across the river. The sun was setting and the darkening sky was a soft purple. And Scott Failor kept right on going. "That's a great horned owl. I'd know that call anywhere."

"Really?"

"Yep. I had one when I was a kid. I found him when he was a baby. His eye was injured. Every one called him One Eye. He'd fly off, kill something, and then come back and land on my arm."

Preston was right, I thought. Scott would be great to have along. We'd certainly always have enough to eat. I was thinking about inviting him along, but I never got much of a chance to ask.

He and Preston talked about cars. I couldn't understand them—cars requiring a language of their own. Then Scott told us about working at a nuclear plant in California. They had a containment breach while he was there, so he quit that job and became a bodyguard for some famous people. He wouldn't say who.

"You've sure done a lot," I said. "Wouldn't you like to—"

"I sure have. I didn't tell y'all about that time I landed in the tree? There was this terrific snowstorm. I was going to see my girlfriend, but a huge drift was blocking the road. I decided to cut across the field to her place. I tore across there at sixty miles per hour. I made it through the trees okay, but then there was this crick. I didn't know about that. I jumped it but ended up going so high in the air that I came down between two trees and the thing just stuck there." He used his hands to show that the trees made a V and that the truck landed wedged into the V.

"How'd you get it out?"

"I didn't. It's still there."

Around ten-thirty, we climbed into our tents. Preston and I tried to write in our journals, but Scott kept on talking. A lot of it centered around his ex-girlfriend: "I'm gonna fix her. When I get down to Louisiana, I'll take everything out of my canoe that I need to get by with and a few things out of my wallet and then dump the whole thing over. The police'll find my wallet and notify her and she'll feel guilty then."

"Uh-huh," I said. This had become my response to him. He kept right on talking. By midnight, I finally quit saying "Uh-huh" but he still didn't stop. The last thing I remember him saying was, "Well, now that's a funny story. It happened when I was up in Alaska . . ."

SIX

━━ ━━ ━━ ━━ ━━ ━━ ━━ ━━

Wild, Woolly, and Full of Fleas

A barge woke us all up a little after 5 A.M. Its horn blared again and again, and someone on board shined a search-light on us. It was as bright as daylight. Scott immediately started talking, something about barges. Preston and I both tried to fall back asleep, but Scott wouldn't shut up. We gave up after half an hour.

It smelled like rain so we took down our tent and stowed our gear in the boat. "Why don't you two stay here for the day? We can go hunting," Scott said. I expected Preston to want to stay once Scott had said that. Although Scott hadn't let either of us talk much, Preston had been able to repeat his desire to go hunting a couple of times during the night.

"I'm afraid we can't," Preston said. "If you're right about that storm coming, we've got to get going." Right then it mercifully began to sprinkle. Although we couldn't see more than a hundred yards in front of us (it was barely past dawn), we started pushing *Sacky* off the bank.

"Don't you two want to stay for breakfast?" Scott asked.

"Wish we could," I said. We shook his hand good-bye, wished him well, and shoved off. It was raining hard.

We were in and out of rainstorms the entire day. It should have put a damper on our spirits, but we were both cheerier than ever. Scott, while a born motormouth and probable liar, had livened up our journey. He was the main topic of the day.

"Did you believe that stuff about living in a cave?" Preston asked me over the whining of the motor.

"At first I did," I said. "When he said the cave was at twenty-eight thousand, I figured he meant twenty-eight hundred feet, but when he told that story about his truck landing in the V of those two trees, I started to have my doubts. Probably about eighty percent of what he said was a lie."

"I know. Everything he said about cars was bullshit. They've never made cars like the stuff he was talking about. But you gotta hand it to him, he's quite a character. I still wouldn't mind having him along . . . if he didn't talk so much."

We thought it best to continue on even after being on the water for eight hours. We had to escape the rain, but every time we thought we'd passed the last front, a new one would appear on the horizon, coming straight for us.

Just short of a hundred miles for the day, we stopped at Huff Access and Camping. It was a Corps-built campground according to our map. We figured it would have showers and nice soft grass to pitch our tent on. Preston badly wanted (and needed) a hot shower.

We slowly motored into the tiny harbor that the Corps had built for the campground. An old man sat at the bottom of the ramp, barely holding the tip of his pole out of the water. He was blocking our entrance. I kept heading toward him, and at the last minute he yanked his line out of the way. He hmmphed as he did it.

"How ya doing?" I called. He didn't answer. I cut the engine and asked again.

"Fine." He was dressed in a red-checked shirt, faded, dirty blue jeans, easy-walking shoes with no laces, and a red and white baseball cap. His skin was tan and leathery.

"How's the fishin'?" I asked. "We haven't caught a thing ourselves." Preston tied us to a tree by the ramp.

"Yeah, the gawd damnt government's messed this river up." The old man spoke quite clearly for not having any teeth. "But I'm gonna get 'em. Gawd damnt, I'll kill 'em if I have to. I'll kill George Bush. I don't care. They screwed up my disability. I'm an American war veteran. I'll kill all them doctors. I went down to that clinic and told that doctor he better treat me right or I'd bust his head open. You shoulda seen his eyes bulging out then." He bulged out his own eyes to describe how the doctor looked, then spit out some chewing-tobacco juice.

All three of us started walking up the boat ramp. The old man stopped and so did I. Preston continued on, saying he was going to check out the campground.

"I worked on this river after the war. I drove all these pilings into the river working for the U.S. Engineers," he said, including the entire river with one sweep of his hand. "That was some hard work, but they didn't mess with me. I told 'em what I thought and they knew." He entered a beat-up old Dodge trailer home that we were standing alongside of. No one else was at the park and so I worried that he would exit toting a gun.

He came out with another fishing pole. He and I stood by his RV looking at the tall cottonwoods that formed a canopy over the campground. "Yep," he said. His lips disappeared into his mouth since there were no teeth to hold them out.

A tiny green frog jumped out from underneath a leaf. I pointed to it.

"Look at that!" he said. "That catfish will love this thing." He snatched the frog up and stuffed it in his pocket.

Preston returned, saying it looked okay but there weren't any showers. The old man said there was a place about thirteen miles up the river that had hot showers. I'd seen it on the map. It was in Decatur, Nebraska, and it looked as if it were in the middle of town.

"Hot showers?" Preston asked.

"Yep. It's a swell, fancy place. Much better than this." We decided to continue on. We thanked the old man, telling him our names. He said his was Bill, Wild Bill. He'd been called that ever since he was ten years old.

"Wild Bill from Squaw Hill, never been kissed nor never will, wild and woolly and full of fleas, never been curried above the knees," he recited unprompted. He started laughing so hard by the end of the rhyme that it was nearly impossible to understand. Preston took his picture and then asked if he could take a picture of his hands as well. They were big, meaty, blotchy things that had been ravaged by weather, fights, and hard work.

We wished him well and took off back up the river. Around five, 113 miles for the day, we pulled in to Beck Memorial Recreation Area in Decatur. There was a boat ramp and a dock. It was our first dock, and although it'd been a long day, I was excited by the convenience and the coming hot shower. We unloaded the boat without bickering. At the top of the ramp lay a rolling hill of green grass and about a dozen RVs. I could make out the communal bathroom farther up the hill. And to my relief, the town was not in sight.

By this time I wanted that hot shower as much as Preston. I hurried through my chores—carrying the bags up to the site, unloading the tent, helping Preston raise the tent, protecting all our gear from the coming rain (gray clouds covered the sky), setting out the food and stove for the evening, etc. As I was making a second trip to the boat, though, Wild Bill pulled up in his RV. He nearly hopped out before it came to a complete stop.

"I shoulda told you I was coming up here, too, but I just forgot it," he said, looking simultaneously sheepish and excited. He unloaded two of his fishing rods. One of them was already baited with the frog he'd caught earlier. After baiting a crawfish onto his other line, he cast them both out into the water with heavy sinkers attached. "I'm gonna catch some carp. There's a lot of carp in here."

"Are carp any good?" I'd always thought they were about the worst eating fish around.

"Yeah, that's a most delicious fish," he said, very serious now, "if you cook it right. First you have to score it—you know, cut some lines into it diagonally. I worked as a cook for a few years in a restaurant so I know all about cooking. Then you just dip it in some Aunt Jemima pancake mix and put it in a kettle with this much oil in it (he measured about one and a half inches with his fingers). And that's good. I cook every fish that way."

"Pancake mix?"

"Yep, it's most delicious that way. Other people do that, too, but it's the scoring that makes it so good."

Preston came down to the dock to tell me he was about to take a shower. I stayed with Wild Bill for a while longer. He talked about his days working on the river and how he'd taken care of the foreman. He'd threatened the foreman until the foreman's eyes bulged way out, and then everything was okay. The foreman knew who the real boss was—Wild Bill.

He didn't catch anything while I sat there, but he kept talking to the fish and me. He filled me in on himself. He was seventy-three years old and his great-grandmother was a full-blooded Omaha so he's registered as a Native American at the reservation. His wife was a school-bus driver and they had seven boys and four girls. He hadn't worked since 1968, "on account of my disabilities from the war. The government has defrauded me. I was discharged with a disability discharge, but now they claim it isn't valid. So I'm suing the government and the veteran's ad-ministration, but I ain't had no luck—been doing it since 1988. They're keeping my records in what they call captivity."

His eyes were a pure light blue and his large ears seemed stretched out from all the years of hanging down. A big mole sat on the outside of his left nostril.

It felt comfortable sitting beside him on the dock, listening to him go on about the government owing him money and his days working for the Corps of Engineers. His face changed from mad to happy depending on the subject, but it was never still. His mood was constantly changing.

I'm not too sure what it was about him, but I knew I liked being with him. He made everything seem possible.

I had to go up for my shower after a while and asked if he was staying the night in his RV.

"No, I'm going home. But why don't we have breakfast tomorrow before you go." I agreed and headed up the hill.

Preston's hot shower had only lasted two minutes, and he was a little upset. He'd also had to pay for our campsite. He was talking to Lea, a woman staying in her RV with her husband, about our trip. She was going to write about us in the Decatur paper.

"I see you've met Wild Bill. He's quite a character," she said.

Seeing that Preston was taking care of being friendly, I continued heading for the bathroom. My hot water lasted all of four minutes before it turned freezing. It was worse than not having any hot water.

Wild Bill stopped by on his way home as I was cooking dinner. He invited us to breakfast again. I told him we would be leaving early and he said he always woke up early. "My feet hurt too much for me to sleep," he said. "I'll be by at six-thirty or maybe even earlier."

A light drizzle began soon after he departed. We ate in the rain and then crawled into the tent for the night. It was only eight. The wind picked up and pushed at our tent, which flapped and shook with each strong gust. But the water stayed on the outside.

"Lea showed me where lightning struck a tree last night," Preston chose to tell me just as we began to hear thunder. "It was less than a hundred yards from here. If lightning doesn't strike twice in the same place, I wonder if it strikes near the same place?"

Since the thunder and lightning continued all night, I didn't sleep very much. But I did pray quite often to anyone who might be listening that I would never be so hypocritical as to pray to live through the night again if I could only live through the night this time. Preston didn't wake up once.

Around five-thirty in the morning, a blinding light shone into our tent. It seemed some townies had finally decided to come rob us.

Preston woke up. "Who in the hell thinks it's a good idea to turn their damned headlights on us in the middle of the night," he mumbled, and immediately fell back asleep.

But I figured out who it was. "It's Wild Bill, I think."

It was. His feet had hurt more than usual because of the weather.

After we ate eggs, home fries, ham, and toast at Denise's Family Dining, Wild Bill took us on a three-hour tour of the area. He showed us the new casino, CasinOmaha, in Iowa near Onawa; Blackbird Hill; some reservation land that Wild Bill claimed was stolen by a local guy and the government; an old trailer home that was placed on the land before it was "stolen"; and the Lewis and Clark Lake where they reenact the expedition every year.

We stopped at the old trailer home. A sign announced: "Boundary Line. Omaha Indian Reservation. No Trespassing—Federal Law Prohibits Damage or Removal of This Sign. Violators Will Be Prosecuted. Omaha Tribal Council."

Marijuana was growing all over the place. We picked some to dry and send back to friends. "I used to smoke it all the time when I was a little boy," Wild Bill told us. "It was part of our custom. It made me healthy. I'm gonna live until I'm two hundred years old. Marijuana is good for many things. They say it cures cancer."

We said we'd heard the same. Then he continued, unprompted, "Now I don't know about hard-ons. People say it's good for that, too. I get a hard-on no problem. I don't need it for that. And younger women, they like older men. I don't know why, but they do." Wild Bill turned to the government. "It makes no sense, the government outlawing something that grows natural on the land, gawd damnt. The government is messing up all this. The land is for getting food. It shouldn't be for anything else."

We tried to find out exactly how the land had been taken

away, but Wild Bill wasn't too keen on the specifics. He just knew that they'd been cheated once again. Somehow we got on the subject of his health. "I had the hiccups for fourteen days once. And you see this bump on my right hand," he said, holding up his big meaty hook, "I got that when four Indians jumped me in Decatur."

"I thought you were an Indian."

"I am." Then we moved to the subject of his wife. "I don't chase after other women, so my wife and I get along fine. I just pick up and go somewhere when I want to. She does, too. Marriage can be hard, though. You just have to know how to work things out."

And then back to politics. "I can run this damnt government better than any of those gawd-damnt politicians. If they'd let me, I'd go run this damnt thing right now. To hell with George Bush." All the time he was talking, Wild Bill was busy smoking cigarettes and chewing Copenhagen simultaneously.

We returned to our boat shortly before ten. Lea was standing by the dock to see us off. She and Wild Bill told us how bad the fishing was ever since the Corps of Engineers dredged the deep channels for the barges. "The barges and the deep channels have thrown off the spawning of all the fish but especially the cats."

Wild Bill was looking sort of sad. He seemed to be upset that we were heading on. So he reiterated how tough he was.

Lea laughed. "Oh, yeah, Bill, you're real mean. That's why I've always heard those stories from everyone else about you giving hungry people the fish that you caught and cooking it up for them even. That's pretty mean." Wild Bill chose to ignore this. It didn't fit the image he'd tried to build in our minds.

After everything was ready for our departure and we'd said our good-byes, Lea turned to Wild Bill and said, "Wild Bill, we probably ought to tell them about the quicksand. Not long back, a boy was pushing his boat off a sandbar up there and he forgot to hold on to something. . . . He died—was pulled under by the quicksand."

"That's right. You two be careful and remember what I said about those lakes. Stay to the east and northeast or you'll end up way off course." Earlier, Wild Bill had confirmed my fears that we hadn't reached the toughest part of our trip. He'd said that the swells and the wind on the lakes above the first dam, Gavins Dam, were not to be believed. And that they were so large that we wouldn't know what direction we were traveling in unless we stayed close to the shore. In particular, we had to watch out for Lake Oahe. We could go hundreds of miles off course and not even know it on that lake. "But from here to Gavins you'll be fine. There's lots of sandbars, but like you said, you don't draw much water."

One last look at Wild Bill as we motored away and we both wished he could go along with us. "He might be crazy," Preston said, "but he's a sweet old fella."

SEVEN

Tornado in Our Tent

The going was easy that morning. Many blue heron loped across the sky at our approach and countless drainage pipes pumped sickly water into the river. One of them spewed white-colored water that had stained all the plants within thirty feet of its outlet. It made us glad we hadn't caught or eaten any fish from the Missouri.

After two and a half hours we reached the south side of Sioux City and stopped at Floyd's Bluff and Monument. It was our major tourist stop of the lower Missouri—the site where Sgt. Charles Floyd of the Lewis and Clark expedition was buried.

Sergeant Floyd was the only causality among the expedition members during the voyage. On August 19, 1804—roughly three months from the start—after an evening of partying with a local Indian tribe, Floyd became ill. "Serjeant Floyd is taken very bad all at once with a Biliose Chorlick we attempt to relieve him without success as yet, he gets worst and we are much allarmed at his Situation, all attention to him," Clark recorded. What he didn't explain was that they probably attempted to relieve him by bleeding and feeding him Dr. Rush's mercury tablets. Dr. Rush was the foremost surgeon of his day, and he had tutored Lewis in medicine before the young explorer set off. Rush's mercury pills were prescribed by Lewis and Clark in many situations.

By the next day, Floyd had worsened. "Serjeant Floyd as bad as he can be no pulse & nothing will Stay a moment on his Stomach or bowels. Passed two Islands on the S.S. and at the first bluff on the S.S. Serj. Floyd Died with a great deal of Composure, before his death he Said to me, "I am going away I want you to write me a letter."

It is thought today that, given the quickness of his death and the symptoms—vomiting and diarrhea—Floyd died of appendicitis. But I imagine the bleeding and the probable ingestion of mercury didn't help much either.

We were able to make out the monument from the water but wanted to see it up close. We tied *Sacky* to a large rock and climbed the steep, eroded bank. A heavy-trafficked four-lane highway blocked our path. We ran in between the speeding cars, leaping the divider in the middle. Then there was a wide railroad track. We crossed it with no problem. A steep hill led up to the obelisk honoring Floyd. It was covered in waist-high grass. I was worried about rattlesnakes but only mentioned all the poison ivy that surrounded us. Preston wore sandals. After crawling through a barbed-wire fence and climbing another hill, we arrived at the monument's base. A nice, paved road led up from the other side—totally unreachable from the river.

A plaque read, "This shaft marks the burial place of Sergeant Charles Floyd. A member of the Lewis and Clark Expedition. He died in his country's service and was buried near this spot. Graves to such men are pilgrim shrines. Shrines to no class or creed confined."

All those men had been in the service of their country.

Preston and I were just gallivanting up the river for our amusement.

Preston looked pained. "It hurts, Captain, it hurts, ahhgh," Preston as Floyd said.

"Here, Sergeant," Preston as Lewis responded, "take these. Dr. Rush recommended them—pure mercury tablets!"

Preston/Floyd ate some imaginary tablets. He clutched his stomach and fell to the ground.

We left a few minutes later, in a hurry to reach well beyond Sioux City. The major channeling of the river stopped there, and we would soon be in the river as it appeared in Lewis and Clark's day. But first we had to stop at a Sioux City marina for gas. I tried to buy a propeller there as well, but they didn't have the kind we needed.

The landscape of the river changed just outside of the city. There were fewer and fewer jetties and the mileage markers also decreased in number. Lea and Wild Bill had warned us about sandbars starting there, but we didn't see any. We sped along as usual.

Within twenty minutes, Pompy (our engine) jumped out of the water and whined at a deafening pitch. I cut the motor off. And at the same time we came to a sudden halt.

"What is it?" Preston asked, a little worried.

"I don't know." He poked the ground with a paddle. We were on a sandbar. That's why we'd been warned. You couldn't see them. And to our regret, Pompy did go deep enough into the water to hit them.

"I guess the proctologist and the gym teacher were pretty smart after all," Preston commented as we pushed off the sandbar, referring to the two guys who'd retraced the Lewis and Clark Trail before us. Their jet boat only drew about six inches of water. Pompy went down well over a foot. "This is going to be tough."

We pulled over to fill the gas tank a little later, and as Preston was pouring in the oil (Pompy was a two-stroke engine, requiring a mixture of gas and oil), I noticed two beautiful larvae feeding on a milkweed stalk. They had yellow, black, and white stripes and were a little over an inch long and about as thick as my pinkie. I marveled at their shape and luster. Neither of them moved, but I imagined their tiny mouths feeding away on the green plant. They were monarch larvae. *Simon and Schuster's Guide to Insects* says, "The larvae feed on milkweed. The larval foodplant is poisonous and both the larvae and the adults are poisonous." Their colorful stripes were a warning.

We hit mile 753—the end of our channel map—around three, and the official end of the Corps of Engineers dredging and channeling work. The river returned to its natural state. We celebrated this milestone by promptly running aground. I lifted Pompy out of the sand and Preston pushed us off with a paddle. We went a hundred yards and I ran us aground again. We were in such shallow water this time that Preston couldn't push us off. We both climbed out of the boat and pushed/pulled her over the sandbar for ten minutes. I couldn't get Lea's words out of my mind: "He forgot to hold on to something. He died— was pulled under by the quicksand."

Full of sass, Preston announced, "We must institute a flogging rule. The first person to beach us three times will be summarily flogged. We must have discipline." I was not amused, but I let him take over the steering. He proceeded to run aground a couple of times within half an hour.

The Missouri appeared no longer to be one river but many. It widened into dozens of canals, separated by reeds or islands, but only one of them was the true passageway. At that time of year even the true passageway was only a foot or so deep in some areas and thirty yards wide at the most. There were no longer any signs of human life either. It looked primitive and forgotten. "It looks like we've dropped off the face of the earth," Preston said, awed. Stands of cattails stood up in what appeared to be the middle of the river.

While one person slowly steered, the other sat on the bow, stabbing the water with a paddle. The bowman would yell out to indicate the depth of the water, "Three feet, three feet, four feet, deep, deep, shallow, two feet, two feet, *stop.*" Sometimes we even avoided hitting sandbars this way.

We both thought we knew which was the correct channel. Preston would say, "Look, I think we have to go over there." We'd follow his direction because maybe I'd led the way before. And the way he'd pointed out would work—for a while. He'd be top dog and then we'd run aground. So then it would be my turn and I'd be top dog. It went back and forth like this all afternoon until neither of us took it very seriously.

Fish began jumping above the surface. They were nearly three feet long and thicker than Popeye's arm. I told Preston that I'd catch us one for dinner. Fishing was one of my responsibilities. A little later we stopped at a stand of cattails so I could pick some for dinner. A friend had given me a deck of playing cards of edible wild plants. Each card has a photograph of a plant on one side and a description and explanation of its uses on the other. For cattail, it reads, "Supermarket of the Swamp . . . Warning: if water purification is in doubt, use purification tablet and soak plant in solution." Euell Gibbons's book, *Stalking the Wild Asparagus*, also highly recommends cattails. So I tasted both the root and the stem pith as directed and neither was adequate. They were sort of rancid even. It was probably the water quality or the lateness of the season. We would stick with Lipton's noodles-and-sauce one more night unless I caught a fish.

"It really looks like we're in another world," Preston said again. Neither of us could get over the dramatic change.

"I wish it were this way the whole time," I said. And then we ran aground again. I asked Preston if he still thought we should flog each other. He'd been steering the boat when we last hit bottom.

There were signs of humanity now and then, but they were of a fairly distant past. Beneath a canopy of deciduous trees, four cars and a truck from the 1950s lay piled on top of and next to each other. Some of them were in the water and the others lay stretched along the bank. Poison ivy grew through the windshield of one car—a crème-colored station wagon. And we passed a couple of derelict fishing shacks. Maybe the water had not been high enough for any boats to get to them for a long while.

We sped around a sharp bend and I nearly fell out of the boat with shock. A man was standing on the shore beside a beat-up old aluminum fishing boat. He wore a checked shirt and green waders. His back was to us. We slowed down thinking he might be in trouble, and the strangest thing happened. He kept his back to us the entire time we were in view. Every single person we'd passed on the river since St. Louis had turned to wave to us. This man was creepy.

"That's weird he didn't turn," I said.

"Yeah, he's probably a poacher," Preston said. Then he turned his head toward the man and called out, *"Poacher!"*

"Preston. Shhh. Poachers have guns."

"Oops." Luckily, the poacher hadn't heard him.

A little later we saw our favorite sight of the day: a lone kingfisher hovering above the water. We killed the engine and floated out of the current and at the same time frantically searched for our binoculars, which we found in time. The bird hovered over its prey (a bug or small fish), then dove straight down, plunging into the water without any hesitation, combining the skills of a hummingbird and an osprey in one body.

Within a few hours, we were beside a farm that stretched along the river mile after mile. The river was still wild and wide (two miles even) as it'd been ever since passing Sioux City, and while there was a farm, no farmhouse was in sight. We docked on the edge of the cornfields to stay for the night.

After making camp, I attempted to fulfill my fishing duties. Preston wandered around the area, looking up the trees in his Audubon book and gathering firewood for the night. The corn, he discovered, was as tough as usual. It had been a long day, but we both felt rested and calmed by the change in scenery.

I didn't catch a thing.

As I prepared our freeze-dried dinner a little later, Preston launched into a recurring fantasy.

"Your grandfather didn't give you that shotgun, boy. You

are lying," he said in a clipped British accent. His hands were placed sternly on his hips.

Then he switched to Scott Failor's voice. He became all bent up and squinted his eyes. He whined, all countrylike, "No, no, mister. It's true, I promise. He did give it to me. . . . Anyway, I've got the gun."

Back to the Brit. "Aha! Not anymore. I've got the gun now. Hod, go slap him a few times across the face like a good chap, won't you. . . . That's it. Harder." Preston paced around the camp repeating this scene again and again to our delight. I told him I'd seen a jar of stink bait in the Sioux City marina that looked an awful lot like Scott's stink-bait jar. No wonder he'd forgotten there was peanut butter in the stink bait; he'd never made it in the first place. We cursed him for the liar he was.

The crickets and katydids had warmed up and were performing at concert level. The river was quietly gurgling just below us. And the mosquitoes, which were a different species from before, were doing their job as well. Preston lit our fire to drive them away. Two carrot beetles landed beside me and began humping.

"The unfortunate part," Preston said, looking across the water to the setting sun, "is that you can in no way capture this in writing or in a photograph." The water had turned purple from the sun, which was now hiding behind a stand of trees. He then bent down to watch the carrot beetles.

The night continued in bliss. A pack of coyotes began barking straight across the river once the sun disappeared, and then another group farther downriver called out in response. The barking gave way to high-pitched howls, which reverberated through the woods and across the water.

Preston and I had talked about the coyotes earlier in the day. He was somewhat used to them in Los Angeles, where they go after poodles and the like. He said they were no danger to humans.

I had come to look forward to their nightly calls. Their short barks and long howls were no longer scary. On the contrary, I found them comforting. Traces of the sun shone violet in the western sky. At the same time, the Big Dipper hung about thirty degrees above the dying light, and the first quarter of the moon rose into view. We had come a long way—not only since St. Louis but just from the morning. At five-thirty we were riding around in Wild Bill's car, and now we were sitting around a fire, listening to the coyotes.

In the morning Preston and I found prints from the Canidae: the dog family. While most dog prints look similar, these appeared to be of a coyote. The measurements were exactly right: two inches by two and a half inches for the front paws and about the same for the hind ones. Many dogs have paws of like size, including cocker spaniels. But the outline, according to *Animal Tracks*, is unique for the coyote. And of course, we'd heard the coyotes all night so we knew they were in the area. Once again there was no scat. In the case of coyotes, this didn't matter. "I sometimes think that the most conspicuous coyote sign is his night song," Olaus Murie writes. "Certainly a camp on the plains in the Southwest or in the Western mountains is cozier in the moonlight. He who would follow the mammals in the wilds should know something of the significance of this. Unaccustomed ears, trained by traditional journalism, might interpret the coyote voice as something doleful, a sad requiem that makes one crowd closer to the campfire. Or a flippant tongue might speak of the 'yapping' of the coyotes. But if the coyote could reflect and speak, he would say this is his song, simply that. However it may appear to human ears, to the coyote it satisfies the universal impulse for expression of emotion, simple as that may be among the furred animals."

We proceeded more slowly in the morning as the water was even lower, and we continuously steered around dead trees and logs jammed into the river bottom. We ran aground a half dozen times, and frequently we both despaired of ever finding the main channel. No other boats were on the river. *Sacky* began to leak again and Pompy choked and sputtered as he was thrown out of the water in the shallow areas.

Eventually, Preston realized the river was deepest below the steep bluffs that overlooked some parts of the banks. So we steered toward the side of the river with the bluffs and were able to make it to Gavins Dam by midday. Just before reaching Gavins, we scared up a flock of bright white pelicans with black-tipped wings. For some reason, I never thought pelicans would be graceful, but they easily climbed out of the water and within seconds were soaring in a V-shaped flock.

The dam elated us at first. It was a milestone, reaching the dammed part of the Missouri. But there wasn't much time for celebrating. We had to get ourselves and all the equipment around it.

On our starboard side was a boat ramp, and after attaching the portable rubber tires to her stern, we began pulling *Sacky* up the ramp. We made it to the edge of the water but reached no farther. We would have to unload her first. We took everything out but the engine—around four hundred pounds of equipment. Three of the full gas cans alone weighed nearly one hundred and twenty pounds.

And then we easily pulled her up the ramp and about one hundred yards. We only had a little over three miles to go to make it around the dam to the Lewis and Clark Lake. Preston suggested we find somebody to help us out.

A good number of trucks and cars were driving by because this was the day before Labor Day weekend. To attract their attention, we scratched our heads a lot and lifted up the front of the bow when they came by. Finally, an elderly couple stopped. We told them what we were trying to do, and the man said maybe he could help out after he dropped his wife off at the campground.

He returned a few minutes later, but *Sacky*'s bow ring wouldn't fit over his hitch, and we weren't strong enough to sit in the back of his van and hold the bow up. He then went back for his smaller hitch. We lifted *Sacky* onto it and Preston held on to the bow line. Her bottom cleared the ground by about 6 inches.

Harold Howard, our savior for the afternoon, drove at about 6 mph and we arrived at the marina on the other side of the dam in about thirty minutes. Harold wasn't all that excited about helping us and didn't say anything but "yep" and "no" on the ride over. Except near the end he remembered helping out some foreigners once, and he became all excited talking about the young woman, excited for Harold, that is. "She was interesting," he said. He left immediately after dropping us off.

We crossed the twenty-five-mile-long lake in a little over an hour. There were swells a couple of feet high, but since the wind was behind us, the lake felt like a soft roller coaster. Having no current was wonderful.

The lake split into a series of canals where it met up with the Missouri, and we had trouble finding the right canal. Most were too shallow. We zigzagged through a maze of islands.

Since Gavins Dam, the water had become clearer, but now it was suddenly crystal clear. We both wanted to drink it, it looked so clean. Instead, we swam beside some bluffs. It was the first time we'd swum in the Missouri that I felt cleaner afterward than before.

While Preston soaked up some of the afternoon sun, I went to carve my name in the sandstone. He immediately berated me, saying I was as bad as the people who threw trash into the water. I argued back, saying Clark had done it everywhere.

"If I'm out here enjoying nature, trying to escape from everything for a little while, do you think I want to come across your or Clark's names on the side of a hill?" he asked.

I stopped carving, not just because he had a good point, but also because he demanded his knife back (I'd already lost mine overboard). The only rocks lying around to carve with were pieces of sandstone, and they crumbled when I tried to use them.

I found a terrific scat, though, full of berries and some sort of nuts. It was hidden in a crevice between two large rocks. Since the ground was all rock, there were no prints. I tried to identify it in *Animal Tracks* but had no luck. I wanted it to be of a prairie dog because we hadn't seen any yet. Lewis and Clark had come across thousands of them, but the family-oriented rodent had been poisoned off its natural habitat over the past two hundred years. "As the rodents competed with cattle for grass—250 prairie dogs consume as much grass each day as a 1,000-lb. cow—they were the object of such fierce extermination campaigns that their number declined by over 90%," explains the *Field Guide to North American Mammals.* The guide goes on to point out that it has now been proven that the prairie dogs actually help improve rangeland for cattle, so many farmers are now trying to reverse this decline.

I put the scat in an empty film canister and we headed upriver again.

The traveling was easy alongside the bluffs at first, but even they failed us after about an hour. We ran aground. We were on the South Dakota side of the river, and we knew we wanted to be on the Nebraska side because I'd seen a campsite listed there on a road map. So we tried cutting across one of the cattail-lined canals. The first one didn't work. We backtracked and asked some fishermen how to get across. They directed us farther back to where we'd come from and said to follow a certain wide canal that Preston had suggested in the first place. I had ignored him.

This canal led us straight across. When we were on the other side, Preston asked if there was a campground on this side. "Why do you think we just spent forty minutes trying to cross this damned thing if there isn't supposed to be a place to camp here?" I answered. It was about six-thirty and we'd been going since 8 A.M. "I told you there was one on this side when we were on the other side, so unless something has changed, it's still here."

"You may not understand this," he said, "but I am distinguishing between a campground and a place that is good for camping."

I looked along the bank we were floating by. There seemed to be plenty of good camping areas. "Since I've never been to Nebraska before," I said, "I can't really say if it's really there, but I did see a campground on the map so that's all I know. Whether or not we can find it is another question." It had been a really long day.

We stopped at one place to camp. It was overgrown with pot. There were five-to-six-foot-high plants growing everywhere. Worried that the cultivators might not like our presence, we decided to go farther upstream. Preston pulled up a four-foot plant before continuing.

We found another flat place about ten minutes later. Cow prints and patties were everywhere. Once we'd unloaded everything, we noticed that pot was growing there as well, but not as thickly. There also didn't appear to be any pattern to the plants. Maybe they were just growing wild; Preston's Audubon guide to the grasslands claims marijuana is an indigenous, wild plant. Preston put his plant he'd swiped back into the soil. "It was just some adolescent whim that made me take this," he said. "I don't want it."

Preston took out the road map before we pitched the tent. To my relief, a campground was indicated near where we were. Even though we hadn't found it, being right was of the utmost importance.

The map also showed we were camping on an Indian reservation. A dirt farm road wound its way straight into our camp, and Preston wondered aloud if we'd picked such a great spot. That was meant as an insult. I think we both worried the pot growers might not like our trespassing. According to the map, it also looked as if we'd now gone about 840 miles, which put us about two days ahead of schedule.

Besides the pot, our campground was distinctly different from all the previous ones in other ways. Dozens of oak trees and thousands of acorns covered the ground. And for the first time, pine trees stood before us. There had not been a single pine along the lower Missouri.

While Preston looked up the oaks (long, flat-leafed) in his tree book, I began fishing with some stink bait that Scott had given us. I cast out a few times with no luck. I cast again, and as the current dragged the weighted bait downstream, something big hit. I started reeling it in furiously. I must've called out because Preston came running over.

I reeled and reeled, and finally it rose to the surface. It was a water-sodden log. To top it off, I couldn't get the stink-bait smell off my right hand.

We made up a little later—not by apologizing but simply by talking with each other. We were now like a married couple with set ways of treating each other. Preston commented, "If the weather holds up, we'll have some good star-gazing in about two weeks, God willing. Until then, this moon's gonna ruin it." He paused. The half moon was beautiful in the black sky. "I don't think it's ever a bad idea to add that God-willing clause."

He lit a fire after dinner. Tired from the long day, he didn't bother trying without gas. The funny thing was it didn't light at first even with the gasoline. He had to pour it on the wood a second time. Still pissed off from our earlier argument, I was happy about his small failure. And that was how we fought—silently and sometimes not-so-silently enjoying the other's mistakes.

We shoved off early the next day. Initially, the main channel was on the Nebraska side of the river, and we followed it along the shore for about twenty minutes—until it ended without warning. We'd missed the correct offshoot. We chose many different canals at random to reach the other side, between the cattail and reed islands. Both of us thought we knew which was best, but none worked.

I suggested we head back to our campsite, thinking we could at least find our way back to the dam from there if necessary. And there was one method we hadn't tried.

"Why don't we climb this bluff here. If there is a way across, maybe we'll be able to see it," I said. Preston was willing to give it a try. "Anyway," I continued, "it will be like the real explorer thing to do. Lewis and Clark were constantly climbing hills to figure out where to go. We'll be just like them—mapping our way out."

So we trudged up the hill, skirting the poison sumac, with binoculars around our necks. And from up above we could see the true canal. We would never have been able to find it from water level. It wove back and forth between the cattail/reed islands blocked by dead-ended canals on both sides. The toughest part would be reaching the South Dakota side where it looked easier. Keeping the image in our minds, we hurried back down to the boat.

Beaming with our newfound skill, we followed the canal through the marshy wasteland to South Dakota, and for a short period we had no problems. But then the same thing happened again. This time there was a nearby fishing boat.

"Is this the channel?" we asked.

"Oh, no," one of the two fishermen answered. They were sun-withered older men. "If you go through here, you'll beach your boat. Look over at the rough water. That's it. You see it?"

We both acted as if we might be seeing it. There was some rougher water toward where he was pointing, but it didn't look much rougher than where we'd pointed.

"You've got to read the water," he said. We nodded our heads, not very convincingly. "Do you have a depth finder on there?"

"No," I admitted. He looked pitying.

"Well, then, I guess you'll just have to read the water."

We motored away from them—both of us cursing his "read the water." But between curses, we started paying more attention to where the rough water was and watching how it looked when it was deep. We didn't run aground again the entire day.

The Missouri, though, had more in store for us. Instead of narrowing into a simple river as it should have, it widened again. It was more of a lake than a river because the cattail and reed islands disappeared as well. And where there's a lake in South Dakota, winds aren't far behind. Unfortunately, these winds came directly at us. We bounced all over the water, and Pompy jumped out of his mount. Staying in the boat as we bounced over each swell took all of our energy.

By the time we made it to Ft. Randall Dam that afternoon, we were exhausted. Our work wasn't over, though. No friendly Harold Howard was around this time. We had to drag the boat a mile over the dam, then carry it over the rocks on the other side before depositing it in Lake Francis Case.

While we portaged around the dam, the weather turned nasty. Increasingly darker clouds loomed on the horizon, and the wind worked itself into a frenzy. Lake Francis Case resembled a stormy sea. Luckily, the wind had shifted and was now coming from behind.

The swells were nearly five feet—more than twice the height of *Sacky*. They started white-capping once we reached the middle of the lake, and the spray quickly soaked us. No other boats were on the water. The swells didn't climb any higher, but they became thicker and more difficult to cut through as the wind was pushing them nearly as fast as we were going. We decided to call it a day after only an hour and headed into North Wheeler, a Corps-made cove complete with a boat dock.

We tied up at the dock but the wind and swells swamped *Sacky* even within the cove. A retired man named Cliff, who kept cussing and calling us fools, drove us to the one establishment in North Wheeler—Zeke's Boat Repair Shop—so we could buy some gas. "And then when you fucking idiots get back here, I guess'll have to show you where to move your boat. There's a more protected place further back where all the other boats are," he said. "People are always coming here to ask for favors. Jesus." We hadn't asked him for any favors or advice, though. He just gave it—complaints included. He wore an ugly brown baseball cap that said I'D RATHER BE FISHIN' and an accompanying white sweatshirt that read HOOKED ON FISHIN'. The sweatshirt had a picture of a guy with a fishing line accidentally hooked on his own butt.

To show our gratitude the only way we could, we told Cliff the entire story of our trip up to meeting him. Despite all his cussing, he seemed genuinely interested.

"Well, I hope it doesn't come to an end tonight," he said. "We're supposed to get a tornado, hail, and lots of thunder. It's going to be bad."

Then he and Zeke told us all about the lake. After 11 A.M.

most days, Zeke said, the lake was too rough to travel on. The wind would pick up and even big-engine boats couldn't handle it.

North Wheeler, our campground for the night, had a sister town called South Wheeler. There used to be a Wheeler. It was now in the middle of the lake, and the bridge that connected North and South Wheeler had been moved farther north for one of the highways.

Zeke talked me into buying some spark plugs, but he also tried to smooth out our busted propeller for free.

We pitched the tent beneath a stand of cottonwoods between a dozen RVs and beached boats. "I don't trust those fuckers," Cliff said, "but you can camp wherever you'd like."

All afternoon older men walked by to check on their boats because of the coming storm, and each stopped to talk. Exhausted, I stayed in the tent while Preston stood out there telling our tale. He must have done a good job because by five-thirty, three different couples had stopped by with food: apples, banana nut cake, sodas, and bread. One couple was Cliff and his wife; we had guessed he was a softy under all that bluster, and now we knew it.

The wind picked up to a fierce pitch and then died down to nothing a few times, but a heavy black front continued to march toward us. We drove our tent stakes in as far as possible, and although the wind buffeted it greatly, the tent held firm for the afternoon.

The mosquitoes stayed away for the first time on our trip. We ate dinner in peace. I worried a little about the weather, but having all of those RV people around made me feel somewhat safe.

It was important to know that I wouldn't be dying alone. Sure, Preston was there, but he no longer counted as somebody else. He was more or less my alter ego, and I'm sure I'd become the same for him. And as far as death goes, I've always been comforted in scary situations when accompanied by other people, realizing that they'd die with me. I could feel brave with all those people around, but set me down in a life-threatening situation on my own, or now with Preston, and I would tremble like a leaf.

Right after supper, we entered the tent for the night, simply to escape the relentless wind. The tent rumbled and quaked. To point out to the Fates without rubbing their noses in it that I planned to live through the night, I began reading *The Grizzly Bear* by Thomas McNamee. We wouldn't be seeing any grizzlies until Montana and I wouldn't be reading about them in South Dakota unless I planned on living through the night. I thought it was very subtle.

Around 2:30 A.M., I woke up with the sense that something weird was happening. I immediately checked if Preston was still there (if anything odd was happening, I figured he'd have a hand in it), but he was dead asleep. I unzipped the entrance to look outside. All clear.

Then I looked up at the sky.

Just a few miles upwind, lightning filled the heavens. The flashes were so frequent that it appeared to be daylight. I'd never seen anything like it. Not a second went by without a strike. And the weird thing was that it wasn't raining.

I woke Preston.

"What? What?" he muttered.

"Look outside. I think we're in trouble."

"Oh, shit," he said, watching the sky.

"What should we do?"

"I don't know." I couldn't help but hate Lewis and Clark at that moment. We were surely going to die when that front hit us.

The wind picked up even more. It was blowing at least 50 mph. The tent buckled and shook but held its ground. I was glad we'd used the curly stakes that I'd brought for just such weather.

"One, two, three," Preston counted between the lightning and thunder.

It began raining—a torrential downpour. The lightning moved closer. The thunder followed within one second. It was all nearly above us. The wind grew deafening.

Suddenly, the storm yanked every single stake out of the ground. The tent collapsed—with us inside. One of the poles bent into a right angle.

The wind swooshed inside and the tent tried to take off. We slid across the ground.

"We've got to get outta here," Preston yelled. I grabbed the bent pole, which was partially erect and receiving the brunt of the storm. Preston quickly threw on his rain gear. Then we switched places. Neither of us thought about how crazy it was to be holding a metal pole in a lightning storm. We were too scared.

We scrambled outside and took turns holding down the tent while the other searched for the stakes. Lightning flashes continued to light the sky, and the entire episode looked like a series of photographs from a natural disaster. Branches flew all around us and we heard larger ones crashing to the ground. Dirt and sand blew into our eyes and faces. The rain pelted us like buckshot.

We eventually found all the stakes but one. Then we managed to reerect the tent but this time facing the storm. (It had been facing the wind earlier, but the front had caused the wind to shift.)

We climbed back into the tent, sopping wet, and within ten minutes, the storm was over. It became completely calm and quiet out. So much so, the mosquitoes came out and we could hear them buzzing outside the tent. I'd never been so happy to hear those thirsty bloodsuckers.

In the morning, one of the fellows from an RV told us the winds had gusted up to 80 mph and that the tornado had flown directly over us. We'd been very lucky, he said. It was hard to believe it'd really happened. Everything was calm and quiet and the sky was clear blue. A light, lazy mist hung over the cove, and a doe and her two fawns watched us as we headed back onto calm Lake Francis Case.

EIGHT

- - - - -

Lewis and Clark Never Retreated

The tree-lined riverside we'd grown accustomed to had completely given way to sloping, bare hills. There were no trees, except for occasional pines clumped together in ravines. Since the weather was nice, we stopped beside one of the tallest of these hills to view the land.

And there were the great plains, gliding along beside us. A strong, heavy fragrance hung in the air, drifting up from the surrounding brush. The scent comforted me and made me want to curl up and sleep. One of our books said it was sagebrush.

A brochure for Lake Francis Case claimed there were all sorts of animals around, including such endangered species as prairie falcons, peregrine falcons, bald eagles, and black-tailed prairie dogs. We didn't see any animals except some cattle way off in the distance. The only tracks on the ground were cattle as well, and it was the same story for scats. Our most important find occurred as we were walking back down the hill to *Sacky*. Something large suddenly rustled in the ground slightly ahead of us. Fearful it might be a snake, we warily approached. It moved again.

"It's a grasshopper," Preston said, but that was an understatement. It was the mother of all Orthoptera. She was queen of the hill. When we were within a few feet, she jumped away, a slow, low-arching flight that seemed more annoyed than fearful. She was nearly five inches.

"Jesus, we've got to catch her." For the next few minutes all three of us took turns hopping along the hill. She was so big that when she landed, the force of her weight knocked her off her legs and onto her side. She was not used to being chased. Finally, I managed to land my cupped hands around her. Her powerful feet pods pinched onto my hand and it felt more like a mammal than a mere insect. I was a little worried that she might start nibbling on my hand. Soon enough she squirted out the brown liquid that all grasshoppers release when they're endangered, and it covered nearly a quarter of my hand. It was the stinky contents of her guts, but since I wasn't planning to eat her, it didn't much matter.

She was speckled with dark green and peach blotches on her abdomen. Now that I had her in my hands I could see she was at least as thick as my index finger. I had never seen such a large grasshopper. I figured it was a she because she wasn't making any noise and the males are the ones who call out.

My hand tickled from her crawling in search of an escape route. I let her go after a few minutes. She took one indignant hop and landed in the protecting cover of some sagebrush.

Back on the water, we were soon downwind of something that drove memory of the pungent sagebrush far away. Something was rotting and it wasn't far ahead. We followed the stench, and as it became stronger, we could make out an animal lying along the bank.

It was a dead steer, lying on the beach at the bottom of one of those stately, rolling hills. Its head was in the water.

"That's weird," Preston said, "the way it has sand all over its body. You'd think it would've washed off by now, especially with all of that rain we had last night."

We moved in for a closer look. "That's not sand," I said, pointing to the stuff that was now obviously moving up and down and all around the carcass. "It's some kind of bugs."

"Yech," Preston said, but then he diligently climbed out of the boat and began snapping pictures. When he climbed back in, he reported they had not just been any kind of bugs but delicious, plump maggots. He didn't eat any.

The waves grew, of course, as the day wore on. Pompy jumped out of the transom a number of times, and our lantern was shattered during the pounding. Early in the afternoon, we crossed another dam—Big Bend.

We were now on Lake Sharpe. We gave the lantern to some fishermen who docked their boat as we prepared to leave. It would've only been in our way. We stood on the public ramp drooling over the fish they'd caught, but they didn't get the hint and offer us some in return.

Just before we shoved off, two Native American men drove up in a beat-up old truck. One of them trudged out of the truck and brushed past me, saying a quick hello. The very next second, he let out a yelp and jumped into the lake with all his clothes on. He splashed about a bit. The other fellow stayed in the truck, hidden behind dark aviator sunglasses. The swimmer walked by me again. "Now that felt good," he said. His clothes hung limp and heavy on his body, but he definitely had more spring in his step. "Use a blue one," he suggested, figuring we were going fishing. "The walleyes bite the blue ones." He went and stood by his truck, and the two of them watched us depart.

Besides Wild Bill (and who knows what Wild Bill was), they were the only Native Americans we'd seen since beginning our trip. Lewis and Clark had had countless encounters with them by this point. Nearly all of them had been friendly, and only a few had given any trouble, even though the expedition was passing through their land.

Lewis and Clark would usually hold a meeting, explaining to the local chiefs that they were now under the protection of the Great Father (Jefferson). To demonstrate the power of the Great Father, Lewis would shoot an air gun he'd brought along. It would "miraculously" knock things over and the natives would be amazed. (Evidently, Lewis had become more accustomed to the gun's workings than when he'd first procured the toy in Pennsylvania. At his departure from Pittsburgh on the Ohio River, a large crowd gathered along the shore. Lewis decided to show off his air gun. Quite unexpectedly, he pegged a female bystander. "She fell instantly," Lewis recorded, "the blood gushing from her temple. We were all in the greatest consternation, and supposed she was dead, but in a minute she revived, to our inexpressible satisfaction.") Lewis and Clark would then give them presents and pass safely up the river.

I had possessed a naive hope that Native Americans had been able to move back to their land along the river—that more reparations had been made.

"Hi, fellas!" Preston said, once we were out of earshot, in a mock-cheerful voice. "We're retracing the Lewis and Clark Trail. You know, those were the guys who made it possible for us to steal all this land from you and completely wipe you out. Isn't that wonderful?" Then he changed to his regular voice. "It's awful, isn't it?"

We pushed on, eventually making a little over one hundred miles for the day and one thousand since St. Louis. We didn't talk about the Native Americans and what'd been done to them. As on every other day, we hadn't the time nor, more importantly, the energy. Nor did we celebrate having reached a quarter of the way. We still had another thousand miles of river and lakes to cross. Then, there'd be the mountains to walk and ride horses over, and finally the rivers to navigate down to the Pacific Ocean. It was too daunting to consider.

As we set up camp on a flat-rock beach, both of us remarked how weak we felt. The ride in the boat had been bouncy and tiring, but I began to worry that there was another problem. We had oatmeal or grits for breakfast each day, granola bars, dried fruit and nuts for lunch, and either rice or pasta dinners. There was some protein in that but probably not enough. While I hadn't counted on Preston's hunting to provide meat, I had thought that we'd be able to catch enough fish to cover our protein needs. So far, I hadn't caught one. And our bodies ached, especially the lower backs.

I was happy, though, that we were getting along so well. We seemed to understand each other and Preston gave me plenty of room to make mistakes. I hoped I gave him as much.

After sitting by the campfire as late as possible—about nine-thirty—we crawled into the tent. Preston went first. As I inched my way in, he said, "Jesus, you smell like the maggots crawling out of that dead steer's ass! Keep your butt out there."

"I haven't done anything. Honest." I really hadn't. He'd been farting earlier from the beans and rice I'd made to give us some protein. It was a freeze-dried, packaged meal from a camping store, and the beans hadn't been cooked long enough by the manufacturer. "You're smelling yourself."

"Really?" he said, looking sheepish, although it was beginning to be difficult to see his face on account of the Vandyke beard he was growing. He then shouted out of the tent, "Who's out there making all that stench?" But we hadn't seen a soul since the last dam. The only answer he received was the call of coyotes a little later.

Preston was bitchy and snide the next morning. That was usually my role. Often, when he would be completing a task, I would make some negative comment, pointing out a mistake. But this morning, he ridiculed me.

After about an hour of running the engine, we stopped along the shore to fill the tank with gas and oil. We had made this a competitive chore because it was quite difficult to pour both the gas and the oil into the tank without spilling. We still didn't have a funnel. It was my turn. I carefully poured the oil in, not spilling a drop. But as I held the gas can in both hands, the tank slipped merely a few inches. About three ounces of gas spilled onto the side of the tank, then onto the log on which it was resting, and finally into the water.

"Oh . . . a minor environmental disaster," he, I believe, hissed.

I ignored him and finished filling the tank, but I felt awful about the spill. As we proceeded along the lake, past the sloping yellow-green hills, all I could think about was his insult. It hadn't been much of one, but it stung. We knew each other now and thus we knew where to strike. I became angry.

"That was pretty snide," I said after about an hour. I didn't need to say what I was referring to. He knew. "You're in a pretty bad mood."

"What?"

"You shouldn't take it out on me."

"You do it all the time." He had me there.

"I know, I know," I said after a bit of time had passed. That seemed to ease the tension.

"I've got a horrendous headache," he explained. "But the worst thing is that I miss Marina badly. I'm so homesick for her. I love her so much. I've fucked up so much in my life, but she's the one thing I've done right. And I don't want anything to go wrong with it. We've been together twelve years and I still feel the same way about her as I did when it all started."

I couldn't stay pissed at him after that.

We passed through the Crow Creek and Lower Brule Indian reservations without seeing anyone who lived there. As a matter of fact we didn't see any other people at all until noon, about ten miles south of Pierre, South Dakota. At that point, the water became crowded with fishing boats. Practically every one of them looked the same—two overweight men, grim faces, puttering along under the power of an electric motor, not deigning to wave in response to our greetings. On the lower Missouri, we'd devised a system of staring at unfriendly boaters with the binoculars; if they didn't wave, we'd binocular them, and sure enough, once those dark spyglasses were trained on the malcontent, a hearty wave would be signaled our way. But there were simply too many of these unfriendly fishermen. Our only recourse was to speed by them, creating as much of a wake as possible to shake them out of their unfriendliness. Luckily, none of them chased us down.

After navigating through a myriad of sunken trees, some of which had exposed tops while others stood hidden just beneath the surface, patiently waiting to rip *Sacky* to pieces, we reached Oahe Dam. It was our fourth dam in four days. While we'd had some assistance on two of the other dams, they were still mentally and physically exhausting. We weren't looking forward to this one; it was the largest of them all. The Lake Oahe brochure explained that the main section of the dam was thirty-five hundred feet thick and that it could release three hundred thousand cubic feet of water per second—quite enough to send us hurtling back to St. Louis.

"There's no way we're getting this thing over that today," I said, but Preston looked determined. The manager of the marina on the south side of the dam told us that the Corps was supposed to help portage any boat traveling upstream that required assistance, and Preston was determined to find a Corps guy to assist us. He scoured the Downstream Recreation and Camp grounds, and within fifteen minutes he'd found us two unsuspecting Corpsmen—Russell and Paul.

He told them what we were doing. " . . . and we're pretty exhausted really—this being our fourth dam. The fellow in the Marina told us that you are required to help us out. We don't want to put you to any trouble, but we'd sure appreciate it." He was all sugar.

Paul was busy cleaning out a mucky, smelly fish-cleaning station while Russell stood by giving directions. Paul wielded a high-powered water hose. Heads and guts were strewn all over the place, and the pressurized water sent them flying out of sight.

"We'll be over to help you as soon as we're done here," Russell said, then pointed out a place that Paul had missed.

They drove us to the Lake Oahe entrance within half an hour, about a five-mile ride. It would have taken us a full, backbreaking day on our own. As it was, we didn't have to pull or carry a thing.

Lake Oahe. Wild Bill had warned us about this lake, and we'd been dreading its arrival ever since. "You've got to be on the lookout all time up there, yep," he'd said. "You could go off on that Cheyenne and never come back. And those waves!" After about forty miles the Cheyenne River meets up with Lake Oahe at an intersection that is nearly five miles wide. It would be nearly impossible to tell which was Oahe and which was the Cheyenne. To top it all off, Oahe is also the largest and longest lake of them all—231 miles running practically north to south. The wind would have ample opportunity to pick up speed and waves and, we imagined, based on the previous lakes, a virtual ocean of turbulence.

Down on the wharf, things looked bad. No boats braved the water and we could see plenty of whitecaps. The wind and the waves blew directly our way. The Corps claimed in its brochure that it had a tree-planting program "recognized by the National Arbor Day Foundation which honored the Omaha District with a 1982 Good Steward Award," but hardly a tree was in sight. What a shame; before the dams were built, they had adorned the entire river.

We hit the whitecaps after twenty minutes. The swells rose high above the gunwale. We estimated them to be four to five feet high, and their spray soaked us through. Their base seemed to be at least six feet thick. Preston steered and I had a knot in my stomach.

The wind gusted, nearly stalling us in the water. "Put on your life preserver," Preston ordered. After doing so, I held the tiller so he could strap his on as well. We'd been using them as cushions up to then, and as we bounced over the waves, I wished we had two more.

The bow lifted a few feet in the air. A strong gust had bullied it off the water's surface. Truly scared for the first time, I stretched across the bow, putting as much weight forward as possible. The gas cans and equipment jutted into all of my soft parts as we bounced along, but the bow stayed relatively low.

Neither of us spoke. I was concentrating on the storm, believing that by concentrating on it and nothing else I could keep it from ripping us apart. Preston was busy just keeping control of our direction. Suddenly, a huge burst of wind swept beneath the bow as we rode over a swell and the boat lifted well past forty-five degrees. Everything went sliding back toward Preston, including me.

"We've got to turn back," I screamed.

Preston didn't answer at first. He looked ahead. "All right, all right," he finally agreed.

"We had to retreat. I can't believe it, but we had to do it," Preston said once we had our backs to the wind and it appeared we were going to live. "Thank God we have these preservers."

Not once in two and a half years did Lewis and Clark ever retreat. We were failing them miserably.

We reached a safe cove within twenty minutes. It had been built by the Corps. We quickly found a protected area for our camp that was sheltered by young cottonwood trees. The tallest was fifteen feet, but densely packed, they blocked most of the wind.

We'd been told by the two Corps guys that two fronts were meeting. That was why the water was so rough. We could see the cold front to the northwest—dense low clouds—and the warm, moist front to the southeast. So far, the cold front was winning where we were, and I hoped it continued to do so. I didn't want another clash of two fronts.

After pitching the tent, I read aloud to Preston from Dr. Gill's *Pocket Guide to Wilderness Medicine*. For some reason, we were particularly interested in the chapter "Lightning Injuries." " 'Lightning is an awesome force,' " I quoted, " 'capable of generating up to three hundred thousand amps of current and two billion volts of electrical potential. That's enough power to shift a five-ton boulder or blast a Douglas fir into toothpicks. You can imagine what it can do to a human being.' " Dr. Gill then proceeds to debunk every known myth about lightning. I read them all to Preston. At the end of the chapter he provides a few lightning-avoidance techniques. These include staying out of tents, putting down metal objects, seeking refuge in an all-metal vehicle. "If you are in the open," he warns, "stay away from single trees, corn stalks, and haystacks. Find a dry cave or a ditch, and crouch down with your feet close together. Or lie curled up on the ground on a rubber or plastic raincoat."

Evidently, Preston noticed there were no dry caves or ditches near our camp because he immediately went down to the boat for the rubber tarp that holds the boat when it's deflated. "I really think we ought to follow those instructions," he said.

"You mean get out of the tent in the middle of a storm and sit on that mat?" I asked, somewhat incredulous.

"Yes." He stalked around our site looking for a suitable place to lay the tarp. I think he found one eventually. I prayed that the fronts would collide elsewhere.

Shortly after a quick dinner of rice-and-sauce, we headed into the tent. It was too cold and windy to stay outside. Preston sat cross-legged and began sewing a hole in his rain pants. Not wanting to read and having nothing to sew, I decided to take an inventory of Preston since he'd obviously become a main focus of the trip for me. His short, greasy auburn hair stuck straight out through the holes in his baseball cap. The cap itself was tilted far forward, though, and oddly, the hair in the back was matted down like drenched seaweed. His hands had become extremely scaly. They were dried-white and patchy. They looked a lot like Wild Bill's. His face was weather-beaten. It was purple, red, and cracking. His nose was peeling. His beard was darker but still full of gaps. He had no sideburns at all. A persistent callus had flared up on the bottom of his left foot. He'd ground it down with a pumice stone a number of times in the last week. He'd actually become obsessed with it: "I've got to keep it down or else . . ." He'd never explained what the "or else" was, but I imagined it to be fairly horrible—blood, pus, pain. I partly hoped he wouldn't be able to keep it contained; I'd get to perform surgery, being the team doctor.

He was wearing his black-and-red-checked wool shirt. It was identical to mine. He became embarrassed whenever we wore ours on the same day. His black cotton pants that had become stained and smelly from being worn nearly every day clung to his legs, and I wondered if he realized they were dampening his sleeping bag. But then again, so were his blue, heavy, always-wet running shoes, which were also encrusted with sand. And then I noticed his eyes. They were light green. No, they were blue. It was nearly impossible to tell. They were, I realized, much like Preston himself—not one thing.

After a little more than an hour, he showed me his sewing job. The tear had only been an inch long so I couldn't figure out what had taken him so long. But the sewing was perfect. There was no trace of the rip at all. I congratulated him. He looked embarrassed.

"I'm lying. That's the factory job. This is what I did," he said, displaying the pants again. The stitching was all out of whack and crisscrossed the seam spasmodically. But the hole was closed.

At that moment a dark beetle landed on my left hand. It was a Sandalid—an excellent flier that feeds on cicada nymphs. I couldn't figure out how it entered our tent since we were all zipped up. He seemed quite content, though, and even appeared to be sniffing the side of my pinkie. He stayed with us for the night.

NINE

- - - - - - -
Lightning Strikes

"We better get out those cold-weather clothes," Preston announced upon awakening the next morning. "It's going to be winter pretty soon." It was only the second week in September. He'd been saying this every single day since the third day of the trip, but for once he was correct. It was cold out—somewhere in the low forties.

My prayers had come true during the night. The cold front had won and no storm broke above our tent. But that was the problem. That cold front was still blowing. Now that it had pushed the other front out of its way, nothing checked it. The wind was blowing harder and the swells— well, the swells appeared to be even higher.

"It looks worse than yesterday," I said. "I think those swells are five feet high."

"Yep," Preston said. I'd wanted him to say more, like

maybe, "Well, Hod, you're right, by golly. It is worse. And there's no sense in our going out there. We don't have anything to prove. We both know we're brave, sturdy fellows. Let's just wait it out here." But he didn't. He looked up at the sky and then across the water. It was hard to see very far ahead because the wind was blowing into our eyes, causing them to water. "We better start practicing with the compass," he eventually said. "We might need to know how."

Once we were on the water, I revised my estimate of the swells' height. They felt more like six feet. And this wasn't even on the north-south section of the lake. We were still in the curved part at its beginning. I was running the boat, and like a fool, I went as fast as possible—dodging higher swells, slowing the engine at the last minute, letting us bounce along to irreparable kidney and back damage. Preston moaned aloud with every painful bang on the water but didn't say a thing. For two hours I drove in that manner, looking for Spring Creek—a Corps-built cove on the eastern shore that had a marina. We needed gas. And I stayed on the eastern side of the lake, as Wild Bill had suggested, even though the Cheyenne wasn't for another twenty-five miles. The marina was only fifteen miles from where we camped, but the wind was so strong we were only going eight miles an hour. After passing the inlet by mistake and heading up the wrong cove until it dead-ended, we backtracked and found the right one around 10:30 A.M. We both tumbled out of the boat, feeling as exhausted as if it had been a full day on the water.

"We made it!" Preston said only half-mockingly. After tying us to the dock, he filled the gas cans while I went to pay.

The Spring Creek Resort smelled pretty nice when I entered. The downstairs was just a convenience store, but I smelled bacon cooking. The odor had drifted down from above. And I heard people laughing up there. And the TV was on, too. They had it turned to CNN. It was too much. I went back outside to see how Preston was doing and to get a breath of fresh air. When I went back inside to pay—after he'd finished pumping—the old woman who'd been behind the counter was gone, and now a beautiful, buxom, blond-haired girl stood in her place. This was definitely too much. Preston came inside about then.

"All right, all right," I said, even before he'd spoken. "Maybe we should get something to eat here." I kept looking at the girl. All I wanted was to nuzzle up to her breasts and have her stroke my head, telling me everything would be okay—that the big bad storm wouldn't get me.

We bravely climbed the steps. Once upstairs, to our left waited the empty, cheerless dining area, but to our right, where all the gaiety and delicious scents began, was the bar. We went to the right. It was a well-lit room with large windows that afforded great views of the miserable day.

After we sat down, I drifted into a daze of satisfaction. We met most of the people in the bar, and they all oohed and aahed over our story. Some were drinking but most were eating breakfast. Working in the kitchen and the bar were the owners of the resort, John and Marlene Brakss, their son, Sean (who didn't seem to be doing much work), and Sarah Kringel, the beautiful blonde, who, it turned out, was only seventeen or so. At one point, after much flirting on Preston's, Sarah's, and my part, Sarah said to us when nobody else could hear, "I really admire what you two are doing. It's so adventurous." It was almost the exact same thing Melissa had said back at Boone Cave. If a person wanted to charm sweet teenage girls, Preston and I were definitely in the right racket.

For two solid hours we ate eggs, bacon, toast, coffee, orange juice, pancakes, and watched CNN. John kept making us extra helpings of pancakes on the house as he cautioned us about Oahe and the coming cold weather. He didn't think we'd make it to Montana before it became too cold to travel.

I didn't talk much except when Sarah was hovering over us—Preston and I babbled ceaselessly to her in our competition to outflirt one another—but Preston kept up a running dialogue with whoever was questioning us. He told some of our more harrowing stories. It paid off, too. An older man named Ed Robinson, with gray hair and a sunken chin, paid for our breakfast without telling us. "I've always wanted to do the trip you're making," he'd said. He was in Spring Creek for a few days of fishing.

When we were about to leave, Ed also offered to tow us a little more than five miles north. Considering how long and difficult it'd been in the morning, we gratefully accepted his offer. Then John emerged from the kitchen with an old fishing rod, giving it to us as a present. We'd mentioned that we'd lost our pole overboard in the high waves.

We said our good-byes. Sarah, I believe, looked deep into my eyes as she wished me good luck and a safe journey. She said the same to Preston, but I knew she was only humoring him. Ours was a true affection.

The weather was the same outside, and I was excited to see Ed's twenty-one-foot, 350-horsepower indoor motorboat. It had a covered, well-protected cabin.

As we puttered along against the wind and waves, Ed displayed all his modern equipment—sonar, global tracking, autopilot. I told him about the "proctologist and the gym teacher" having the same equipment to retrace the Lewis and Clark expedition. "This stuff is pretty good," he said, sweeping his hand over the control panel, "but the way you guys are doing it is the best."

He set the autopilot on and turned away from the tiller. "An old riverman once told me that more than three hundred and sixty-five steamboats lie buried beneath the river between Sioux City and St. Joseph. That's a lot of history."

"We can believe it," I said. "Before we reached these lakes, we got stuck so many times we lost count. Those sandbars are impossible to see."

"There's a trick to it," he said. "When you're in a suspicious area, send your wake ahead of you by sharply turning the boat and stopping. You can tell by how the waves act whether or not there's a sandbar." I recalled how the water had rippled over the sand whenever we'd been suddenly stuck, and knew what he was talking about.

"Of course," he went on, "it doesn't always work. I've had to dig myself off of countless sandbars. Those steamboats were something, though. They would dig their own channels when they were in shallow water. They'd just back them up and use the stern-wheel to dig their way out."

When we reached the island Ed wanted to fish around—he swore he could catch walleyes in those high seas, but it seemed doubtful—Preston and I hesitantly bid him farewell. It had been so intoxicating in his boat. We were all safe and warm there.

"Sort of makes you wish we had a better boat, huh?" I said to Preston. He gave a sad smile.

Preston drove first, cautiously. We'd agreed not to push it as I had earlier in the morning. We went about five miles an hour.

"Sarah was something," Preston said, beginning the inevitable conversation.

"Man, I just wanted to wrap myself around her," I said. "Those luscious breasts. Mmm!"

"I bet Sean has intense masturbation sessions over her," he added.

I became miserable, despite memories of Sarah or simply because of those memories. It was just as cold out, and no matter how slowly we went the spray kept bombarding us. It soaked us. Our rain suits sucked and we only had on tennis shoes.

For some reason, Preston chose to point out more things we needed to start doing. They included stirring up the fire in the morning, making more headway on good days, drinking more water, eating more food, and mooching off strangers. Maybe he was right about every single point, but I just didn't want to hear it.

I didn't respond.

Around three, we finally gave up on making more headway and pulled into another Corps-built cove. We'd only gone thirty-five miles, but we were both chilled to the bone. Preston rightfully insisted that we peel off all our wet clothes immediately after we tied *Sacky* to some large rocks. My stomach was hurting pretty badly, and soon enough I had a bad case of diarrhea.

Preston built a fire. "Days like this just show we've got to start using the compasses," he said as I came to join him by the fire.

"Listen," I snapped, "we'll each do what we want, you know what I mean?" I was in a very bad mood and it was easy to take it out on him. I was sick to death of his telling me what we needed to do. And as the day came to a close, I hated him more than anything. I'd completely forgotten how good I'd been feeling about him the day before. That no longer mattered.

After dinner, we sat around the fire drying our clothes and writing in our diaries. A lone, small bird began shrieking in a stand of shrubs about twenty yards away.

"*Shut up!*" I screamed.

"What, *you* are annoyed with nature?" he said with heavy sarcasm, irony, and bile. The bile probably wasn't truly there, but I was in no mood to debate the point in my head.

"Just that one," I said defensively.

He started chuckling then. God, I wanted to kill him. And then I noticed him madly scribbling in his diary. He was writing this whole episode down in his diary! Didn't he have anything better to write about? I wondered—ignoring all of the inane things I'd ever recorded about him. It was too annoying, I thought, that he was writing so extensively. Two writers on a trip was one too many.

I stayed in this mood for a few hours until the Pepto-Bismol tablets kicked in, and by eight the sky had cleared, the wind had abated, and the moon was shining brightly upon us. It even felt warmer. I didn't say anything to Preston, but I felt a little warmer toward him as well. Probably what had lifted my spirits was that one of his shoes had been burned as it dried before the fire. The inner pad that had been pulled out to dry as well was burned beyond recognition or use. The shoe, however, was salvageable. Preston said it was my fault, that it had been my job to watch the drying socks and shoes while he prepared dinner. Maybe it had been. I don't know. It was the only time since the first night that he'd cooked dinner. Maybe I had been too busy watching him to make sure he didn't mess up. My controlling instinct was in full force.

As we turned in for the evening, I noticed that my lower spine now hurt to the touch. That was not a good sign. And

I tried to ignore the fact that for the fourteenth night in a row my hands and fingers were swollen to about one and a half times their natural size.

The wind shifted again during the night, coming directly from the south.

"Preston, we finally have some good luck. Today'll be easy. All we have to do is get around this point, fight the wind there a little, and then it'll be smooth sailing," I boasted.

Neptune or some other god must've heard me. Things *were* easy—for about fifteen minutes—but once we turned southeast to get around that point, it felt like *The Poseidon Adventure*. Gust after gust blasted us, nearly to a standstill at times. That wasn't the worst of it. The swells were higher than ever and as thick as the length of our boat. I was so scared that I couldn't even complain and Preston was probably even worse—I was driving. But he didn't make a peep.

Without being asked, he stretched himself across the bow, and even with his weight we couldn't keep the boat down. We were bucked again and again. And when we came crashing down—usually into the side of another wave—gallons of water would come rolling over him.

The spray drenched me quickly enough, and although every wave soaked Preston, I was the one who started to shake from the cold. When he took over Pompy, he suggested we stop so I could warm up. And even though I protested—my mind had become mushier than usual—he started heading toward the shore, which was a mile away.

Thank God. For the very next minute, I punctured the boat.

My hand rested on a bungee-cord hook over the starboard pontoon. The hook faced down, into the rubber. At some point when we came crashing down off a wave, I must've pressed down too hard.

The pontoon was leaking fast. While I slowed the flow with my hand, Preston guided *Sacky* to the nearest beach.

He was doubly careful because the waves could now roll right into the boat on my side.

We made it ashore, but it took an hour to fix the leak. I was in the way, shivering and dripping water onto the hole. It couldn't dry. My fingers fumbled with the patch. I couldn't get it to stay in my hand. I was even having trouble ordering Preston around, mumbling more than usual. Finally, Preston suggested I go sit between the rocks to escape the wind.

I continued to shake and feel completely befuddled. We'd read the section on hypothermia in *Wilderness Medicine* recently, and I took some solace in recalling the distinction between mild and severe hypothermia. "The most reliable sign of mild hypothermia is shivering. But you must be sensitive to some of the more subtle signs, such as thick or slurred speech, confusion, difficulty keeping up with the group, and incoordination." For severe hypothermia, I'd have to quit shivering and probably piss in my pants. I kept shaking.

With me out of the way, Preston patched up *Sacky* in about ten minutes. Then, hidden behind a dune, Preston made us change into dry clothes and eat some sardines to generate heat. It worked.

Back on the water, our lives changed. We floated in the air with Tinker Bell and Peter Pan. What had been hard water and torturous winds now gave way to marshmallowlike waves and strong breezes at our backs. Nothing had changed, though, but our direction. We'd turned the bend and the wind literally pushed us north.

"I think we can make it to Mobridge today," Preston announced. We'd been planning on not reaching Mobridge, one of the few towns along Lake Oahe, until the following day. "And anyway, we've got to try. Who knows what direction this damned wind will be coming from tomorrow?"

So we pressed on and by seven that night we made it to the Mobridge campground, with less than a gallon of gas and fading light.

We spent the next day in town, eating a couple of hot, heavy meals. The wind had shifted during the night and was sweeping down from the north, directly in our path. Black clouds hovered over the area all day long. The farthest we could've gone that day was twenty miles, if we didn't flip over.

We washed our clothes and bought more groceries in town. We bought more contact glue (because it was obvious that we would be getting more holes in *Sacky*), pens, film for Preston, and food: sardines, tuna, beans, freeze-dried noodles-and-sauce, Ziploc bags, and hot sauce. Preston bought a wool hat at a thrift shop because his was lost. The hat was light blue and white and looked completely out of place above his bearded face.

We also bought trash bags to wear on the inside of our boots. Preston had tried out this technique the day before. I had howled with laughter at the sight of him, but his feet had stayed warm and dry all day.

Mobridge looked as if it were straight out of a western. Many of the buildings had those high fronts that seem as if nothing is behind. Everybody came to the downtown for business and eating. There was no local mall. And I actually saw tumbleweed blow along the highway as we rode back to our campsite in the back of a pickup truck. It came barreling along the road, skittering in front of us, and eventually came to a stop in a ditch. Preston had seen tumbleweed in California and wasn't much impressed. It was my first sighting.

That evening, I read aloud to Preston from *The Grizzly Bear* as we lay in the tent. It was our best book and we'd both become obsessed with grizzlies. He'd read to me a couple of other evenings. He'd performed willingly, merely wanting to share various good sections with me. I had to be cajoled into it.

In the scene I read, a young man and his girlfriend go camping in Yellowstone Park in the backcountry. They are warned not to camp because the weather is bad and the grizzlies are out: "As far as the young man was concerned, that settled it. He was damned if he would let some wimpy ranger or a rumor of bears stop him. Just to be on the safe side, however, and since there didn't seem to be anybody around, at the trailhead he strapped to his backpack's hip belt his tooled-leather holster with the big blue .357 magnum inside. . . . He felt better right away. This was against the law, and his girlfriend, although she didn't say anything, was obviously annoyed."

They have a terrible hike and become soaked in a cold stream. Neither of them sleeps well that night, hearing noises the entire time. In the morning, a mother bear and her cubs hear the man cursing. The cubs run toward the noise, never having seen a person.

"With a single peremptory huff and a furious slap to each cub's head, the mother grizzly puts an immediate stop to their curiosity. One cub bawls, and she bashes him again, and he falls obediently silent. She rises on her back legs and takes a few heavy steps forward, tilting her head to one side and sniffling . . . she smells man. With a quiet grunt to the cubs to go ahead of her, the mother grizzly races up the slope and over the ridge, and the three bears vanish into the shadows of the spruces."

Just before I fell asleep, Preston said, "I was praying that the guy would be eaten by the grizzly—that he'd try to pump her full with his .357 and then spaz out. Too bad."

By midafternoon the following day, Lake Oahe gave way to the Missouri again. There she was—twisting and turning, gurgling and breathing: alive as those damned lakes could never be. This happened ten miles beyond Ft. Yates, one of the other few communities along Oahe. I hadn't been happier in weeks. Where there had only been waves, a current now flowed. Barren, rolling hills gave way to tree-lined shores. Of course, we became stuck a few miles later, but it was more than worth it.

And there were animals. We came across one of those startling white pelicans with the yellow-orange beaks and black-tipped wings. It didn't fly very far away as we approached, so we followed it in the boat, cutting across the river. As we approached the second time, it merely paddled away, looking over its back at us. Preston fumbled with his camera bag, which had been stored away, protected from the water. The pelican continued to swim, instead of flying away. Its head looked all bald and worn out. I figured it was old and that was why it wasn't flying away. But then it began to fish—at least that's what we thought it was doing. White pelicans are more buoyant than brown pelicans and cannot go completely beneath the surface. It ducked its head underwater, once, twice, then looked back at us in a disgusted manner. Resigned, it finally flew away.

Something large floated downstream from where the pelican had been. It slowly rolled and shimmered in the water. It drifted alongside us. It was a dead two-and-a-half-foot-long fish. It was a carp. We both let out a groan.

"It was in its mouth the whole time. I can't believe we did this," Preston said.

"We're idiots," I added. The poor bird had caught a feast and had been holding it in its beak and throat the entire time we'd been harassing it for a picture.

"I hope he finds another one," Preston said.

We tried fishing ourselves a bit later. For more than an hour we slowly trolled along the river with some lures I'd bought in St. Louis. We had no luck.

I even tried fishing that evening at our campsite and still caught nothing.

Our campsite was a real one that night. We were not more than fifteen miles south of Bismarck, but it was our most natural site in a week. The Corps hadn't built it. It was just a clearing in some woods. There were owls, mice, bats, and bugs all around. Preston pointed out a spider that was missing a leg and labeled it a brown recluse. But then he'd been labeling everything a brown recluse ever since I'd read from the wilderness-medicine book.

After the sun set—a glorious sight because the moon rose simultaneously—a coyote bayed at the night. Another joined in and then another. Soon more than half a dozen were barking and crying all around us. It sounded as if they were within two hundred yards. We felt better. We named our site Camp Solace.

The next day on the river was heavenly. Preston and I

could actually hold conversations as we rode along instead of having to fight for our not-so-dear lives.

Preston told me about a restaurant he'd worked in in New York. He was an assistant cook. "That means I chopped up stuff and sometimes fried things. But it did give me my big, onetime meeting with Andy Warhol. It was Vitas Gerulaitis's—you know, the tennis player whose best ranking was maybe seventeen in the world—birthday. We had a cake for him. We didn't make it ourselves, of course. It would've been too much bother. As the party went on, they started taking pictures. The owner was having his picture taken with Vitas and Andy. They needed somebody to hold the cake and called me to do it. We were waiting for the picture to be taken and Andy says to me, 'That's a nice cake. Did you make it?'

" 'No,' I answered somewhat coyly, 'we don't make cakes here. But we do slaughter our own chickens.'" Preston stopped talking for a second and then went on to tell how he always squawked like a dying chicken whenever anybody ordered it. He said it was loud enough to be heard outside the building.

"But, Preston," I asked, "what about Warhol? What did he say back to you?"

"Oh . . . he laughed, I think."

The land resembled the lower Missouri more than anything else. It was flat along the river, covered with trees, vines, and bushes. There were turkey vultures and blue herons everywhere.

After passing through Bismarck and only staying long enough to buy gas, we stopped at Fort Mandan. We'd been looking forward to the fort for a few days.

Fort Mandan was built by the Lewis and Clark expedition to wait out the winter of 1804–5. It was named Fort Mandan in honor of the Mandan Indians they were living among that winter. Sacagawea joined the expedition there as the wife of a French Canadian trapper named Toussaint Charbonneau. Charbonneau himself was not much of an asset to the expedition and was nearly left behind when he claimed he was going as a free agent and would not be ruled by Lewis and Clark. They dismissed him, but "Mr. Chabonah Sent a frenchman of our party [to say] that he was Sorry," recorded Clark, "for the foolish part he had acted and if we pleased he would accompany us agreeably to the terms we had perposed . . . we called him in and Spoke to him on the Subject, he agreed to our tirms and we agreed that he might go on with us." Considering the role Sacagawea would play in the success of the expedition, it is a good thing that "Char Bono," as Preston and I called him, wised up.

The fort is not marked along the river and we had to scan the shoreline for nearly ten miles before we happened upon it. And we were in for a big surprise.

First of all, it was only a replica. That was understandable. The inexcusable part was that it was nowhere near the original site, which was more than ten miles upriver from the replica.

We first entered the "gift shop"—a shack—because that was where the gap-toothed woman managing the fort led us. We told her what we were doing, but she was completely unimpressed. The proctologist and the gym teacher—the guys in the jet boat—had been there during the summer and swept her off her feet. She showed us pictures of their boat, as well as the support van pulling the canoes and bikes. "Those men were important," she told us. There was a weathered buffalo head on a wall selling for $1,150 and an antelope next to it. Another wall had a mounted beaver, and a deer looked out from a third. Lewis and Clark did send specimens to Jefferson, but somehow all of these dead animals seemed out of place with the spirit of the expedition. They certainly had nothing to do with our trip, and they weren't from Lewis and Clark's day.

The replica looked much like the original fort with twelve-foot-high walls and ten rooms on the inside. One of the rooms housed two bullboats made by a twelve-year-old local girl. Constructed of buffalo skins, they were about the only authentic things around. Native Americans had used these round, quick-made boats for centuries for short outings on the river. They were usually made and used by women and girls.

The walls of another room were covered with graffiti: "I love Swenk, Dyke from Hell," "Nicole B. loves big dicks," and my favorite one, "Jerome is gay, He fucked Preston."

We'd been planning on sleeping in the fort, but since it was so depressing, we continued up the river for another two hours and found an isolated but well-forested island. We hit many sandbars on the way as well as a large log. Our propeller was bent out of shape, and Preston worked on it while I set up camp. His good deed didn't pay off, though, because I saw something magnificent.

I stood between two sand dunes, apparently well-hidden by them and the tiny cottonwoods that stood all around. A large hawk swooped down within six feet of my head. At first I thought it was after me, then I saw the tiny sparrow it was chasing. I followed the hunt for a full minute. The sparrow got away.

The hawk had an orangish underbelly, black wings on top, a blackish gray head, and a white stripe near the middle of its tail. According to *Grasslands*, an Audubon Society nature guide, it was a northern harrier. It is on the Society's Blue List, which means it is in a state of decline. Roughly twenty American birds are Blue Listed right now—the harrier because of pesticides and loss of habitat.

Emboldened by this sighting, I went looking for scat. It had been so long since we'd camped at a place with animals. I quickly came across a dish-shaped turd that was lumpy and about one-half inch thick. It appeared to be made of numerous Hershey's Kiss–shaped droppings that had dried together. Prints of some canine were all around it. Yippee!

I flipped through my tracking book to identify what it might be, but as I did so, something else on the ground caught my eye. Right beside the dog tracks were human footprints. And I realized that the scat was most likely either a domesticated dog's or even worse—the human's. I went back to our campsite, a defeated naturalist.

We did finally live off the land that night, though. A few miles before we reached our campsite, we had beached *Sacky* beside some cornfields. Preston scaled the bank and came back a few minutes later with half a dozen ears of corn. It was juicier than any other we'd found so far but was still feed corn. Since he'd picked it, however, we decided to eat it anyway.

It was delicious. "This is hearty stuff," Preston said. "I love it." It was the same corn I used to eat every week while in Kenya as a Peace Corps volunteer. At first I found it odd that the Kenyans preferred their tough white corn. They hated the imported "yellow maize" from the United States. It was even rumored that the American corn was full of contraceptives to make the African men less virile and that it was animal feed. I tried explaining that just the opposite (about the animal feed) was the truth. That we only fed the tough, dry corn to our animals and that they should grow the sweet, juicy kind. I never succeeded and I soon began to love their corn instead. I eventually came to realize that the "feed" corn made much more sense as a crop there because of the harshness of the weather.

Nearly everything worked that way while I was in Kenya.

Preston had begun waking up first in the morning, and the next day was no different. He also made his usual announcement: "I've got one working. I can feel it." Shits had become a major topic of discussion, and we often described them. Mine were always identical to his. The odd thing, I thought, was that Preston always had to go even as he lay on the ground; he didn't need to move around, eat some granola, or drink some coffee. He simply woke up and it was waiting. He'd never have to worry about colon cancer, at least.

It was cool that morning but at least it wasn't freezing. We reached the dam for Lake Sakakawea (the North Dakota spelling) by midmorning. It was sad to say good-bye to the river.

I believed I knew the shortest way around the dam and

so Preston followed my orders. First I had us carry all the equipment—in two shifts—more than a mile along a dirt and then paved road that went around the east side of the dam. Preston then hooked up the harness and we began towing the boat. More than a dozen cars passed without even a wave. We eventually started cursing them. North Dakota was not a friendly state.

Couldn't they see that we were two valiant adventurers who would condescend to accept assistance from local villagers?

Finally, a man in a beat-up van pulled to a stop. We had not had the chance to curse him. He asked us where we were going.

"Around the dam," I answered, a little short.

"Well, you've gone about a mile and a half the wrong way. It'll take you forever to get there this way. Let me help you," he said. What a good fellow, I thought.

His name was Mel Herman and he had a big belly. He looked as if he hadn't bathed in days. We were definitely in good company.

He swung open the back door to his van. I was so excited I yanked the boat forward, trying to wedge it in too quickly. The front pontoon hit the edge of the door, which was rusty and, as it turned out, quite sharp. That horrible sound of air escaping through rubber broke the morning's silence. The bow deflated in seconds.

Preston and I had to patch it up right then because we couldn't even make the boat stay on the tailgate without any air in the bow. I apologized to Herman for how long it was taking.

"What are people for," he said, "if not to help each other? I've got all the time in the world, anyway. Just the day before yesterday, I got some gastritis." He paused and rubbed his stomach. "I went to the doctor about it and it turned worse. The doctor said a hernia had developed from all the pressure of the gastritis. I just got out of the hospital last night. And the doctor said to take it easy for a while, and there's nothing easier than helping you two. You're doing all the work."

"We were beginning to get worried about North Dakotans," Preston told Herman as he was driving us around to the other side. "People don't wave to us on the water and nobody stopped to ask what we were doing until you came along."

"Well, I guess we're pretty independent. People don't mess in each other's business," Herman explained. "I once lived in the East—in Philadelphia. I had enough of that in six months. I cleared out of there."

"It was that bad?"

"I couldn't understand why people weren't allowed to carry guns. Young punks would shoot somebody in a robbery, and all those city people didn't give a damn. They just stayed in their apartments. If I could've had my guns, I would've done something. But people in the city just don't care. If they did, they'd all own guns. If all the good people had guns, they could clean up the city in just a couple of weeks, isn't that right?"

"Well, uh, it just wouldn't work that way . . . ," I began.

"I'm not a racist or anything, but those blacks just don't know how to raise their kids. They don't have good family values," Herman blurted out.

"It has more to do with the conditions they've been forced into," Preston said. "If I were living in the inner city, you can bet I'd be doing the same thing."

But Herman didn't see it as an environmental thing. He went on and on about cleaning up the cities with guns. Preston and I both eventually tuned him out until he dropped us off at Lake Sakakawea.

We had to repatch the new hole arguing about which method would be better—a large patch or a small one that barely covered the hole. First we tried it Preston's way and then we tried it mine. As it turned out, neither worked because we couldn't give the patch enough time to settle. It leaked around the edges, so we smeared Shoe Goo all over the patch. This slowed the leak but didn't stop it. We were both happy to note that Shoe Goo had only been shown to cause cancer in California.

A lightning storm chased us all afternoon across the

lake, but we were able to stay ahead of it thanks to a fortu-
itous tailwind. It was clear we had the storm beat by five,
and the water calmed down to a glassy, flat surface.

"This is how I always pictured these lakes to be," Preston
said. "I imagined flat lakes that we would just mow across
and bikini-clad women skiing in circles around us. We'd
mooch some food and drinks. Get a tow now and then." I'd
imagined the same.

"It smells like fish," I told Preston. "Let's give it a try." We
could see things breaking the surface all around us. Preston fished while I captained the boat, trolling at the slowest
possible speed. He caught a shiny, silvery fish in about five
minutes. It was slightly more than a foot. I caught one next
and then he snagged another. They were biting lures we'd
bought at the last marina.

Later, I fried them up in pancake batter for dinner, scoring them first, just as Wild Bill had told me. They were extremely bony, but neither of us thought we'd ever had
better-tasting fish.

Our campsite that night was in a steep ravine that came
straight down from the hills that towered over the lake. The
hills were different here. They were beautiful, stratified
with red, white, and yellow layers. Thick bushes of sagebrush covered the lower slopes. They even had trees on
them, evergreens mostly. I climbed one of the hills. The
ground was made of clay and petrified wood. Deer droppings dotted the ground. It was altogether much prettier
than South Dakota.

Around midnight, I woke Preston. The tent was quaking
and bending and the lightning was within one mile according to my count. He'd been sleeping through the entire
storm.

"Hod, we've got to get out of the tent. That book said so,"
Preston said. I cursed myself for ever having read aloud
from the wilderness-medicine book. The section on lightning had explicitly stated that one must get out of a tent
during a thunderstorm and rest on a rubber or plastic mat
far away. Preston had taken it to heart.

"What?"

"I brought the rubber boat-cover up. We can lay it down on that flat area."

"You think we have to?" He was already putting on his rain gear. Fear made me follow him—nothing else. I got dressed, and for half an hour we squatted in the rain and wind as lightning struck the hills around us. Our useless rain gear did no good as usual, and we were soaked to the bone.

And as the worst of the storm blew over, I decided that next time I would rather stay in the tent and die, especially since the tent remained untouched by the electrical storm.

We stopped in New Town to buy gas the next day. There was no town, only a few trailer homes. And there wasn't a soul about, except at the marina.

"I wouldn't go out on that lake today," the shopkeeper told us. "It's bad out there. The wind's blowing over thirty-five miles per hour." We thanked her for her advice but said we were on a mission.

Curious about the fish we'd eaten, I described them to her.

"Those were either silver bass or shiners," she said.

"Probably shiners, whatever those are," I said. "I think I can identify bass."

"I don't think it was shiners. We never eat those. They're pretty bad."

"What do you mean bad? Bony?"

"Yeah."

They were definitely shiners. They'd only tasted so good because of Wild Bill's recipe.

PART 2

A CAR HELPS

TEN

- - - - - - - - - - - - - -

When You Have Nothing Else to Eat, You Eat the View

"We respect our elders not because they're old and feeble but because they've walked all those years," Anson Baker Sr. said on the radio of our shiny blue Dodge Dynasty. Baker himself sounded like an elder, speaking calmly with the heaviness of many years past. "We have a saying: Do not criticize another until you've walked in his moccasins for seven days and seven nights." He was reading a prepared statement to his fellow members of the Three Affiliated Tribes near Williston, North Dakota. He wanted their votes for three councilmembers in the coming elections. It might have been mere politics, but if so, he fooled Preston and me. We sat mesmerized by his voice.

Having our own car with heat and air-conditioning might also have played a role in our trance. It was two days later, September 15. Our plans had changed dramatically.

We'd fought the lake for the rest of the day after learning

about the shiners. Mostly, we'd lost—lightning and hailstorms tore into us. The morning after, we rose early to beat the wind on the lake and were heading west by seven. The swells were already fairly high, but we hugged the shore like the previous day and reached Lewis and Clark State Park—thirty-five miles away—by ten. There was supposed to be a dock, but it was pulled far up onto the bank. We'd hoped to buy gas there but the marina was closed down. And the cove leading into the marina was completely dried up.

We returned to the lake, headed for Williston, which was only thirty-five miles away. The water had calmed down considerably. This was odd because the lake wasn't supposed to turn back into the Missouri until Williston. But we weren't complaining; the ride was smooth.

Within a few minutes, Pompy started bucking in the water, hitching up and shaking every few minutes. Since I didn't want Preston fiddling with him—he'd want to take him apart to show off his mechanical skills, I thought—I didn't say anything. We kept going.

About ten minutes later, we suddenly came to a halt as Pompy reared out of the water whining to a deafening pitch. I looked back and there was a mile-long trail of muddy wake behind us. We'd been churning up mud the entire time Pompy'd been shaking. Preston stuck a paddle into the lake. It went deep, all the way up to the handle.

So why were we stuck?

"It's not water, Hod," Preston explained, and then he strained to pull the paddle out of the water. What was this? Maybe he was playing with my head. He knew I was always worried that something awful would happen to our adventure, some unforeseen catastrophe. He finally lifted the paddle up, though, and it was covered with slick, gooey mud. I'd stubbornly motored us right into the middle of a mudflat.

We tried to paddle toward the shore, which was more than a mile away. No way. *Sacky* didn't budge ten yards after ten minutes of paddling. Preston then attempted to pole us off the mudflat with one of the long oars. The oar merely sank deeper and deeper into the mud. We were stuck.

"Why don't you try walking us out of here?" I suggested. He had on his tennis shoes, which were already wet from the day before. Mine were dry. That was the excuse I told myself, at least. He consented.

He slid off the bow on his stomach to ease his way in. And he kept going until only his head was above the mud/water. A sickening look of utter horror streaked across his face. I dove from the stern toward his hands, which were slipping off the bow, but before I could reach him he found the bow line and held himself steady. With my pulling and his scrambling, we eventually got him back into the boat.

"Good idea," he said.

There was no bottom.

We sat there for a while, but no one came to rescue us. And now that we had to think about it, we realized we hadn't seen a boat for two days.

Preston suggested raising Pompy so that the propeller was barely in the mud/water. The first couple of inches were mostly water. It worked, but silt shot through the water pump and the going was extremely slow. This wasn't good. We eventually found an area with more water. It was a few feet from the shore and only lasted a hundred yards.

For three hours we crisscrossed the lake in front of the Lewis and Clark State Park, looking for the true channel through the mudflat. We both believed there had to be one. There wasn't.

Giving up, we went back to the park. The ranger's husband, Frank, filled us in: "I haven't seen a boat go up there in over a month." He was fed up with the Corps. "This is the lowest the water's ever been. It's dropped twenty-five feet in the last six years. It's the Corps of Engineers' fault. They've drained all the water out of here so those towboat companies can run on the lower Missouri. We've got a lawsuit against them. I think every state up here does."

"I don't understand how it can be so low, even if they are letting out too much water. There's been so much rain this summer," I said, showing my ignorance.

"It's not the rain that matters. It's how much snow they get in Montana in the mountains. There was hardly any last winter. The Corps should've kept it here instead of releasing it all for the barges. But I guess money has its power."

We were lucky we'd made it as far as we did. The park was closing the next day. Frank led us to a campsite. He'd told us there was no way we could make it to Williston by water, and so we planned to stay the night.

I called the Corps to find out if they'd be releasing the water in Montana anytime soon, and if not, I asked them if they could tow us through to the other side of Ft. Peck Dam. It was a couple hundred miles away. "Absolutely not," was the exact answer. "It's against every regulation to assist boaters in that manner." The Corpsman also told me that even their jet boat wasn't able to travel on the upper Ft. Peck Lake (where we were headed) and that it would be impossible for us to travel up the Missouri any farther. "You can try and put in at James Kipp Landing, but from what I understand there isn't enough water there for a canoe. Even the paddlefish aren't getting through."

I didn't tell Preston the part about there not being enough water for a canoe or paddlefish and that it was impossible to go any farther. I just said we should find a way to get to James Kipp Landing. I knew it was deceitful, but sometimes you have to omit some truths to keep up team morale. Lewis and Clark had probably done it countless times.

There was only one problem. The James Kipp Landing was about three hundred miles west of where we were and we had seven hundred or so pounds of equipment. Hmmm.

We needed a real Sacagawea. As I mentioned earlier, she was a great asset to the expedition, especially when they reached the Continental Divide and ran into her brother. He provided—at a cost—the team with horses and a guide. Sacagawea also helped feed the expedition as well.

Within the first few days of her joining the expedition, Lewis wrote, "When we halted for dinner the squaw busied herself in serching for the wild artichokes which the mice collect and deposit in large hoards. this operation she performed by penetrating the earth with a sharp stick about some small collections of driftwood. her labour soon proved successful, and she procured a good quantity of these roots."

That was what we needed: a good woman to show us the way. I called the only person I knew who lived anywhere near the Lewis and Clark Trail: Temple Richardson in Livingston, Montana. Temple and I had worked together in New York and had even thrown a red-beans-and-rice party together once. She was a pure city girl, raised in Chicago and made for New York. She would be dying for company and would do anything to see an old friend.

"It's about time I heard from you. I have letters and maps waiting for you here. When am I going to see you?" That was the first thing she said to me. I could almost see her blond hair shining and her smile spreading from ear to ear just because she was about to see us.

"It's funny you ask that, Temple," I said, and then I briefly recounted our escapades and present predicament.

"Hah!" she screamed out. "Hey, John, guess what happened to these bozos. They ran out of water." She was all heart. "Some Lewis and Clark you two make. Using a motor to get up the river."

I let it all slide over me. I had forgotten how sarcastic she could be.

"Do you know anyone who would be willing to come get us and take us farther up the Missouri—to the Wild and Scenic section in Montana?"

"How much you willing to pay?"

Pay? Did Sacagawea ask for payment?

"Maybe fifty?" I offered.

"Hah!" This definitely wasn't going as planned.

"Well, could you do it?" I finally asked.

"You're crazy. I'm not driving over three hundred miles to see your sorry butt . . ." She went on and on from there. I stopped listening really. At one point I said, "I'll write about you someday," and she started laughing even harder.

We'd had plans to meet in October along the river, and I told her we'd still be there on time, no thanks to her. But there was no making her feel guilty.

We had to switch to Plan B. The next morning, after long showers in which we shaved and made ourselves slightly presentable, we hitched into Williston. It was less than thirty miles by road, but it took us more than two and a half hours. For nearly two of those hours not a single car stopped. Only two dozen went by, but still, it was shocking that all those cowboy-hat-wearing Dakotans were too chicken to pick us up.

One woman in a blue station wagon finally pulled over for us. Was it my hands clasped in prayer or Preston's blatantly displaying his camera (we thought that'd make us resemble tourists)? She lowered her window two inches.

"Is anything wrong?"

"Well, we ran out of water on the river. We're trying to get to Williston so we can rent a car."

She had a cute little daughter in the front seat.

"I'm awfully sorry. I'm afraid I can't take you. I've got my daughter to think about. But do you have someone I could call?"

As she drove away, Preston said, "You can't blame her. Look at us." He had a point. He looked like a psychotic killer and I guess I looked the same. His Vandyke beard was his most sinister feature.

Finally, a farmer named Lawrence Urban picked us up in his rusty old Pinto. His car was full of flies, but he didn't pay any attention to them. I swatted at a couple to see out the windows.

"I picked up a fellow who was hitchhiking through here last year. He was going across the country that way," Lawrence said. "We don't get very many hitchhikers around here."

After being asked what he did for a living—farming—he told us about his favorite hobby. "I grind rocks. I make them into smooth balls and things like that. I've done thousands and have used rocks from all over the world. That woman at the *Williston Herald* wrote all about me. She was a good writer."

We eventually told him what we were doing. He suggested taking us to the paper: "They'll definitely want to write about you two." Since he was driving, we let him take us there but said we weren't really interested.

Lawrence told a young reporter what we were doing and then she came over to us. The newspaper's offices were in an old brick building and looked disheveled enough for it to be a good local paper. I began to think it might be fun to be interviewed.

"So you two are retracing the Lewis and Clark Trail?" she asked. "To tell you the truth, we've done a lot of these river stories. We had two guys come through here last summer in a jet boat, and then last month I did a story on a kayaker who was going down the Missouri. But let me go ask my editor." She came back a few minutes later saying she could write a small story on us in about an hour. We told her we'd return after eating breakfast.

Lawrence left us then, happy we were to be written up, and we hitched to the car-rental place. Once there we decided to blow off being interviewed, considering the lack of enthusiasm. We had some pride.

After renting the car, we drove back to the Lewis and Clark State Park to load up all of our equipment. That was when we heard Anson Baker, Sr., talking about the importance of elders to the Three Affiliated Tribes.

This was our plan: we would drive everything to James Kipp Landing in eastern Montana. After spending the night there I would drive the car back to Williston (a 650-mile round-trip), and then I would hitchhike back to Preston the same day.

Besides the whole hitchhiking ordeal, the only difficult equation in all of this would be my fast.

Mr. Baker had reminded me of a goal I'd had for nearly half my life. I'd always wanted to go on a vision quest since first reading about them in a high school class on Native Americans. In all Great Plains tribes and many others, an adolescent boy would complete a three-to-four-day fast in the wilderness in search of a vision. It was his initiation into manhood. His fasting experience determined his image of himself in the physical world, and it usually meant a new name. After the fast, the boy would return to his people and a medicine man or elder would interpret his vision. A man might seek many more visions throughout his life, whenever he was in need of answers or spiritual cleansing. The spirits that come in a vision bestow some of their powers upon the seeker.

I was well past the right age for a first vision quest but was young in spiritual years. Maybe it would still work. Since we were in the Great Plains, I had to give it a try. As we drove toward Montana, I told Preston I would begin my fast that night, after supper. After the third day of fasting I would leave our camp for the night and climb the tallest hill to seek a vision.

In an uncharacteristically serious manner Preston turned to me while driving. "Hod, I have to tell you. I think that's really stupid. You're already exhausted from everything we've been doing. It shows more and more each day. And for three weeks we haven't been eating enough food. This isn't the right time."

"I'm going to do it anyway."

We were both silent for a long while. I didn't think about it at the time, but I was certainly being quite selfish, treating him as if he were a private and I was Captain Lewis or Clark.

"But Preston," I eventually said, "you get to interpret any hallucinations or spiritual dreams that I have. You're the one that has to give me my vision-quest name. You're my shaman."

He brightened considerably. "Oh, good. I actually love to interpret dreams and I can't wait to name you. Like that dream you had the other night. You know, the one in which I didn't want to have sex with those women but you did want to but didn't do it in the end? I think that means you actually trust my decisions—despite most evidence—or at least some of them. And that incest dream you had last night? It means you want to sleep with me."

This wasn't exactly what I had in mind, but he was all I had. It was my destiny.

We covered more than three hundred miles that afternoon. In the boat it would have taken four days. We caught sight of the Missouri sporadically. It was low. We could see mudflats and sandbars everywhere. There were no deep channels. It was sad not to be on it, though, and I couldn't help but feel as if we'd failed. I buoyed my feelings by reminding myself that it was late in the year. We wouldn't be able to cross the mountains by foot if we stayed and slugged it out with the low river. The snow would be too high. And the river was only going to get lower, according to the Corpsman I'd talked to.

Paul Harvey blared out of the radio. I hadn't heard him since I was a kid, and I'd sort of liked him back then. It took me a minute but I finally realized that he was doing a commercial for Total cereal. He was using the same voice and style as his news and was presenting the cereal information as if it were facts. And when he returned to the "news," I realized that Paul Harvey was not worth liking. I hadn't known how much of a slant he put on everything. He stated that car sales were down, and in the same breath he stated as a fact that it was because people were waiting for the new models to come out. He was maddening.

I didn't calm down until we saw the herd of sixteen pronghorn standing two hundred yards from the road. I hadn't even known there was such a thing as an American antelope, but there they were. They had adorable little white butts and ran away from us in a straight line—one right after another. They picked up incredible speed within seconds and no wonder; they are the fastest animal in the Western Hemisphere, able to reach 70 mph and sustain 35 mph for long periods of time. My tracking book explained that the pronghorn has "no dewclaws and therefore has the most streamlined foot of all, with the exception of the single-toed horse." Lewis and Clark had called them goats (thus their Latin name, *Antilocapra americana*) and had first seen them in North Dakota. Back then, though, they were plentiful. "Soon after I discovered great numbers of Goats in the river," Clark recorded on October 16, 1804, "and Indians on the Shore on each Side, as I approached or got nearer I discovered boys in the water Killing the goats with sticks and halling them to Shore, Those on the banks Shot them with arrows and as they approachd. the Shore would turn them back of this Gangue of Goats I counted 58 of which they had killed on the Shore."

Pronghorns no longer abound. Our guns had been a lot more effective than the Indians' methods.

From Clark's description I imagined the running of the pronghorn had once been akin to the annual migrations of the wildebeests in the Serengeti, in which millions of those gangly animals come charging through the same area year after year, even drowning each other in various crossings of rivers and streams.

My last meal was at the Hitchin' Post in Malta, Montana, that evening. We'd been looking for a place with buffalo meat, thinking such a meal would be fitting for a vision quest, and the Hitchin' Post had seemed a likely spot. Also it was one of two restaurants we'd seen the entire day. The other one had been more than a hundred miles back. As it turned out, the Hitchin' Post only served beef steaks. We ate there anyway.

"I'm glad I don't have to be with you tomorrow," Preston said as we stuffed our faces. "They say the first day is always the worst."

I was pretty grumpy the next morning. The James Kipp Landing was right beneath the highway, and the road noise kept us awake most of the night. Also, every once in a while some idiot would veer off the highway and come cruising through the campground. This happened all night long.

Preston gave me some last-minute advice about hitchhiking, which mainly consisted of not entering the car of anyone who looked too weird. He also suggested that I keep a knife in my pocket.

The drive back to Williston, North Dakota, was simple and fast. Not being with Preston was odd, though. The longest we'd been apart in the last three weeks had been about half an hour. I missed him. That seemed even odder.

I was out hitchhiking for the return by one-fifteen. My stomach was beginning to grumble. I tried drowning it with water. For one full hour, nobody stopped. Three weeks of sleeping outside was definitely not good for catching a free ride. And then a guy in a beat-up old red Mirada started waving frantically at me, pointing toward the side of the road. He seemed to be yelling at me as well, but I couldn't hear him because his windows were rolled up. What the hell, I thought, and shot him the bird. I'd had enough of these people. He pulled all the way off the road and stopped. I walked in the other direction.

"Hey," he called. "You need a ride?" At first I didn't answer. This guy might be crazy. I kept walking. He called again. I walked toward him for a better look. His car was filled to the ceiling in the back with all sorts of junk. But I saw a pair of skis and he was wearing a beige fishing hat—like some old grandfather. Do psycho-murderers of hitchhikers travel with skis and grandfatherly hats? I wondered. And quickly decided not. It just didn't fit together.

I climbed into his car, but as he drove erratically onto the highway, I began to regret my decision. He had no control over the car and it jerked from side to side, constantly crossing the traffic lines.

The Book of the Vision Quest, a frighteningly New Age guide by Steven Foster, advises all questers, "It is important that you realize you are ceremonially free to bury, burn, smash, change your name, bathe, vow, draw blood, cut your hair, heap stones, chant, rattle . . . or behave in any other way that is meaningful to yourself."

So I worried.

He was dressed in faded blue jeans, a checked shirt, and pseudo-Birkenstocks. Could I trust this guy? As he told me where he was heading—clear across Montana and then up to Canada—I continued to inspect him. He had yellow, chipped teeth and dirty salt-and-pepper hair where his hat wasn't covering. He was wiry and short—too much like a spring ready to pounce. He was chain-smoking Marlboros.

"I only drive fifty-five. That's it. Don't want to attract the cops," he was saying as I tuned back in. Why didn't he want to attract the cops? He asked me where I was going. I said I was meeting up with my buddy in Malta, although Preston was at James Kipp. I didn't want this guy knowing exactly where I was going. Could I jump out of a car going 55 mph and survive well enough to run away after a short tumble?

He talked and talked as we drove along. Sam was a Canadian from northern Ontario and was heading out to British Columbia for the winter, where he was a ski instructor. He was driving through the United States because gas and cigarettes were cheaper here. He lost $200 in a casino the night before on a reservation in Minnesota. "I was doing fine until I started drinking all those beers, and then my money slowly crept away. I was up until 4 A.M. trying to win it back. Which reminds me of going out to Las Vegas last spring with my dad and uncle. My dad died of a brain tumor in June, and he'd just been diagnosed in March. I tell you, when my time comes, that isn't going to happen to me. I'm going to say my good-byes, write some letters, and then I'll end her. I wanted to give him a morphine overdose and that's what I want. Quick and easy, aye? And my uncle. I couldn't believe it but he had that priest give my father his last rites. My dad was a lifelong atheist, just like me. He wouldn't have wanted that done. I wanted to stop him but I knew my uncle needed it."

Oddly enough, I was beginning to like this man. Sam was incredibly straight, and eventually he let on that some of his craziness might have been exaggerated. "You can't be too cautious when you're picking up hitchhikers and hitchhiking. You have to circle the truth and exaggerate some," he advised me. Eventually he returned to his Las Vegas gambling story to say that it was a great treat for his dad. "It was the best time. Last of the big spenders, we were. Living high and mighty," he said, and laughed softly.

He dropped me off in Malta, Montana, where I had to start heading south to meet up with Preston. I asked him what his last name was and his address so I could send him a postcard when I finished the trip. He hesitated a bit and finally said his full name was Sam Inch, then gave me an address in British Columbia. It wasn't too clear if he was telling the truth.

It was after 5:30 P.M. by then. Not only was I starving but it looked as if I would be camping alongside the road for the night. It was ninety miles to Preston and the James Kipp Landing. Hardly any cars passed for more than an hour, and those that did were filled with cruising teenagers. Surprisingly, none of them threw anything at me. Just as I was about to give up and look for a hill to pitch my tent behind, a minivan pulled over. It was nearly seven.

John McClaren was the driver. He was a displaced Californian and dressed the part in a blue-and-white flowered shirt, hiking shorts, and real Birkenstocks. John was living in Billings, Montana, now and serviced ultrasound machines throughout the state. He missed California. I tried building up Montana in his mind to kill the time, telling him there was plenty of wildlife to see in the state and certainly enough mountains to hike in the western part. He agreed but thought the people simply weren't the same. They were too distant in Montana.

We saw deer and pronghorn before the sun set. I was falling in love with those antelope and hoped to see more and more of them. I told John everything I'd read about them, pretending I was an expert.

When we were only a few miles from James Kipp, John told me why he wasn't too worried about hitting any deer. He had devices on his van to scare them off. "They're ultrasonic whistles so the deer don't come running out. They hear those things and run away. I'm just afraid it's going to happen anyway one day."

Either he shouldn't have bragged about the whistles or he shouldn't have doubted them. It's hard to say which did him in, but the very next minute, a huge stag darted out in front of us. John swerved and slammed on the brakes, but he couldn't avoid the collision. My side of the van smashed directly into him.

John pulled over. "Do you think he ran off?" he asked me since we couldn't see him on the road.

"No," I said, holding back nervous laughter. The impact would probably have killed a dinosaur. We'd been doing sixty-five. "He's probably back on the side of the road somewhere. But you'd better come take a look at this." The passenger door was crunched in more than half a foot, and the grill was torn to bits as well. Even the fender was dented.

"I can't believe this happened. I'm going to have nightmares tonight. This is awful," he blurted out. "What should we do?"

"We should go back and check on it. Make sure it's dead." Poor deer. We found it within a few minutes about fifty yards back. Its neck was snapped and he'd died instantly.

John drove me the last mile to James Kipp very subdued, only going 45 mph. Preston had a fire going and we fed John a granola bar and a cup of tea. He seemed a little better after half an hour and left for Billings. He had many hours to go and I knew he'd be watching for deer the entire time.

The rednecks drove through our campsite all night again. Thanks to the tiring day and my fast, I became extremely crabby and planned countless ways to sabotage their trucks—digging preposterously deep holes, ripping their hair out while Preston held them down, dropping them in the outhouse, etc. Catching myself in these fantasies, I realized it was going to be tough to make it seventy-two hours. I was spiritually about as far away from the essence of a vision quest as one could be, at least according to *The Book of the Vision Quest*: "You can make any place holy if you find it yourself, occupy the space there, and truly respect what is happening all around you."

The land and river around James Kipp Landing were much as they must have been in Lewis and Clark's day. The banks were free of any Corps of Engineers handiwork. Deciduous and evergreen trees hung over the shore, and the river rippled through narrow passages and then meandered over widened flats. In other words it was unpredictable and alive—what a river should be. The Missouri hadn't been this natural except in the area just north of Sioux City—before the first dam. It was exactly how I'd pictured the Missouri as a boy, reading Richard Neuberger's book about the expedition. This was where the rattlers had been along the shore and the men had literally to pull the boats over the rapids, wading through the water and walking on rocks until their feet were covered with carbuncles and cut to shreds. I had wanted to do the same—forge my way through the wilderness.

But in my dreams, I never expected to attempt it when the air temperature was in the low thirties and a frigid fall was fast approaching. Neither had I considered what all those rocks making the rapids might do to our propeller. We found out that next morning.

After waiting out a morning rain shower, we pumped *Sacky* back to life, attached Pompy to her transom, and loaded her down with all of our equipment. Even in my weakened state this was a simpler task than it'd been in St. Louis. Despite ample evidence to the contrary we'd learned a lot. We knew our boat.

As we traveled through the rapids, it appeared we'd learned something else. We knew how to read the water. We cut through rapid after rapid that morning, only missing rocks by inches. The going was slow as we read each section of the river. Eventually, though, our skill and luck ran out. After about ten miles we began hitting more and more rocks.

We tried every possible passage up certain rapids, but there was no winning. The lack of snow had taken its toll. The Corps guy had told me it would be too low, but I hadn't wanted to believe him. I now told Preston that the Corps guy had warned me against trying. He just laughed. But the situation had become a little too serious. We ripped up the good propeller on a boulder that turned out to be the size of a couch.

I was beginning to feel weakened by this point, so Preston had to do all of the work in replacing the propeller with the old one that was already damaged.

Careful to protect our remaining propeller, we began pulling *Sacky* through the more precarious spots. The deepest parts were less than a foot. Even when we both climbed out to pull her through these shallow areas, *Sacky* would scrape the bottom.

As we pushed and pulled her to deeper water, the rapids rushed over our rubber, knee-high boots—a purchase we'd made in North Dakota for just such an occasion—and filled them with cold, wet water. Sometimes we would make 150 yards in half an hour this way. Streamlined, *Sacky* was not.

I became weaker and weaker. Preston implored me to eat, and it was difficult not to as he wolfed down his granola bars and dried fruit directly in front of me.

At one point we had to beach *Sacky* to change into dry clothing and stomp around in circles to warm up. We were both shaking from the cold and our feet and hands were numb, despite wearing thick gloves and waterproof mittens. We had purple and orange spots all over us. It didn't help that there was a 20-mph wind blowing.

In the middle of the afternoon, we busted our auxiliary propeller on an impenetrable set of rocks. Completely unbalanced, Pompy shook and rattled, barely able to make any headway against the current. At full throttle, we could only make a couple of miles an hour.

"We can't make it this way, Preston," I said. "We'll run out of gas before we've made it twenty-five miles, and there's nowhere to get gas until more than a hundred. I think we've got to turn back."

There simply was no debate, not because I was dictating our course but because nature and the Corps of Engineers were. If we decided to pull the boat upstream from this point until we reached the mountains—five hundred miles or so—we wouldn't complete the task until . . . fifty to a hundred days had gone by. That would mean pulling it through the water when it was snowing—something even

Lewis and Clark didn't try to do. So then we'd have to winter over in Montana and wait for spring to continue along the river, then cross the mountains and ride down the Columbia in the summer. The only problem was we didn't have the money to stay somewhere for that long or the capability (or land) to build a winter home. We had to turn back.

So that the day was not a complete failure, we climbed some cliffs on the southwest side of the river. Coniferous trees dotted them, from the base up. The cliffs were sandstone and clay—difficult to climb—except where the trees grew. There, the clay gave way to hard, jutting rocks and we worked our way up through the trees.

The view from the top was magnificent. We could see the river that we would no longer be traveling on for tens of miles. It curved and twisted through the landscape—a living mass of water and surrounding greenery—so distinct from the nearly dead, rolling hills of the prairies that led away from the river valley.

The climb had been necessary—to show what we would be missing—but it took a lot out of me. I hadn't eaten for nearly forty-eight hours, and the exertion was great. I began to feel extremely spacey and weak. So much so that I even thought I understood Nature. Nature wasn't this serene element laid out for our benefit. It wasn't a soft, peaceful place to escape to that so many writers and poets would have us believe. Nature was a living, breathing taskmaster that was simultaneously rich and tumultuous. Nature never bent to our whim or fancy. We bent to Nature's—again and again. The only way to survive was to bend. If that meant waiting out a storm, battening down the hatches, or even retreating and changing plans, then that is what we would do.

We drifted halfway back to the James Kipp Landing that evening and camped in the middle of an island. Sixty-feet-high cottonwoods soared above us. They swayed in the wind as if they were grass. Another front was coming through; this was supposed to be the first real cold snap. The heavy aroma of sagebrush swirled around us.

"Hod, you should stay on a fast for the rest of the trip," Preston said as I stood mutely staring at the fire he was building. "You haven't told me what to do all day. It really makes you a much gentler person."

I laughed softly. He was right. Although we'd been defeated by the river, I felt extremely calm and wasn't telling him what to do as much as usual. It was easy to notice, now that I wasn't, how much I usually berated him.

But I was still attacking him in my head. "All you get is the view. And because you have nothing else to eat, you eat the view," explained *The Book of the Vision Quest*. Watching anybody eat when you're on a self-imposed fast is fairly upsetting, but watching Preston devour his food was disgusting. The worst part was hearing him slurp. Since I wasn't eating, he ate out of the pot he cooked his noodles in, sitting cross-legged before the fire. He sounded a lot like a pig and poured in way too much Worcestershire sauce. He belched five times at the end, ruining any chance of our seeing deer for the evening. (I'm sure both of us had thoroughly scared them off well before then, but that's how I was thinking.)

"Man, those sardines come back on you with a vengeance," he said. He'd eaten a tin for lunch and drunk the oil. "I'm not having any more of those for a long time."

I wanted one badly.

Before sunset a blue-headed kingfisher hunted the river in front of us. It would hover a good twelve feet above the water for nearly a minute, then plunge straight down—not as crazed as a seagull but somehow slightly more controlled. He dove again and again and finally flew out of sight. I hoped it was with a full belly.

ELEVEN

"I Bid Adieu to My Boat, and Her Expected Services"

"Pres, I had a spiritual dream last night. I think tonight when I walk off alone for my final quest will really be something," I said when we woke up. We were lying in our bags longer than usual because there was no rush. Also it was freezing out; there was ice on the tent.

"That's great, but could you turn the other way when you tell me about it. Your breath smells like four-day-old road-kill. I think it's your stomach eating away at itself. Please?"

"Really?" I asked, breathing into my bag and smelling it for myself. I nearly gagged. "Sorry. Anyway, I was in the future. I never dream about the future so that in itself must mean something. I remember walking into this modern building and passing Captain Picard from 'Star Trek: The Next Generation.' He lived in the building and greeted me. We didn't know each other. This woman—I think she was a girlfriend or something—and I go up to an apartment and decide to have a look at the balcony. Suddenly, an errant . . . Hey, are you awake?"

"Yeah."

"Okay, this errant Klingon ship starts firing at the building—at the balcony actually, but it wasn't having much luck. The woman and I were scared, though, anyway. Out of the blue, a superman—who looked a lot like William Riker from the show—appears on the balcony dressed only in a swimming suit. He quickly explains that the ship was weak and useless and that we'd be okay. To demonstrate, he allowed the phasers to hit him repeatedly and nothing happened. The woman and I then felt safe, even though he left. The Klingon ship continued to fire away. . . . The weird thing was that it was a Klingon ship. In the 'Next Generation' the Klingons are allies of the Federation."

"Oh, that's really spiritual," Preston blurted out. "You're dreaming about a syndicated TV show. Some fast. Maybe you should go ahead and eat this morning."

He obviously didn't know spirituality even when it was thrown in his face. Poor soul. Should I also point out to him, I wondered, that my stinking breath might be a sign that I was getting closer to nature? That maybe my vision-quest name should be Bear Man? Pliny the Elder—one of the world's first naturalists—wrote of bears in the first century A.D.: "Bears' breath is unwholesome. No wild animal will touch things that have come into contact with a bear's breath, and things which bears have breathed upon putrefy more quickly." And thus, was Preston decaying even faster than before I'd begun my fast?

These questions would have to wait. We returned to James Kipp Landing after a short float down the river, left our equipment, then hitchhiked south to Billings, Montana. There, we rented another car at the airport. Our plan was to keep the car for a week and see Glacier and Yellowstone parks. Lewis and Clark split up on the return trip, and both of them went to areas near these parks. Also, this way, we would see many of the animals that they saw, most of which had been wiped out from all other public (and private) lands. "The buffaloe Elk and Antelope are so gentle that we pass near them while feeding, without apearing to excite any alarm among them," Lewis wrote on April 25, 1805, not far from the Yellowstone River. "And when we attract their attention they frequently approach us more nearly to discover what we are and in some instances pursue us a considerable distance apparently with that view." In Montana today, only domestic cattle, thinking you are about to feed them, would do the same.

According to our original itinerary, we didn't need to begin our hike across the Continental Divide for another week. If we started any sooner, we'd arrive in Lolo, Montana, too many days before our rendezvous with the horse people.

Everyone in the airport gave us a lot of space. Young mothers gripped their children close to their bodies as we walked by, and even the cowboys wouldn't come near us. We looked like homeless men. At one point, as I was signing all the papers for the rental, Preston squatted in the middle of the airport beside a gleaming column. He drank some water out of one of our dirty plastic jugs and pulled on a strip of beef jerky.

It was a scary sight even to me. He looked uncivilized and out of place in the modern airport. I realized I looked the same.

After renting the car, we drove back to James Kipp and packed up all of our equipment. Preston kindly performed most of the heavy work. When we were done, we couldn't even see out the back window.

We followed the river that evening, taking the car on an unimproved dirt road that was only meant for four-wheel-drive vehicles. It was the sort of road one only drives a rental over. We scraped bottom many times but stuck to it anyway. Neither of us was quite ready to surrender the river yet, and I still had my night of isolation ahead. I wanted to be on a hill near the Missouri.

Around seven, we stopped at the confluence of the Judith (Clark named the river after his future bride) and Missouri Rivers. I only had a little more than an hour until sundown and a good forty-five-minute hike to the hills overlooking the valley. I packed a tent, sleeping bag, flashlight, knife, and water. Preston became very protective.

"Hod, maybe you shouldn't do this. You're really worn-out. Can't you just stay here and have a vision? You said yourself you're already not doing it the right way," he pleaded. I noticed then that I was wobbling a bit. I said no and began walking away. "Here, I know," he continued, easily catching up to me. "Why don't I drive you over there?"

"No."

"Well, then, at least take a granola bar for the morning so you can make it back here."

"Make it three." It would be over by then. He dug into his bag and handed them over.

"Good luck," he said. I found out later he was truly worried and had to fight off the impulse to follow from a distance.

It was nearly a three-mile walk to the hills I'd chosen and so I hurried to beat the sunset. I had my heart set on the highest hills covered with pines, but as I reached the base of the hills, breathing much too hard considering the lightness of my pack, I realized that a long, high barbed-wire fence blocked my path. I settled for some adjacent, lower-lying hills.

Cattle patties and sagebrush covered the hill I climbed. This sign of domesticated animals upset me, but at least the cattle themselves were not around.

My heart pounded and my legs ached when I reached the top although it was only a few hundred feet up from the base. I quickly made camp before the sun set. I then sat outside the tent and watched the sky as all light vanished. It was quite cold—somewhere in the thirties—and I wore only a light jacket.

Oddly, considering two rivers flowed beneath me, I heard no coyotes call that night. Everything else appeared normal—the stars were in the sky and the ground was hard and cold. But the land seemed dead. I tried to concentrate on things that constantly circled in my mind—my family, friends, even religion—but nothing would stay put. I couldn't hold on to any solid thoughts, and when I let my mind drift, it drifted away so that nothing was in there.

I entered the tent, somewhat discouraged and extremely cold. Maybe, I thought, my vision would arrive in a dream. For many Native Americans there traditionally hasn't been much of a distinction between visions and dreams. I fell asleep instantly and did not wake until sunrise.

"If you are young, your vision will lead you toward fulfillment in your adult life. If you are an adult, your vision will guide you through the necessary changes ahead in such a way that you will grow and your people will be blessed. If you are very much older, your vision will prepare you for the ultimate transition and give you the power to die victoriously and with dignity, enriching the lives of those you love and leave behind." So says *The Book of the Vision Quest.*

For one of the few times in my life, I had no dreams—not one. My vision quest, I thought, had failed. I hadn't eaten in more than eighty hours. I ate my three granola bars and, with the rising sun, headed back to Preston.

On my return I came upon four mule deer munching on greens not more than fifty yards away. They all bounded and hopped away into some wooded marshland. One, though, a buck, stood at the edge of the woods and stared at me for nearly ten minutes. I stared back, until eventually he, too, bounded away.

Back at Preston's camp, I ate a large breakfast of grits and sardines that he had waiting for me. I also told him my entire experience because it was his job to name me. He had a hard time holding back his laughter when I told him I hadn't dreamed a thing. To his credit, he chose a higher path. He said he needed some time to consider an appropriate vision-quest name.

It wasn't until I had a full stomach and we were on the road again that we fought. While Preston had to be kind to me during my fast because of my weakened state, I, even though calmer than usual, had been difficult to deal with.

He'd held back much resentment. I, on the other hand, was prepared to erupt simply because I hadn't had the energy to bark orders at him for so long.

"What did you do with the map of the Wild and Scenic section?" I demanded of him as he drove toward Fort Benton, Montana—an old outpost on the Missouri. We'd been sight-seeing along the way, watching the world go by at a much faster pace than we were used to. "Do you know where it is?"

"Is it in your pocket?"

"Of course it isn't," I snapped. "Would I ask you where it was if it were in my pocket?" I started rummaging through his knapsack to show him I knew he'd lost it.

"I'm sick of you always accusing me of losing things," he said, watching me more than the road. He was driving.

"You do it, too. You're just sneakier about it and won't ask outright." My voice had sped up. I felt as if I were in an argument with a lover. "Instead, you say things like, 'Where is our toothpaste?' implying that I misplaced it. Why else would you ask that out loud?"

"I'm seriously tired of your whining about the things I do wrong," he whined. "And—"

"I can't help it if you're always doing something wrong."

"And I'm sick of your ordering me around. I don't need you telling me what to do—"

"Then, why don't you fucking go back to California. I can make this trip without you," I nearly screamed. There was a sudden stop to all conversation.

A few seconds went by and then we both broke out laughing. This spat had been waiting, not since my fast started, but since the very first day. It let off a lot of steam and we both apologized for the next thirty minutes.

We drove until Great Falls—site of the L&C expedition's month-long portage around what were then unchecked, terrific waterfalls. Of the five falls, the largest was nearly ninety feet. They overwhelmed Lewis's imagination and he wrote: "I wished for the pencil of Salvator Rosa or the pen of Thompson, that I might be enabled to give the enlightened world some just idea of this truly magnificent and sublimely grand object, which has from the comencement of time been concealed from the view of civilized man."

The falls have now been tamed and beaten by dams that help control the upper Missouri. We skipped visiting them.

This was also the scene of one of Lewis's bitterest disappointments on the expedition. Before heading out, he contracted the Harpers Ferry armory to build him an iron canoe to be employed on the upper Missouri. The boat was his design. After portaging around the falls, he decided it was time to employ this modern vessel. The men attached skins to the frame for several days, and Lewis launched the boat on July 9.

It sunk immediately. There had been no pitch to seal the skins with and the water pulled them apart. Lewis, admittedly mortified, handled this defeat with aplomb: "I bid adieu to my boat, and her expected services."

Preston and I concluded, considering our bad luck with the low water, that the area was ill-fated for all who followed the Lewis and Clark Trail.

We camped that night along the Great Falls' commercial strip in a Kampgrounds of America, replete with Kamper Kitchens, Kabins, and Tent Villages. I once swore that I'd never stay at a KOA, and it was only fitting that in my time of failure I even failed at that.

We headed north for Glacier National Park the next morning. On the way, we stopped at the Bob Scriver Museum in Browning, Montana, on the Blackfeet Reservation. A large section was devoted to stuffed wild animals, and a sign claimed that the exhibit existed to acquaint visitors with all the wildlife that Montana offered. But the placards below each animal gave away the real sentiment; the descriptions boldly claimed how each animal had been "taken" and were often accompanied by descriptions of the kill. As I walked by each stuffed carcass, all I could think was how there was one less of each of these creatures: bald eagle, coyote, wolf, mountain goat, elk, grizzly (shot thirteen times by three men), prairie dog, badger, beaver, and on and on. We had been unable to glimpse any of these animals but they had been plentiful in Lewis and Clark's day.

A large, brown grizzly, however, greeted us as we entered Glacier. Actually, it wasn't large. It was gigantic. We instantly knew it was a grizzly by the telltale hump at the back of its shoulders. We'd been patiently waiting to see this creature for nearly a month and there one stood.

"Just think," I said, "we might be seeing one of those as we hike across the Divide." Most information we had claimed there might be a few grizzlies scattered throughout the national forests along our route. "Wouldn't that be great?" The bear continued to lumber along the stream slowly heading our way. It was not in the least perturbed by our presence. Not a good sign.

According to McNamee, a truly wild grizzly would most likely run off at the smell of humans. But the ones that weren't concerned with humans presented a problem. They were usually the ones that would maul you. They've been trained over the years by campers' trash and idiot tourists who entice them with food to take a picture. They knew humans were a food source.

Our favorite story concerned just such a tourist. He and his family were supposedly (supposedly, because while many people know this story, no one has ever verified it) camping in Yellowstone. They had a cute little boy named Bobby who loved the bears. Wouldn't it be great, the father wondered, if we could get a picture of Bobby with the bear. They smeared peanut butter or honey (depending on who is telling the story) on the boy's head. And shoved him toward the bear. Poor little Bobby.

Lewis and Clark had run-ins with grizzlies as well. They had heard much about these bears from the Indians they encountered along the way and quickly learned respect for them. After the first few encounters, Lewis wrote, "I find that the curiossity of our party is pretty well satisfyed with rispect to this anamal, the formidable appearance of the male bear killed on the 5th added to the difficulty with which they die when even shot through the vital parts, has staggered the resolution of several of them." And later he summed up his own feelings: "I must confess that I do not like the gentlemen and reather fight two Indians than one bear." There are many entries about the bears chasing the men, even after the bears had been hit numerous times.

The funniest aspect to all the grizzly lore, though, was the advice on dealing with a grizzly that various "experts" handed out. McNamee was the most honest. He wrote in *Grizzly* that there is always one grizzly who fails to recognize the surefire way to ward him off. Climbing a tree to escape a grizzly is great because the bear's long claws and tremendous weight make it difficult for him to climb—until you come upon the one grizzly who loves to climb trees. The same goes for flashing a multicolored golf umbrella in the bear's face. That was the preferred method for a while until there came a grizzly who had a keen interest in just such an umbrella.

The most interesting suggestion to Preston and me was the oft-quoted tip to curl up in the fetal position. The park service, all guidebooks, and even McNamee recommend this tactic. Play dead, they say. That seemed fine to us; the grizzly would realize that you are not a threat and then leave you alone. Right? But then Preston got to thinking:

"Hod, everything we've read in McNamee's book points out how much grizzlies love a carcass. It's always being shown that a grizzly would rather eat something that is already dead than chase after it, kill it, and then have dinner." I was beginning to see where he was going with this and was glad we were back in the car, heading to our campsite. "Now, what could be more appetizing than a curled-up, fleshy human who, to all appearances, is dead?"

Grizzly-bear warnings hung throughout the park campsite and included restrictions on food preparation, cleaning camp, etc. Campers could be fined for not keeping food properly stored.

After pitching the tent, we hiked toward the nearest glacier lake—only a few miles away. Preston had a tree book and I had my tracking book. He identified the yellow-leafed trees, which we thought might be birches, as quaking aspen. They are called quaking because the leaves quake when the wind blows them. It was much more difficult to identify the various conifers. We'd think we had learned what a Douglas fir was, for instance, walk along, point to a tree and label it a Douglas fir, look it up, and find out it was a something spruce. This happened again and again. I gave up and only looked for tracks and scats.

A young woman happened along, whistling. She was attempting to warn grizzlies of her approach. She also had a bell attached to her knapsack, and I refrained from pointing out that this might lead the bears to think she was a defenseless cow. We were walking so slowly that she wanted to know what we were doing.

"Well, Preston is failing to identify all these trees and I'm looking for shit. This book shows you all the animal shits, see." I showed her the book.

"That's really a great book," she said. Was she mocking me? There was a twinkle in her eye, but maybe it was simply the lighting. She told us her name was Jan.

"You see," I said, pouncing toward Preston's foot, "this is a marten shit that Preston just stepped on. Now I know there's a marten around here. It's really much better than seeing the animals because you can use your imagination to guess what the martens are doing here."

" 'Marten scats may be found on rocks along mountain trails, and in the trail itself,' " I quoted. She stood even closer to me. Preston looked on in envy. I really wasn't positive it was a marten scat but was not about to admit it.

"Well," Jan said, preparing herself to press on, "you two are certainly weird. I like that." We walked with her to the lake, where she waited for her friends. They were going to lie on the beach until dusk. It was probably forty degrees out.

"I've got to hand it to you, Hod. That book is a great magnet for women," Preston whispered to me as we continued on the trail. He was whispering because we were being as quiet as possible, contrary to all advice. We both hoped to see a grizzly while walking.

We turned a bend and there on the rocks not more than a hundred yards above us were four mountain goats. We couldn't believe it. We ran back to tell Jan.

"Oh, yes, you're right. Those are mountain goats," she said, not impressed.

"Have you seen them before?" I asked.

"A whole pack of them stood on a trail in front of us yesterday and wouldn't even move out of the way. It was amazing. They weren't more than ten feet in front of us."

That night, Ken—a young man from Japan whose name means "health" in Japanese—ate dinner with us. He was camping at a nearby site, having arrived on his motorcycle when we were out hiking. Watching him set up camp, Preston and I decided he needed a full meal. He was frighteningly skinny and looked as if the winds had taken much too much out of him.

That was the first thing I asked him, how could he handle the wind on his bike? He simply shrugged and said it wasn't difficult. He was obviously some sort of daredevil because I had a hard enough time staying upright on a motorcycle in a dead calm.

As I prepared dinner, I decided he was the right fellow to confide in—to talk to about my fast. A lone guy on a motorcycle among all these glaciers had to be spiritual. His wispy facial hair marked him as sensitive. I told him everything. I knew he was listening by all the faces he made, but at the end of my story all he said was, "Oh." Preston, who was supposed to be busy collecting fallen wood for a fire, laughed.

"You still have to give me my name, asswipe!" I yelled at him. I wish I hadn't. He loves an audience.

"Well," he said, nearly winking at Ken, "I just happen to have come up with two apt names. Based on your dream the second night, you know—Captain Picard, Klingons—the one that you thought was so spiritual. Your name could be Watches Too Much Television."

Ken started laughing and choked on the hot chocolate I'd made, the ungrateful wretch.

I suppressed a smile.

"But based on your behavior during the entire fast, I believe I've come up with something more pertinent—something that gets to the heart of your quest."

"Yes?" I asked, trying not to sound too eager.

"Needs a Meal." Again, Ken spewed hot chocolate on the wooden picnic table. Didn't he know the grizzlies could smell that spilled stuff from miles away?

"Very funny," I said. "But I refuse both of them. You have to go back to the drawing board. Neither of those take into account my last night of fasting." Thanks to Preston's ribbing me—I refused to believe he really meant those names—Ken came to life.

He told us all about his bike—a 650 Suzuki that was falling apart. He'd bought it secondhand in Montreal two months back, upon arriving from Japan, and had been touring Canada and the United States since. Because he arrived in the summer, he didn't have any winter clothes.

"I'm working at a ski resort starting in November. I'll work in the ski-rental shop. They'll have warm clothes for me. This works very well. The job sucks [he'd done this two years earlier so his English was better than Preston's or mine] and pays shit, but I get a free ski pass. If I worked in a hotel or restaurant, I'd make more money, but I'd have to buy the thousand-dollar season lift pass. The only reason why I'm here is to ski. I want to be in the ski patrol, but I need more practice."

"Do you have a job back in Japan?" I tactfully asked. He was twenty-six.

"I majored in economics but it was not for me. In Japan, everything is along a line. Family, high school, college, a good company . . . Once you step out of that line it's very difficult to go back in."

"That's awful," I said.

"I don't have to worry, though, I was never in line."

During dinner—pasta with a can of tuna and spices—we asked him the typical (read stupid) questions one asks a visitor. One of which was what he thought of Americans, compared to Canadians.

"In Canada, people are more humble. Here, they boast

all the time. I can do this better than you and so on."

I felt I had to defend America. "Maybe all they're doing is stretching the truth."

"What does this mean, 'stretching the truth'?"

It's an expression. Stretching the truth is when someone tells something that isn't necessarily true, but at the same time the person isn't bad; he is just trying to make the story better."

Ken looked slightly less confused, but Preston howled his head off, nearly. "Boy, I better write that one down," he said as he reached for his journal. "So that's how you think of it—the stuff that you do. Ha, ha, ha—'just trying to make the story better.' " Of course, Ken started laughing, too.

A few hours after sunset, the three of us were exhausted and called it a night. We invited Ken for breakfast the next morning. At first he accepted our offer, but when we told him we'd be waking around seven or so, he demurred. He wouldn't be up until ten or eleven. We also suggested he brush his teeth at our camp and spit his toothpaste into the fire. "Grizzlies love the smell of toothpaste," Preston warned him.

His was a nice way to travel, I thought as I readied for sleep—not at all like the hectic pace Preston and I were setting. And it seemed so contrary to all the stereotypes about the Japanese.

I fell asleep to Preston's reading aloud from the grizzly book: "Most hiker injuries have been inflicted after the hiker was charged by the bear . . . [and] charges occurred primarily on trails with little human use. The findings of this research, together with records on human injuries in the park, suggest that habituation of grizzly bears to high numbers of hikers in their habitat may reduce the rate of injuries resulting from fear-induced aggression. . . . As long as they perceive people as bell-wearing, predictable, harmless, ungenerous with food, and unacceptable as prey, grizzly bears are—even at close quarters—going to leave us alone. Well, okay . . . most of the time."

We continued as tourists for the rest of the week. We

hiked through Glacier National Park the following day to a glacier lake, spotting bighorn sheep for the first time in our lives. Walked past pearly everlasting, which is good for diarrhea, huckleberry bushes, which bears love, mounds of bear grass, which disinterests bears, and scat after scat. I was able to identify some as either goat or deer pellets, but had trouble with some larger ones. They had been stepped on by other hikers. We did identify a set of black-bear prints. So maybe the large scats were bear.

In the afternoon we drove back to Browning to visit the Plains Indian museum. The museum had been our legitimate reason for heading to Glacier because we figured we could learn more about Lewis's encounter with the Blackfeet there.

On the return trip from the Pacific Ocean, Lewis and Clark split up. Lewis took a northerly route back to show that one could reach the Great Falls without having to take the long mountainous route they'd used on the outward journey. On this route, he passed near the mountains that now make up Glacier National Park.

Up until then, the expedition had been lucky in its encounters with natives. But by this point, Lewis was anxious to be home again, having admitted in his journal that he missed society. He was also beginning to see evil omens in nature: "There seems to be a sertain fatality attached to the neighborhood of these falls," he wrote, not two weeks before the clash with the Blackfeet. And the day before the encounter, he wrote that he was apprehensive that he would not reach the United States soon enough.

Lewis, and the men who were with him, came upon the Blackfeet during the tribe's buffalo hunt. Lewis did not have Sacagawea with him (she was a sign that they traveled in peace), so he and his men were instantly perceived as a threat. Lewis also did not help matters any. He, in turn, perceived the Blackfeet as threatening and wrote that he preferred death to "being deprived of my papers instruments and gun."

Not surprisingly, there was trouble. After a long night of peacemaking with the Indians, Lewis was awakened the next morning by one of his men shouting, "Damn, you let go my gun." Another of his men had already stabbed a Blackfoot who had attempted to steal a gun. The Blackfeet made off with other guns and started to chase off the horses.

Lewis and his men pursued them and retrieved all the guns. They also killed two Blackfeet. Lewis shot one man himself.

We hoped the Plains Indian museum would shed a little more light on the entire episode. But we weren't there for more than fifteen minutes before being told to leave. According to the hours posted, more than half an hour remained before closing, but two Native Americans ushered us out. I complained to Preston, suggesting we go back in.

"Hey," he said, "what are you going to tell them? It's their place. They get to at least make the rules here."

I shut up.

The next two nights we camped at separate but equally miserable sites along the Missouri. Both were dirty and full of trash. One was near a granary that had trains loading and unloading all night long. The engineers blew their whistles every single time they crossed an adjacent bridge.

The only things we accomplished those days were sending the motor back home and losing Preston's down vest. We intentionally disposed of the engine because we wouldn't need it to travel down the Clearwater, Snake, and Columbia Rivers once we'd hiked across the Continental Divide. The downstream current would do all the work, just as it had in Lewis and Clark's day. Losing the vest was a mistake; Preston left it in a restaurant. He'd been counting on its keeping him warm during our mountain crossing.

On the third day, we stopped at my friend Temple Richardson's home in Livingston, Montana, on our way to Yellowstone. I wanted to meet her husband, pick up some maps, and give her one last chance to be our Sacagawea. We still needed to find someone to cart our boat and extra equipment over to Idaho for us; we couldn't pack seven hundred pounds across those mountains on our backs.

I couldn't quite figure out why Temple and John had

moved to Livingston. A lot of other city people had moved there, she'd told me, including a number of writers. So I'd thought it was going to be a mountain town covered with pine trees and flooded with streams. It wasn't. Livingston was a plains town—dry, windswept, and charmless.

All the lawns were brown, defeated by the sun, and only a few trees dotted the roadside. But Temple and John's house was genuinely inviting—thick white walls and solid wood floors. They were renovating it when we arrived.

Had Temple's attitude toward us changed? I wondered as we toured their home. We walked back outside to eat lunch down the street and ran into one of her friends. She introduced us by saying, "Yeah, these guys are *driving* the Lewis and Clark route!" I kindly did not point out that it was a trail—not a route. I did start to explain that we were only driving a very small portion of it when her friend, oblivious to Eastern sarcasm, said, "Oh, how nice. That must really be something."

After lunch, John pulled out some maps and we showed both of them exactly what we were doing, pointing out again and again the difficult three-week hike ahead of us. Somehow, Temple began to soften—maybe the real Sacagawea had to warm up to Lewis and Clark as well?—and offered to locate someone to drive our equipment over the mountains. We could leave our river equipment and excess clothing with her.

She even went so far as to offer to wash our clothes. Preston said she didn't need to do that, but I kept my mouth closed. Our clothes stunk.

From Livingston, Preston and I drove down to Yellowstone Park, where Clark, without Lewis (nor any mishaps), took the Yellowstone River through on the return trip. Temple and John would meet us in three days in western Montana for a night of camping before we set off on our hike.

Our two nights at the park were calm and restful. Yellowstone was not nearly as dramatically beautiful as Glacier, and it seemed tamer. That probably had something to do with the multitude of paved roads and the numerous RVs.

We found a campsite at Slough Creek, thanks to John, that was only for tents.

Sadly, we acquired game-parkitis. It is a common disease that befalls nearly everyone who visits national parks or African game parks. People become numb to the wonderful sights around them. How often would Preston and I get the chance to see hundreds of buffalo running or even lying around? Not very, but after the first time, we picked up the habit of simply remarking, "Oh, some more buffalo." We did the same for elk, deer, and antelope. There were so many of them, and yet we sped by them as if they weren't even there. Once, I couldn't even wake Preston to see a herd of buffalo; he just muttered, "Let me sleep." I wasn't any better. Conscious of game-parkitis, I pretended to be interested in the huge herds of animals, but I was always itching to speed on to the next sighting.

This numbing indifference did not occur with solitary animals, though. A reddish brown coyote that Preston spotted within some woods held our attention for as long as we could see it. What was it doing out in the daytime? Why was it so healthy looking? Was it not scared of our car or had it not seen us? And the same went for a large hawk that flew a few feet away from the car. We slammed on the brakes and watched it dive into the tall grass before us. It looked like a red-tailed hawk in its light phase, but some markings on its tail suggested it might be a crossbreed of a red-tail and a Harlan's. They were both common to the area. We watched this great hunter scanning the grasses for as long as she stayed in view.

One of the evenings, I went tracking with my book, walking along a path that followed Slough Creek. A friend had sent a lucky Peruvian amulet vial to Temple's, and I had it with me on my walk. Figuring it alone would keep the grizzlies away, I disobeyed all grizzly rules and kept quiet. Maybe I would see something live. I followed a branch of the path up into a meadow. It was covered with buffalo and deer scats. The buffalo patties measured (my tracking book has a ruler imprinted on the inside of the back cover) more than a foot in diameter.

I returned to the creek bed and began looking for tracks in the shallows of the creek. First I found canine tracks that fit a coyote. They could also have been a camper's dog. Then in about one inch of water I discovered my favorite tracks yet. There were six of them—separated by the animal's stride, perfectly shaped and quite distinct. No one had disturbed them. I peered closely and hovered over them while I whipped through my tracking book. The front prints had four digits and the back, five. Finally, I came upon them; they were wood-rat prints—measuring just under half an inch each. They resembled miniature hands, minus a finger.

A wood rat is also a pack rat, so I began looking for his bulky nest that would be filled with trash from past campers, maybe an odd plastic plate, a dried buffalo scat— anything that might be worth collecting. But I didn't find it.

I next came upon some blue heron tracks—our old friend from the Missouri. I followed them along the creek bed for a hundred feet when suddenly a great blue flew out of the brush in front of me, sending my heart racing as I imagined not this startled bird, but a crazed, human-conditioned grizzly. I was lucky the great blue was merely hunting and not protecting a nesting site. His sharp beak could easily have ripped my flesh.

Worried that the Peruvian vial I carried would not protect me in the fast-approaching dark, I began retracing my steps, spotting some six-inch beaver tracks along the way. I came upon Preston fairly soon. He was fishing for trout with a spinner.

I saw five huge trout about eight feet in front of him.

"Preston, look. There's trout!"

"I know. I'm trying to get them," he whispered back. His casting had improved greatly since tangling up Scott Failor's line, and he tossed the spinner just on the other side of the fish, softly enough not to frighten them. I could see the spinner shimmering in the water, catching the last of the fading light. It was going to pass right before their hungry mouths. One turned to watch it coming. The spinner came nearer. Nearer. Nearer. And it kept right on coming until it was out of the water.

The trout hadn't even nudged it.

"Those damned fly fishermen with all their fancy equipment and wading boots spooked these suckers," I complained. The fly fishermen had looked at us with disdain when they walked by our camp and saw our spinning reel.

A husband and wife, Kevin and Jeannie, were fishing with spinning reels nearby. Preston had been talking to them and so we all walked back together.

"One of those fly guys told me he thought I couldn't fish here with a lure. What an asshole," Kevin said.

"Ha! A fly is simply a glorified lure," Preston responded. "Where do they get off?"

As a topic of conversation, we all four cursed fly fishermen as we ambled back to the camp.

"Shh," Jeannie said. I thought she was sick of the conversation, but she pointed straight ahead. "Look."

Standing on the bank about thirty yards ahead were a mother mule deer and her three fawns. The mother hopped across the stream, stepping on various rocks. The first two fawns followed. The last—much smaller—tentatively worked its way across and then stopped in the middle. It was really much smaller and appeared bewildered.

"The last in the pecking order," Kevin reflected. The fawn's family didn't wait, so he eventually mustered up the courage to finish the crossing. It was lovely watching them.

Kevin and Jeannie visited our camp after dinner, bringing some beers with them. They were on an extended vacation—something like five weeks—and were driving across the West. They were from New York so we were all able to complain about the locals.

I egged Preston on when they offered some pot. I would get a vicarious pleasure from his wasted state, and we had to be hospitable. Preston had not smoked for years but finally gave in. Once they were all high, the conversation rapidly made no sense.

After they departed and we readied for sleep, Preston

continually stated, "I feel so stupid. This is why I hate pot. I feel so stupid." It was a wonderful evening.

I read from *Housekeeping*—a novel by Marilynne Robinson that a friend had loaned me. *Housekeeping* was a book to be savored and read slowly, not because it was difficult but because it was rich and sweet. Before falling asleep I came upon this underlined passage: "For need can blossom into all the compensations it requires. To crave and to have are as likely as a thing and its shadow. For when does a berry break upon the tongue as sweetly as when one longs to taste it, and when is the taste refracted into so many hues and savors of ripeness and earth, and when do our senses know any thing so utterly as when we lack it? And here again is a foreshadowing—the world will be made whole. For a wish for a hand on one's hair is all but to feel it. So whatever we may lose, very craving gives it back to us again. Though we dream and hardly know it, longing, like an angel, fosters us, smoothes our hair, and brings us wild strawberries."

The words played with my heart, and as I packed the book away for the evening, I couldn't help crying a little.

At the end of the third day we drove to Butte, Montana. We'd be returning the car there the following day and figured on camping somewhere nearby. Yet, we couldn't find any suitable place to pitch our tent. All the land was private and our car would be too visible if we trespassed. We drove into town to look for a camping guide in a bookstore.

They didn't have one but the woman who was helping us look asked why we needed it. I told her.

"I'll call my husband. He knows the directions to a wonderful place called Racetrack," she said. How could a place called Racetrack be wonderful? I wondered. "It's full of trees and there's a creek right next to it."

Considering there were hardly any trees in Butte, this did sound good. Her husband gave us simple directions. "You'll love it," he said.

After I hung up, we talked to the woman again, thanking

her. She asked what we were doing, and to explain why we were in the car we complained about how much the rivers were messed up.

"We've heard the Columbia fishing is destroyed, too," I said.

"Oh, I don't know. We're always so hard on ourselves, when, after all, we're just poor little feeble humans, trying to get by. We can't help making mistakes."

Our campsite for the night was wonderful. It was nestled in a valley in the Deerlodge National Forest. A cold, fast-running stream sped by our tent—not more than ten feet away. Tall conifers stood nearby, and the roaring of the water reassured. It was great to be away from Yellowstone and all the people. The fact that it was raining, sleeting, and snowing only added to the beauty.

Some lone animal whistled every few minutes. "It sounds almost like a flute being played," Preston remarked. I imagined a pied piper deep within the woods, beckoning us to enter.

It called throughout the night and by morning we realized what it was. Once when I was camping in Maine, I heard something much like it but of a deeper note, bellowing across Lake Pemadumcook. It had been a male moose in rut. It, too, had been forlorn and beckoning. The animal from the night before was not a moose but an elk. Its call was higher pitched—one of the most beautiful sounds in nature.

We returned the car that morning and began hitchhiking to the Clark Canyon Dam reservoir in southwestern Montana. It was the point where Lewis and Clark left the Beaverhead River and began their arduous crossing of the Continental Divide—a crossing that they thought would only be a day's portage. Of course, there had been no dam or reservoir in their day, but the location was the same.

The backpacks were cumbersome—not a good sign considering we had three weeks of wearing them ahead of us. Preston's weighed fifty-eight pounds and mine was forty-eight. I somehow convinced him that his should weigh more since he weighed twenty pounds more than I. Also, as soon as I filled the water and gas bottles (for the stove), mine would be roughly six pounds heavier.

We had to walk a few miles along the highway without a ride. All of my muscles ached. Finally, a beat-up van pulled over. Actually, it didn't so much pull over as run us off the shoulder. The front-seat passenger rolled down his window. I could tell from twenty feet away that he was wasted.

"Hop in," he said. I prayed that Preston would give them some excuse why we couldn't get in. He didn't. We climbed in.

This is a mistake, it's a mistake, I kept telling myself. The driver is going to bang us on the head with a shovel. He's going to shoot us. They're going to sodomize us. Why is the driver leering? Why isn't he getting back on the road?

The van smelled like dead fish. "We've been fishing at . . . ," said the driver, slurring his words.

"Mostly drinking," said the passenger.

"My name's Reverend Joe," the driver said. Lordy, no, I thought, don't let him be a crazed cultist or something. He slammed a tape into the player and cranked the volume. "L.A. Woman" by the Doors rattled and blared out of the blown speakers.

I couldn't hear him or the passenger talk anymore although I could see their mouths moving. A hell of a lot of saliva and other muck gathered at the corners of their mouths. Meanwhile, Reverend Joe was not staying between the traffic markers.

He turned down the music because he'd evidently asked us a question. "Where you going?" he repeated. I tried to send a telepathic message to Preston not to tell him, but it didn't get through.

"Clark Canyon Dam."

"Hell, why don't we just take them there?" Reverend Joe asked his passenger. "You don't have nothing better to do." I could smell the alcohol on his breath from the backseat. He cranked up the music again.

The next thing I knew, Reverend Joe pulled onto an exit

ramp. We'd gone about a mile. I was scared. This is where he was going to dismember us.

"We're going home," he said. Oh, God. But he stopped the van. "You fellas are going to have to get there on your own. Have a safe journey." Before Preston had a chance to do anything crazy, like plead with them to take us farther, I threw open the side door.

We were alive.

Another ride took us to the connecting highway we needed to head south on. A fellow hitchhiker was already there. He was heading for Salt Lake City, according to his sign. Like us, he had a backpack, but his was so full that items were spilling out of the pockets.

"I've been staying in Butte since March," he explained, unprompted. He looked sad and washed-out. "But I'm outta there now. Old lady troubles . . . Yeah, it's pretty bad—divorce and all that, I guess. I just took these things here"—he pointed to his pack—"and let her have the house."

"Saves you the headache," Preston said, trying to lend some male support, figuring he was a Scott Failor type.

"Heartache's more like, I'm afraid . . . yep," he answered, and looked off, back toward Butte.

We walked on—so we could both get our rides—but his sorrow stayed with us the following hour. That is, until we got our next ride.

A skinny, nerdy fellow picked us up. He was from Yankton, South Dakota—near Lewis and Clark Lake. That was the first dam-created lake we crossed. He was studying to be an X-ray technician—"one of those guys who turn on the X-ray machines, not fix 'em."

He told us he likes to hike a lot: "I really like to check out a place and approach it from a knowledgeable perspective. First, I walk around the perimeter of a piece of property for reconnaissance. I don't let anyone see me. Then, I dress up in my diving suit, fins, and mask, put my stuff in dry sacks, and then sneak across. See, that's why all my stuff is camo." His clothes and backpack were all camouflage designed.

"You see, I always wanted to be a Navy SEAL. I even joined the Navy and was training to be one before I was discharged on account of my shoulders. . . . To be a good SEAL, you have to be able to do a special sidestroke. It's the most efficient stroke and the most silent. They teach you to just lift one eyeball and your mouth out of the water every couple of strokes to keep you hidden. I was really good at it."

I laughed out loud then, imagining this skinny fellow with the huge Adam's apple silently sputtering along with one eyeball sticking out of the water. I couldn't stop and Preston looked back at me worriedly. His face said, "Shut up. This guy could be crazy." "Could be" wasn't the half of it.

He dropped us off less than thirty miles short of our destination. Soon after he departed, a car with two guys dressed in camouflage passed. Their faces were painted in camouflage as well. What was happening?

We eventually snagged a ride that took us within a mile of the reservoir. The place was a pit. Trash surrounded the lake and it was at least thirty feet low. It was drying up. The only place to pitch our tent was at a "developed" site on the western edge of the lake.

There were no trees, so a sandy, belligerent wind blew at us the entire time. The campground was a pigsty and the ugliest place we'd found thus far. Two RVs were there and only one site remained. It had what appeared to be a human shit in its fire ring. I figured it was human since toilet paper accompanied it. We collected the surrounding trash and two huge logs that were hidden beneath a picnic table and lit the whole mess on fire—with a little help from our gas bottle. As the fire rose more than three feet high, the place brightened considerably.

I finished reading *Housekeeping* that night and then debated giving it to Preston. It was such a gem and I felt like having something separate from him. But I handed it over, knowing he'd especially enjoy the drifting aspect of the book.

His astronomy teaching paid off that night and I was able to identify both Cassiopeia and the great square of

Pegasus for him. He then tried to teach me more, but I began humming so as not to hear him. More lecturing would make me forget the ones I'd finally learned.

Temple and John arrived the following day. Temple was decidedly beginning to resemble Sacagawea. While we were visiting over lunch in a nearby town, she made numerous telling comments: she was eating more; she'd had her milk for the day; she could only do so much heavy work; she was in a hurry to finish renovating the house.

"Hey, Hod," Preston whispered to me when they were out of earshot, "do you think she's pregnant?"

I didn't know so I asked her.

"Yes," she said, "but don't tell anyone. It's a surprise."

Whom were we going to tell on the Continental Divide?

Sacagawea had been pregnant when she first joined the expedition. As a matter of fact, she almost died during delivery. "Mr. Jessome informed me that he had frequently administered a small portion of the rattle of the rattlesnake," wrote Lewis, "which he assured me had never failed to produce the desired effect, that of hastening the birth of the child; having the rattle of a snake by me I gave it to him and he administered two rings of it to the woman broken in small pieces with the fingers and added to a small quantity of water." Sacagawea gave birth to Pompy promptly thereafter. I made a mental note to suggest this method of childbirth when Temple's time was up.

Temple was beginning to resemble Sacagawea in her contributions to our expedition, as well. Not only did she bring us marinated steaks, Vidalia onions (to bake in the fire), avocado-and-tomato salad, and Häagen-Dazs chocolate chocolate-chip ice cream, but she also decided to take our equipment to Idaho in one month's time.

She and John were cute together and extremely patient with one another. Although they disagreed on how to set up their tent and how to cook the meal, neither one sniped at the other. Some of it was a little strained:

"Look, honey, I think we ought to put the stakes in first. It's what the directions say."

"No, no, it will be okay. The ground is too hard anyway."

"Well, how about if we put in a couple? The wind might blow hard tonight. Hodding said it took their stakes out last night."

"Um, honey, we have to get these poles up first, then we can worry about the stakes. Okay?" And the one who was worried about the stakes went about pushing them into the ground, and the pole-person continued to set the poles up. There was no fight.

I gathered some wild mustard for all to taste, using my edible-wild-plants playing cards to identify them. John and Temple declined. Preston and I found them quite mustardy and too bitter to eat much of. I also collected some willow leaves, catkins, and bark to make a tea for Preston's headache. The nickname for willow is the aspirin tree. The warning on my cards read: "DO NOT USE AS BULK FOOD; USE SPARINGLY FOR MEDICINAL PURPOSES." But by the time I had the concoction ready, he claimed his headache was gone.

PART 3

TWO HUNDRED MILES AND FOUR FEET

TWELVE

Tom Jones Crosses the Continental Divide

"I guess this is what they mean by 'living off the land'!" Preston announced as he popped the second piece of chocolate into his mouth. He'd been walking faster than I along the narrow country road and spotted things on the ground first. He'd found a bar of chocolate, Aver Baumstamm chocolate—a cocoa-creme-filled wafer, produced by Rudolf Aver, A-1183 Vienna, Austria, and imported by the Sterling Candy Corp., Moonachie, N.J. 07074. The wrapper suggested, "Keep cool and dry." It was gold and glittering.

This was definitely a perfect place for keeping dry. We were walking through the last stretch of the plains. There was supposed to be a creek running beside us, but it had withered away long ago. Clark's opinion of the plains struck a chord: "This Countrey may with propriety I think be termed the Deserts of America, as I do not conceive any part can ever be settled, as it is deficent in water, Timber & too steep to be tilled."

We'd marched off under the gaze of Temple and John a few hours earlier, dressed for the freezing morning that it was: long underwear, wool hat, gloves, and a fleece jacket. But within an hour both the day and we had heated up. We'd stripped to shorts and T-shirts.

Our hike across the Continental Divide had begun. Lewis and Clark had buried their excess baggage and sunk their canoes (to be gathered on their return) at this point.

Temple and John took our goods and would bring them to Idaho in a month. In the meantime, we would cross the Continental Divide at Lemhi Pass on foot, then head down into a valley, up some more mountains, down into another valley, over another mountain pass, and then (switching to horses) down into the Columbia River system that would take us to the Pacific. There was an easier place to cross the Divide—back at Great Falls—but Lewis and Clark didn't learn about it until later. They had to suffer through this torturous hike and horse ride, and so would we.

Preston had seen the first chocolate bar glittering in the dirt, picked it up, and when I caught up to him, announced, "I'm gonna eat this. Want half?"

I'd never been fond of eating candy found beside a road before and considered his question for a full thirty seconds. Was it laced with PCP? Or did it have a razor blade tucked in there, like a Halloween apple? What was more important, the possibility of being poisoned or extra calories?

"Yeah," I finally answered. Then he found the second one. We ate it without any talk, and the same for the third. The last was cappuccino flavored. They were all better than most American chocolate bars. We figured a shipping truck had lost a box of them after hitting one of the many bumps in the road.

If these things were in our path, what else might we find? We studied the ground more closely. Over the next hour we came across a crowbar, a plastic jug of windshield-wiper fluid, two pairs of women's underwear, one pair of men's, two T-shirts, many cans, and many bottles. A few things be-

came obvious. The litterers preferred Bud Light, Budweiser, Busch Light, and Busch over all other brands. The
brewing companies for these brands can feel good about
that, but what does it say about the kind of people who
drink their swill, considering it was all litter? They liked
sleeveless, ribbed T-shirts. Plastic, sixteen-ounce bottles
were their favorite containers for soda. Pepsi appeared to
be their favorite brand, but generic fruit-flavored sodas
were a close second. I saw only one Coke can. Copenhagen
was their favorite chew, although I did find one old bag of
Beechnut.

"I sorta like seeing all this garbage," Preston commented
when we stopped for a lunch break, "seeing what people
like to use."

Well . . .

After I'd recovered a little more from the hike—the pack
weighed me down and sweat blinded me—I asked Preston
what he'd do if he found a wallet with money in it.

"If it was something like ten dollars, I'd send it all back,"
he answered. "What would you do if it was six thousand
dollars?"

"I guess I'd keep two thousand dollars," I answered.

"Oh, yeah. That'd work. 'Here's your wallet. All there
was was four thousand dollars,' " he joked. "They'd believe
that! But then again, if you gave it all back, they'd just give
you a fifty-dollar reward. That's what they always do."

"Yeah, you're right." Neither of us had ever been in such
a situation, but we knew how it'd come out.

From that point we were on the lookout for money. Instead, we began to see animals. We saw five jackrabbits.
They were so big and fast; I could see how the jackalope
joke started.

We also spotted a herd of pronghorn. When the buck
who was in charge of his harem saw us, he sent them running off in one direction. They sped away in single file. He
stood his ground watching us, but once all was in order, he
charged past the line running at nearly twice their speed to
reach the head. After about a mile, he turned the entire
group at a right angle, allowed his charges to run for about

another mile, and then brought them to a halt. They were well away from us and all were accounted for. He held his head high, pranced around, and appeared proud of himself as the dust settled down.

By midafternoon, we arrived in Grant, Montana. We'd already walked 10.7 miles.

Grant wasn't so much a town as it was a filling station/welding shop and the site of a run-down hotel called the Horse Prairie Hilton. The Hilton looked as if it came straight off a movie set. It was dark and weather-beaten, and a crooked sign hung from just one hook. The sign said showers and kitchen were available, but the place looked more like a stable than a hotel.

We went to the gas station to see about filling our water bottles. Our four bottles held a gallon of water all together, and we'd used up more than half of that in the morning.

A slim, young guy dressed in tight-fitting camouflage clothing was filling his truck with gas. He had sideburns like the guys on "Beverly Hills, 90210." It turned out he was in the area for hunting.

He introduced himself, looking me squarely in the eye: "My name's John Best."

He was up from California, bow-hunting for elk. He was from "L.A.," and when Preston said he was living there as well, John said, "I used to be a model but now I make my living doing commercials." Preston didn't volunteer that he was an actor as well, so I kept my mouth shut.

I asked about bow-hunting. Wasn't it a worse death for the animal?

"If you do it right, you'll hit some arteries. Hit him in the lung. The deer will run thirty to forty yards and then fall down. . . . What happens is they smother to death," John explained. "I was a little concerned with what kind of death it was, but the scientists assure me it's more humane than shooting them. I looked into it all."

"What if you make a bad shot?" I asked.

"Well, if you gut 'em, then it's awful. They can go on forever. But my buddy and I know how to track them. We've taken courses in it."

Courses? That sounded like something a quack nature-man named Tom Brown would teach. I'd come across some of his books while preparing for our trip. He has written about eight of them—on topics ranging from wilderness survival to having a vision quest. (His vision-quest book was even goofier than the one I'd read.) I'd bought two of them because I was interested in the topics. But a multitude of sections in *Tom Brown's Guide to Wild Edible and Medicinal Plants* scared me off. For instance, on amaranth he wrote, "I have learned much about my amaranth brothers over the years, both from watching Stalking Wolf and using my own instincts about the plant. I have grown to know it as a brother. . . . Its essence and spirit become a part of me." In the same book he also declared, "Once the feeling of equality with Creation is assimilated into the very essence of your being, and the reverence for all spirits becomes a reality, then the doorway to a deeper communication with the earth opens." Yikes.

"You mean like the kind Tom Brown teaches in New Jersey?" I asked.

"Yeah, exactly. That's who I studied with. I've taken two of his courses. My buddy and I did his intensive one last time."

"Don't you think he's a lot of hype?" I blurted out. "I think he's hokey. I haven't taken one of his classes, but I've tried to read his books. He says he was raised by an old Native American, but I don't believe it. It just makes him sound more spiritual to say that."

John wouldn't agree with me, except to say Brown was a big storyteller. "But I think he's humble. He says he's no guru."

"What kind of feather is that?" Preston asked, pointing to John's arrow bag and changing the subject. A large, mottled feather hung down from it.

"It's turkey."

"Did you kill it?" I asked.

"No, I bought that. I'm still waiting to get one." He then went on to tell us he taught archery back in California, but it seemed odd that an archery-instructing hunter had not killed his own turkey yet. Maybe this was all a part he was playing in a commercial and he was doing "research"—the way an actor might hang out with physically handicapped people to prepare for a role? I saw Preston looking John over whenever it wouldn't be noticed.

About then, Jack, the owner of the shop, came out. He was a lean fifty-year-old with thinning hair and a well-worn face. He asked John why he hadn't come to the barbeque.

"Barbeque?" Preston asked, lighting up. He'd been awfully quiet ever since John told us he did commercials.

"Oh, yeah," Jack said, "we had a firemen's benefit barbeque. Had two whole hogs one hundred and fifty pounds each. One was filled with eighty pounds of chicken and the other was stuffed with the same amount of Polish sausage. We turned them over the fire for five hours on a spit. That was something. And there wasn't a bit left at the end."

I could hear Preston's stomach grumble.

Jack, John, and I went inside. I wanted to fill the bottles and John had to pay for the gas. Preston chose to stay outside. While I was filling the bottles, I noticed a large woman standing near Preston, just looking in the window. I didn't think much of it and stood around talking to Jack and John, spinning our story. When I attempted to buy an onion, Jack wouldn't let me pay and then handed over four ears of corn left from the picnic. He then suggested John tote us to the turnoff up the road. It was about eleven miles away and was the only place we could pitch the tent and have running water.

We weren't supposed to accept any rides during the hike according to my rules, but if there wasn't anywhere to pitch our tent before there . . . I accepted Jack's offer to have John drive us up the road even though it would put us a day ahead of schedule.

"Hod, did you see that woman say hello to me? She was big," Preston said when John and I went back out.

"That wasn't a woman," John said. "That was the Horse Prairie Fairy. That's what everybody around here calls him."

"It's weird to have a cross-dresser all the way out here," I said. "He must get abused a lot."

"Well, I don't know. I think they treat him fine. No one bothers him. Things are more relaxed out here."

"He came up to me and said, 'Awfully nice day for this late in the year, hmmm?' " Preston reported.

"Yep, that's old Horse Prairie Fairy for you."

On the drive toward our camp, John Best spoke about his motorcycle. "Yeah," he boasted, "my Harley's great for picking up chicks. I just cruise around on it. It's the life, but I've got a serious girlfriend now so I guess I'll have to sell it."

"Did you meet her with the Harley?"

He didn't answer but gave us advice for camping. "Now what you've got to do is set up camp on the upwind side of any water source. That way you won't have any condensation in your tent. In this area that is generally going to be on the western side. Now, to keep out camp raiders—"

"What are those?"

"Birds, like gray or Steller's jays. You can set a string trap for them. My buddy and I've tried to do it—we learned it from Tom Brown—but we haven't caught any yet." He had taken on the role of our mentor, explaining everything to us greenhorns. I guess he thought our questions about bow-hunting meant we knew nothing about camping. His voice dipped an octave or two in the process.

We came to the turnoff soon enough. "Just walk down that road about a mile," he instructed us, "and you'll find the streambed. And remember what I said about setting up around a water supply." We thanked him for the ride and started walking off.

After we'd gone a hundred yards or so, Preston let loose: "I hate sideburns and I hate yuppie guys who ride Harleys. He seems just like the kind of guy who'd do something like that to get girls. He's all that I hate—as if doing commercials is better than modeling! I don't trust that guy. Anyone who wears camouflage can't be trusted. God!" Preston glanced over his shoulder then and I did, too. John was still back there. He seemed to be watching us with binoculars. "Shit, he's probably got a surveillance gun and can hear every word we're saying."

I thought John was fairly smarmy myself, but I didn't really hate him. He was just too full of himself.

"I guess he just represents everything about L.A. that I detest," Preston summed up. I glanced back again and John was gone. We came to the stream in about fifteen minutes, but the land was fenced in on both sides. This was a rancher's land. We squirmed our way between the barbs, taking turns as the other held the wire apart.

Willows bordered the stream, and we wove in and out of them until we came to an area that could not be seen from the road or the hills above. Cattle skeletons littered our campground, and Preston named the site Dead Cow Gulch. He then cracked open a skull and extracted souvenir teeth for us both.

The sun set soon after and immediately the temperature plummeted. The horizon was a rich orange and the hills turned purple-black. An owl checked out our campground, sweeping slowly through the low-lying willows. Since owls have wings that disrupt airflow in a manner to eliminate all flying noise, one of our nature books explained, we only saw and never heard him. He took one, two, three passes and then flew out of sight soundlessly.

"Why, that's a great horned owl," I said.

"No, I think it was a screech owl."

We looked it up and we were both wrong. What it looked most like was a short-eared owl. They weren't supposed to be common in the plains. Maybe the willow woods and stream made up for the surrounding barrens.

A truck stopped out on the road near where we'd crossed the fence. Was it the landowner? I worried.

"I bet that's John Best," Preston said. "I've got a creepy feeling about him. He may want to play some hunting game—with us as the prey." At first this seemed a little crazy to me, but then I got to thinking about that movie *The Most Dangerous Game.* They had been befriended by the hunter and then later mercilessly hunted down. Why couldn't John do the same? Maybe he'd already tracked down his "buddy" and done him in. After all, John was wearing camouflage.

The truck went back and forth on the road, making three or four passes. It was the only vehicle to go by, so we could easily distinguish its sound. Finally, whoever it was gave up. Preston and I both set down the rocks we'd unconsciously been holding. If it had been John, maybe he was unable to track us because we hadn't taken his advice about making camp upwind of the creek.

The coyotes began calling to one another soon thereafter. We'd seen their burrow holes while looking for a spot to pitch the tent, and now they surrounded us. I wanted them to come closer. They were like family and I laughed to myself for having once been afraid of their calling.

We took it really easy the following day since John had driven us so far. We only needed to hike about six miles. Our bodies were a little sore from the day before, and we ambled those miles. When we stopped for a snack of dried fruit, Preston read to me about the lynx, mountain lion, bobcat, gray wolf, and coyote from one of the Audubon books. The most astonishing fact was that coyotes can leap up to fourteen feet. What an amazing feature for a canine. The mountain lion only leaps six feet more. The leaping ability clinched it—I was in love with coyotes. I would miss hearing them when our expedition was over.

We arrived at our campsite for the night by one in the afternoon. It was another minivalley with its own creek— Trail Creek—and a cover of willows. The site we chose was across a barbed-wire fence and well away from the road. Being away from the road probably didn't matter much since only three cars had passed us all day.

We were smelly, dirty, and hot and decided to bathe in the creek. A beaver had built a dam, creating a perfect pool for a dip. It was warm and dry out, somewhere in the eighties, but the water was freezing. We couldn't stay in longer than thirty seconds. Preston looked down in the water and announced, "My penis is blue." I couldn't even see mine it'd shrunk so much from the cold, and my balls stung as if sea nettles had attacked.

We'd hop in, submerge, splash all over, climb out, scrub with biodegradable soap, jump in again, and then repeat until all was clean. We rinsed our clothes off as well, not wasting any soap on them. They'd been sticking to us like honey.

The last time I'd swum in a beaver pond, this huge papa beaver had come barreling across the water like a Trident submarine, slapping his tail to warn me off. But this beaver never emerged. At first, Preston and I guessed some rancher had killed him earlier in the year. I found a perfect scat, though, at the bottom of the pond that I thought was a beaver's, so we changed our theory. Maybe our beaver simply wasn't bold.

Amazingly, its scat was still intact. Beaver "droppings are not often found, since they are deposited in water," explained my tracking book. "They consist of oval pellets of coarse 'sawdust.' " The scats now in my hand matched this description and looked just like the illustration. Bare-butt and blue from the cold water, Preston and I did a little dance for joy over this stupendous scatological find.

Emboldened by my discovery, I went off on a scat hunt while Preston read *Housekeeping*. I clambered over rocks, crossed the creek dozens of times, and stuck my hands into many a crevice. I found the best ones on top of a two-hundred-foot-high rock that stood about a half mile from our tent. The thing was covered with jackrabbit pellets and some ptarmiganlike fowl shits. The "ptarmigan" scats matched the ones in the book and were in a deep crevice below a four-foot-high boulder on top of the two-hundred-foot rock. They could also have been the scat of a prairie falcon, but I forgot to smell them to see if they stunk of rotting flesh. (If they were falcon and not ptarmigan, the bird would have been eating birds, rodents, and other small animals and would probably have a stinkier shit. Ptarmigans eat berries, seeds, and insects.) There were no prints.

Next to one scattering of jackrabbit scats I found the shit

of what I thought was bear. It was pure grass and massive. The tubular shape of the scat was nothing like cow or horse (which also eat grass), and since there had been a dismal berry crop on account of the extremely dry year, it was likely a bear could have eaten only grass. They were a little over an inch in diameter, about one and a half inches, and while they were all connected, they appeared almost to separate at intervals of three–four inches. The overall pile was more than five inches wide and three and a half inches tall. I also found some elk droppings, but they were down on the prairie.

On my way back to camp, I put three samples of these scats—I left out the ptarmigan's—in my pockets. It took a while finding the camp because the head-high willow trees and healthy sagebrush created a maze out of our little valley. I entered a couple of dead ends but didn't mind because they were usually embedded with elk and deer prints.

On returning, I showed my scats to Preston. He had to agree that the jackrabbit and elk were what I said, but he remained skeptical of the bear scat. He thought it might have been from a horse, but a horse couldn't have climbed up that steep rock. He also accused me of putting dents in the elk scats to make them match exactly the ones in the book.

We decided to catch our dinner that night. For the next hour Preston whittled away on a long, heavy stick to make a spear. He ran around the camp, throwing the spear into the ground and screaming out, "Ha! Take that you wily willow ptarmigan." I whittled at a small piece of wood and made a hook (Temple had our fishing gear). I'd seen a drawing of it in *How to Stay Alive in the Woods*, and although it is one of the most unintelligible books I've ever attempted to read, the hook had seemed useful. I then caught a cricket and hooked it up.

We crept (of course we'd scared everything off hours before) to the stream, and as Preston scoured the banks with his spear, I attempted to catch some foot-long darting fish. They never came near my bait. Part of the problem might have been that my hook floated and that it was twice as large as the cricket.

As we sat around the campfire, simply staring at the flames, smelling the nearby mountain air brought down by a easterly breeze, and talking about Marina (Preston's wife), Preston said more than once, "This is so sublime."

And I couldn't help agreeing. We'd finally come into our own—walking along the old road at our own pace and seeing as many animals and scats as we could wish for. It was a far cry from New York City, L.A., or even a small Montana town. We even knew how to get along with each other. When we were in a good mood, talk. When we were in a bad mood, keep quiet and walk separately.

Coyotes serenaded us to sleep that night at Camp Sublime.

The sun took its time reaching us the next morning. True, there were hills around us blocking its path, but I worried it was a sign of approaching winter. We'd been warned by Barb Opdahl—she and her husband would be leading us across part of the trail by horse in less than three weeks—of early winters in the mountains. "It can be downright mean up there," she'd said. "So just be prepared. You have to be ready for any type of weather. It's really hard. . . . You're not having a car follow you?"

Preston was unworried about our future. Before we ventured out that morning, he reported, "I just walked over to the same area where I took my first shit yesterday. I lifted up the cow patty I'd buried it under and dumped exactly on top of it. That way, when fifty years or so from now, when they send a team to retrace our expedition, they'll lift up that patty and be amazed at what big men we were." His heart was in the right place as far as burying his feces went, but I don't think Kathleen Meyer, author of *How to Shit in the Woods*, would approve. But then she didn't have to worry about leaving behind markings for future researchers to unearth. I kept quiet.

Once again we began the hike with too many clothes on

because ice and frost were on the ground when we awoke, but within the hour we'd peeled everything off. The landscape was slowly changing. Rolling, yellowed hills no longer surrounded us. In their place, the foothills of the Bitterroot Mountains darted up, speckled and sometimes covered with pines.

This simple change of scenery lightened our loads, and we walked up in altitude as if we were on level ground. Our destination for the day was Lemhi Pass, not more than seven miles away. Lemhi Pass was an old Native American trail that the Lewis and Clark expedition used to cross the Continental Divide. But for them to do so, they needed to procure horses from the Native Americans in the area. A task more easily said than done since the Shoshones were completely afraid of the white men.

Lewis tried in vain to approach one Shoshone: "I made him the signal of friendship known to the Indians . . . which is by holding the mantle or robe in your hands at two corners and then throwing [it] up in the air higher than the head bringing it to earth as if in the act of spreading it, thus repeating three times. this signal of the robe has arrisen from a custom among all those nations of spreading a robe or skin for their gests to set on when they are visited. this signal had not the desired effect. . . . I got nearer than about 100 paces when he suddenly turned his horse about, gave him the whip leaped the creek and disapeared in the willow brush in an instant and with him vanished all my hopes of obtaining horses for the present."

I had wanted horses for this section as well, but in this century the problem was a little different. Much of the land was now private—except the road we were walking along. The national forests we'd be walking through were public, but the government required horse outfitters to buy licenses for each forest. One outfitter quoted me a price of $20,000 for the four-hundred-mile overland trip, and all the others outright refused. That was why we were walking most of it.

Thanks to Sacagawea, Lewis and Clark were able to trade for horses. Lewis finally persuaded the Shoshones of his peaceful intentions and led them to his rendezvous point with Clark and other members of the team. They brought Sacagawea to translate, and as it turned out, she was the sister of Cameahwait, the chief of this tribe. From that point on, their dealings with the Shoshones improved. They eventually received horses and a guide, enabling them to continue their westward march.

Our being horseless had its benefits, though. We were able to collect dandelion flowers as we went along. Dandelions are rich in vitamins and calcium, and I planned to add them to the night's meal.

"Maybe you shouldn't add them to the food," Preston said as he stooped over to collect a handful. "You could simply fry them separately, and that way, if they taste like shit, our whole meal won't be ruined."

"I don't know . . ."

"We can't afford to miss a meal, Hod."

About an hour before we reached Lemhi Pass, we came upon two old trapper huts. We figured they were trapper cabins because they were at the turnoff for Trapper Creek, according to the posted sign. They were made of old but sturdy, weathered logs. The roofs were long wooden planks covered with sod. Grass was growing on top of them.

"Now, these would be great to build," Preston said. "They're so sturdy and simple. And they're hand-hewn."

I didn't know what *hand-hewn* meant but pretended to understand. "Yep," I answered. Later, he explained that it meant they were cut, shaped, and fitted with a hand ax.

In one we found a three-foot-high mound of drying mushrooms. Who would do that? I wondered. Was this someone's cache of edible mushrooms. I was excited about the possibilities of borrowing such fungi. Something suddenly began thumping on the floor.

"I think that's from a rat," Preston offered, and just after he spoke an eight-inch rat scampered across the floor. We looked closer at the mound and noticed it was surrounded by rat turds. Many tins and other garbage were in the pile, and what looked like a nest was on top. This was the work of an industrious pack rat.

We looked for a more specific sign—"an accumulation of dung that has a homogeneous, tarlike consistency, black in color. . . . In some instances this black deposit drips over the edge of the rock and extends down the face as a somewhat sticky overflow for a distance of a foot or more," according to my tracking book. But our rat had only deposited tubular, half-inch scats.

The road switchbacked up to Lemhi Pass from that point and our hiking became more labored. We checked our pulses at one point and they were well over 140. It didn't matter to us (well, I complained but Preston persevered) because we also wound our way into the national forest. We were leaving the Great Plains!

By one, we reached Lemhi Pass. A couple of commemorative signs provided the history of the crossing. They were all about Lewis and Clark. On the other side of the pass a tree-lined, level valley led to Idaho. A clear stream ran through it. Since we'd be hiking in the valley the following day, it was good to see there would be no water problems.

It wasn't all that exciting to have reached the Continental Divide because we knew we were following Lewis and Clark's route. It'd been an exciting moment for them because they thought a river would be waiting within a day's hike to take them to the Pacific Ocean. What joy!

But it hadn't worked. The Salmon turned out to be unnavigable. That's why they headed north and then west to reach what is now called the Clearwater River. We'd be doing the same.

A developed campground (in this case, that meant there was a fire ring and a picnic table for each site and one portable outhouse for the entire grounds) was a couple hundred yards away. We would be sleeping beneath pine trees for the evening. It seemed so luxurious.

Preston wandered around our forest, identifying the trees. After much debate (with himself) he finally decided on Engelmann spruce and lodgepole pine. I joined him for a bit but it was too difficult, even with the trees themselves and the pictures and descriptions in the book directly in front of us.

His Audubon book also described the water bugs that were in a nearby stream. They were common water skimmers, known in some areas as Jesus bugs and others as scooters. They have two long middle legs, shorter back legs, and even shorter front ones. Their bodies are shaped like an orzo noodle and have ridges at the end of their backs. One of them had caught a smaller, rounder water bug and appeared to be attempting to murder it. He failed and eventually dropped it by the side of the stream. As it started to clamber up a grass stalk, a tiny black water spider tried to catch it. The spider pulled at it with two of its legs, but the tiny bug tried a little bit harder and escaped.

A sign was posted by the stream. It quoted Lewis recording an incident that had occurred along this stream: "McNeal had exultingly stood with a foot on each side of this little rivulet and thanked god that he had lived to bestride the mighty & heretofore deemed endless Missouri." McNeal was wrong in thinking that this was the headwaters of the Missouri as the real source of the Missouri is Upper Red Rock Lake and its streams, west of Yellowstone National Park. Lewis made the same mistake a few hours earlier: "The road took us to the most distant fountain of the waters of the Mighty Missouri in surch of which we have spent so many toilsome days and wristless nights. thus far I had accomplished one of those great objects on which my mind has been unalterably fixed for many years, judge then of the pleasure I felt in allying my thirst with this pure and ice-cold water."

I went deeper into the woods after we pitched the tent to practice my compass reading and simply be alone. I marched in straight trajectories based on my readings until I was well away from the campground. Dead and fallen trees abounded, and I found myself peering over my shoulder and whirling around to catch a glimpse of any advancing predator. But I wasn't too sure what it might be. No grizzlies were left in the area and nothing else would really bother me. A mountain lion would run off if I stared it down, but it was hard to imagine that in the dark woods.

An annoying chattering/chirping pierced the air. I circled around with my binoculars in place, and on a limb not more than fifty yards away was a Clark's nutcracker, named after our very own William Clark. It was such a large bird—the size of a crow and so stately with its silvery gray head.

I searched for its cache of seeds, since its favorite food is pine nuts (they'd be great in some future pasta). They hide more than twenty thousand seeds through the summer and fall, but I didn't find a single one.

On my return, Preston was talking with a man who'd arrived in a dark green truck. His name was Tom Jones and he was retracing the trail, too.

"I'm not doing something as adventurous as you guys," he said. "My wife wouldn't let me be gone for so long. I'm just following along from Three Forks to the Portland area, stopping along the way and seeing for myself all of the important places. To get some feel for what those brave men went through. When I drove by Beaver Rock—did you see it?—well, that's too bad. It was such an important landmark for them. When Sacagawea saw that she knew where they were and that they could make it safely over the mountains. That must've been something."

"Ah, yeah," Preston and I both muttered. We'd been so busy trying to hitchhike down to Clark Canyon we hadn't even noticed. We'd also skipped Three Forks—the place where Tom had started his retracing and where three rivers formed the headwaters of the Missouri in southern Montana. Lewis had named the three rivers: the Jefferson, the Madison, and the Gallatin (named after Jefferson's treasury secretary—Albert Gallatin).

Tom had worked for the Forest Service for sixteen years. "I'm a road finder," he explained. "That's not the fancy name they give it. They call it 'transportation developer.' But it's what I do. If they want a road through a forest, I go out there and figure where it ought to run—given points A and B."

"Have you had to fight fires?" I asked.

"Yep."

"You must've fought some pretty bad ones, huh?" Preston asked.

Tom just shrugged. He wouldn't brag, and I think that's when Preston and I knew we liked him. He was in his mid-forties. He had slightly graying hair—what we could see of it from beneath his baseball cap—and was a skinny, shorter fellow.

As we stood there talking, eating some stale chips he had in his truck and drinking ice-cooled sodas, a large owl landed on a tree not more than twenty yards away. We watched her with our glasses, and Preston and I tried to guess what she was. "That's a great gray owl," Tom told us. "You hardly ever see one of those." She swooped down among some tall grass, tussled with something, and then flew deeper into the woods. Preston looked up the bird in his book and Tom was right.

"I was pretty lucky there," Tom said. "If it'd been any other kind of owl, I wouldn't have been able to identify it."

Preston and I had seen many marks in the local trees that looked as if they could be bear scratchings. Tom took a look and pronounced them natural splits in the bark. "But this is black-bear country," he added, "even though they're probably all down in the valleys right now on account of the bad berry crop this past summer."

Tom ate dinner with us a little later. I fried the dandelions in some oil and salt as an appetizer. They were awfully bitter, but no one complained until I said they were inedible. I'd made such a big deal out of them. "Don't you think we'd be eating dandelion flowers all the time back home, considering how many there are, if they tasted good?" Preston asked.

We discussed the Forest Service with Tom. The only drawback to our campsite and the forest was the cow patties all over the place. I'd always thought, in my ignorance, that national forests were places for the public to enjoy. I'd never known that the government let ranchers use the land for grazing. Tom explained that the forests were used by many private enterprises: cattlemen, miners, oil companies, farmers, and lumbermen. How was that public usage? I wondered. It seemed more like a sweet private deal for certain companies, farmers, and cattlemen to get rich off .

Why should they get better treatment than anyone else?

Tom agreed with the questions.

But he defended the Forest Service's lumbering projects. "You see . . . ," he said, rubbing his index finger along his cheek and gazing off into the sky. There was a substantial pause while he thought. "Forty years ago the public was clamoring for wood products. So the Forest Service set things up to supply wood. Now, in the last ten years everyone is saying, 'Leave the forests as they are. We want them to be pristine and wild.' But no one is cutting back on his usage of wood products. Everyone is still using just as much paper as before, and they still want wood in their homes. There has to be a change. . . . Now, we are obliging this most recent outcry. We're making less timberland available. It'll be interesting to see what happens."

Preston said that maybe the Forest Service had decided to do this, but that with all of the bureaucracy in D.C., he doubted the decrease in lumbering had really started.

We moved to a subject we could all agree upon and traded turns recounting events from the Lewis and Clark expedition. Tom became enraptured with the stories— leaping up to act out the confusion the men faced when they reached the Marias River in what is now northern Montana. "Should they follow this large river that obviously led west or continue on what seemed to be the Missouri?" he asked in a hushed manner, peering around as if he could see both rivers in front of him. "What to do? They'd come so far but now had the ultimate choice to make. By sheer luck—or was it instinct?—they chose the right river and stayed on the Missouri. Otherwise they would have been stuck for another winter." I might've worried about his obsession if it hadn't been for the Yukon Jack that he and Preston were drinking. A little later, Preston read aloud from the Yukon Jack label, " 'Canadian liqueur. One hundred proof. Yukon Jack is a taste born of hoary nights, when lonely men struggled to keep their fires lit and cabins warm.' Ah, good ol' Yukon Jack."

"I can't believe you two have never heard of Yukon Jack," Tom said.

And when Tom went off to take a piss, Preston whispered, "This stuff is awful, Hod. It tastes like syrup."

Tom had a ruddy complexion, but it had turned outright red. Preston was looking about the same. They continued relating events from the expedition, as if no one had ever heard or spoken of these things before. They were drunk. Eventually, one of them had the bright idea of going on top of the pass and looking down at both valleys. They went and I stayed behind.

As they walked off, I heard some stumbling noise and then Tom said, "Sorry about that."

"That's all right," Preston said. "I'm stumbling, too."

While they were gone, I lay on our picnic bench looking up at the sky through the trees. Their limbs and trunks were darkly silhouetted against the lighter night sky. Not a cloud was out and the stars shone nearly enough light to see by. I felt we were on top of the world. I continued lying there, watching the unmoving trees.

The minute I climbed out of our tent at seven-thirty the next morning, Tom came scrambling down the little hill that led from his truck. He had an armful of food: oatmeal, coffee, and bananas. He seemed no worse off but Preston was hurting. From inside the tent we could hear him scream, "Yukon Jack! Hoary nights!" and then he'd moan and groan. "Now there's some nasty stuff!"

"I just have to say that I think this is something," Tom said as we gathered around our breakfast. "Here we are at Lemhi Pass and I run into you two. It seems so perfect. All three of us sharing the same interest. And I want you two to have something. I picked it up at Fort Clatsop [the expedition's winter fort on the Pacific Ocean—our final destination]. I had this thing at home and I thought, 'Well, I'd sure better bring it along considering where I'm going,' and now it's fitting I have it to give to you. Good luck." With that said, he handed over a replica medallion of a coin Jefferson had minted for the expedition to give to the Indians. He also gave us Army MREs (meals ready to eat):

peanut butter and hardtack, beans, and peaches. Whenever there was a fire, the Forest Service gave the MREs to
the firefighters. Tom had collected many over the years.

We parted company soon after breakfast. Much like Wild
Bill back on the Missouri, Tom seemed sad to see us go.

The first three miles of our hike that morning were on a
rough trail that led through the Salmon National Forest. It
purported to be the Lewis and Clark Trail. It crisscrossed
various streams and often completely vanished from sight.
Our only guideposts were occasional signposts depicting
the figures of Lewis and Clark. Towering lodgepole pines
kept us hidden from the rest of the world, and the only
other signs of life were numerous scurrying chipmunks
and a couple of soaring hawks. It was difficult going but
worth every step: no cars, roads, or signs of modern life
(garbage).

We reconnected with the road all too soon, but at least it
was a dirt one. And unlike in Montana, trees grew all about.

Two men approached us in a dark, covered pickup.
"Where you going?" the driver asked.

"We're following the Lewis and Clark Trail to the Pacific."

"Well, we can't take you there, but we'll give you a lift to
Tendoy," the driver continued. He was older than his passenger. They appeared to be father and son and were both
dressed in camouflage.

"Um, no thanks," Preston said. "We're walking all the
way to Lolo, Montana."

At first I thought their faces were covered with camouflage as well, but then I realized the boy simply had a
bumper crop of pimples. Were their hands covered with
camo? The boy's weren't but the man's appeared to be. I
looked more closely.

It wasn't camo. His hands and arms were covered up to
the elbows with something all right—real blood and guts.
The colors were red and yellow. They'd obviously had some
success, but the boy looked petrified. Maybe it had been
his first kill.

Preston gave me a look, indicating he'd noticed the
same thing. The man was still trying to press a ride on us.

He was awfully eager about it, but finally he gave up and continued down the road.

We found the trail of another hunter soon afterward.

These days, it is the rare human who spots America's largest cat, the mountain lion. It once roamed throughout the United States, but its territory has been confined mostly to mountainous regions, thanks to the encroachment of modern society. The lion covers up to twenty-five miles in a night's wandering and needs an abundance of undisturbed wilderness. They were once the natural predators of deer, whose population is now out of control in many areas of the United States.

Preston and I happened upon not a lion but something nearly as good: its tracks. We'd been following elk tracks for some distance when we spotted them. They were perfectly preserved, having been made when the road was muddy. They measured four by four inches and the scalloped pads were quite distinct. According to my tracking book, they could only be mountain-lion tracks. For sixty-eight feet (we measured them), the tracks stayed on the edge of the road. Sometimes the tracks were two and a half feet apart and other times they were right on top of each other. It was erratically changing its gait: preying on something.

What was this lion doing walking right out in the open? Then we noticed it was walking on top of the elk tracks. It was after them. A mountain lion will hunt anything from elk to grasshoppers.

All of a sudden the tracks simply disappeared. It must have pounced into the grass and brush growing between the road and the creek. But where? We backed up to where the tracks began.

Lying just within the grass was a piece of porcupine tail. I picked it up. "Maybe this is what it ate," I announced, but neither of us felt so sure about it. I dropped it back down to the ground, and when I did, something on the other side of some willows caught my eye.

We cut through the brush to investigate, and there lay the rest of the porcupine. All of the meat and innards were gone, but a lot of the pelt was still left. Flies were buzzing around so it couldn't be that old.

"Do you think the lion was hunting this? With all the elks around?" I asked. It didn't seem likely.

"Well, something had to have made this big turd," Preston said, smiling. He pointed to a five-inch-by-three-inch mound of hairy scat that looked exactly like the drawing of lion scat in my tracking book. There were scratch marks in front of the scat as well, nailing shut any doubt about who ate this porcupine. Also, as it turns out, porcupine is one of the mountain lion's favorite meals.

Farther into the brush and up where the tracks ended, we found more porcupine hair and quills. "So the lion circled the porcupine along the road," Preston theorized, "grabbed it somewhere near the creek, and then dragged it screaming to this kill site. How amazing."

We were overjoyed with having figured this out and rested in a cool, green glade just a few hundred yards away. I suggested to Preston he spread out and take it easy— lounge around a bit. "You have a hangover and all, Preston," I sympathized, "I'll get our snacks out." I was hoping his fleshy body, stretched along the ground, would draw the mountain lion, but Preston was on to me.

"That's awfully sweet of you, buddy," he responded, "but I'm feeling fine now. You're looking a little peaked, though. Why don't you take a little nap?"

Although it was October 1, and more than five thousand feet in elevation, the black cottonwoods shading our area all had their green leaves. That and finding those tracks were a good sign for our mountain hike.

For dinner we dumped the MRE beans Tom had given us into some beef-flavored rice. It tasted great.

Within twenty minutes, however, Preston was squatting not more than fifty feet away.

"Whoa!" he called out. "A big fat cork just popped out and now it's a dire situation." He'd been squatting for some time by then. What a joy to be able to share his bowel movements with him.

"So it's pretty fluid, huh?" I asked.

"Yeah . . . uh, fluid movements." He paused. "Aw, come on now. I can't believe it. It looks just like those MRE beans. Wow. That's pretty spectacular."

I gleefully recorded his every word in my diary and even teased him about it when he returned: "Nothing like a good diarrhea to brighten up the day?" Suddenly the rumbling in my stomach turned more "dire" as well, and I got my just desserts a few minutes later.

Oddly, our upset stomachs were just the panacea we needed, making up for some earlier bickering. Maybe it served as a reminder that we really were in this together— no matter what. We had a pleasant evening.

THIRTEEN

- - - - - - - - - -

Hobo Scum

"What should we do?" I asked Preston for the third time. Up until then, the morning had gone fine. The air was thin and cool. No clouds hung overhead. Everything was perfect. My feet weren't even sore from the day before. We'd passed other cattle all morning, but they had run off the road into the safety of the surrounding brush long before we drew near.

This big, bad bull had other ideas. He stood his ground in the middle of the road.

"Just pretend you're not intimidated," Preston instructed. "He'll back off." So we marched on, ever closer. The bull wasn't having any of it. He shook his head from side to side and stomped a foot. I was hoping that the myth about bulls charging red objects was true. Preston wore a red backpack and mine was blue.

"Maybe we should try something different," Preston added. "Let's walk along the hill."

The hill was a sharply angled rock slide that stretched along the road for nearly a mile. We had to climb up a ten-foot drop-off even to stand on it. So there was no way the bull could reach us. But once we were up there, the going was slow and labored, thanks to the steepness and sliding rocks. I fell a number of times and was barely able to see, much less follow, Preston. He skipped along the rocks as if he were a damned mountain goat. But the bull stayed even with him the entire time. Preston walked; the bull walked. Preston ran; the bull ran. Eventually, Preston had had enough and climbed back down to the road and scared the bull into the brush. He even warded him off with his red backpack as I gingerly approached. I begrudgingly thanked him.

By midmorning we were thoroughly in the valley and we hit civilization again: Tendoy, Idaho. It was a one-shop town. The grocery store served as a caterer for road crews, a filling station for highway traffic, a gathering place for locals, and a post office for everyone. The elderly woman who ran the general store had dyed-brown hair, but her eyes looked young.

"You know," she said upon hearing of our trek, "Sacagawea was born three miles away at Panther Creek. But the one thing about that whole story I can't figure out is, how come Sacagawea was kidnapped at Three Forks? I've never been able to figure out how that happened. She was there with her father and she was a Shoshone. The chief, her father, was killed. His son was knocked off his horse. So Sacagawea gave her horse to her brother. She was kidnapped, along with another little girl, who later made it back all on her own from North Dakota. If her brother stayed alive, how'd she get taken?" (Sacagawea was eventually traded to Charbonneau, who brought her with him on the expedition.)

I didn't have an answer.

Why was she so interested in all the Lewis and Clark lore?

"You can't help but care about it, living in the area," she answered, and then slowly shook her head. "But so very few people pay any attention to it anymore—it's real sad."

From this point on, our route followed a major highway that ran from eastern Idaho up to the western border of Montana. Lewis and Clark had woven their way through here crossing and recrossing the mountains to find the way to the Columbia River. Their hardships had been snow, ice, and little food. Ours would be the modern world. We'd be walking through towns like Tendoy and even larger ones. Telephone and electric wires would accompany us. Cars and trucks would leap out at us, and roadside trash would be ever present.

From Tendoy, we had a day and a half's hike to the next town, Salmon, which we started that same afternoon. We took the old highway that runs for about fifteen miles on an escarpment overlooking the new one down in the valley.

The landscape was magnificent. Before, there had either been rolling hills or rising mountains, but now, we had both simultaneously. Snow-covered peaks rose to our east and rolling hills ambled beside us. A water-fed valley lay below. The only drawback was that the trees were beginning to thin out again; we were walking out of the national-forest boundary.

Preston established new hunting rules while we hiked along. He was tired of seeing all the hunters in their trucks and camo clothing, people like John Best in particular. "It goes like this," he explained. "Anyone who wants to hunt grizzlies must use bows and arrows only. For lions, you can only have a spear. And you can't wear any camouflage. Camouflage will be outlawed forthwith. Let's see, turkey hunters have to have their feet and one hand bound behind their backs. This is all to make it more sporting. It's much too easy as it now stands, don't you think?"

What about elk, deer, pronghorn, and moose hunters?

"Simple. They can use their hands. Nothing else."

Preston and I hadn't had much conversation during our hikes, but he talked a lot on this afternoon. Something was on his mind and he finally let it out. "I've been having such intense dreams about Marina. Last night, I dreamed she didn't love me anymore. The worse thing was there was nothing I could do. I even begged to her on my knees, crying around her legs, but she still wouldn't love me. It was awful."

There wasn't really any way to console him since it was only a dream. I think it helped just to tell it. When we found some watercress growing in a creek beside the old road a little later, there was no hint that the dream was still lingering in his mind. "We need the roughage," he commented. "But do you think this stuff is polluted?"

"Of course it's not. We used to eat watercress from my grandmother's that grew in a stream right by the road as well. It'll be fine." I wasn't really sure it was watercress, to tell the truth, but it tasted somewhat like it and neither of us felt sick after sampling a few bites. Preston even admitted it tasted good. But it was spicier than any cress I'd ever had. We gathered two large bunches.

We rested beside Kenny Creek a little later to eat lunch and rinse off our bodies. The people in the Tendoy store had all been friendly, but we'd noticed that none of them stood too close to us. I'd also been sticking to my sleeping bag the last few nights, and my crotch was perpetually damp and sticky from sweat. It was impossible to sleep with a mildewing crotch. So we rinsed off extra carefully. It was over seventy degrees out and the cold mountain water was soothing.

We hiked a few more miles, stopping when we'd completed about eleven miles for the day. Once again there was no public land suitable for camping, so we trespassed through someone's barbed-wire fence and set up camp beside a two-foot-wide creek that lay hidden by a thick growth of quaking aspens. We were completely hidden from the road, as well as the ranch house that was down in the valley.

First thing after setting up camp, we filtered water, washed the watercress, and ate a plateful each. By the end of this green meal both of our mouths were burning. If it was watercress, then it had aged to a powerful point. Preston trotted off behind the nearest, thickest bush.

Just to make sure he was feeling better, I threw stones at him while he was taking a shit.

"How could you throw stones at me while I'm having a diarrhetic attack?" he yelled. The watercress had been a might too powerful. "Ouch!"

He came limping back to camp. "Did one of those stones hit you?" I asked.

"No, you're a lousy shot, but I'll get you back anyway. . . . You caused me to step on a cactus spine, though. As the doctor, you have to take it out."

What was he doing walking around without shoes on? He stuck his foot in my lap.

It was weird how in varying ways he really did resemble Clark and I, Lewis. Clark had also had trouble with cactus spines. Would Preston's foot become swollen with a festering boil on account of this cactus, just as Clark's had? Unsure of what ailed him at first, Clark recorded, "I have either got my foot bitten by Some poisonous insect or a tumer is riseing on the inner bone of my ankle which is painful." A few days later Lewis added, "The tumor on Capt. Clarks ankle has discharged a considerable quantity of matter but is still much swollen and inflamed and gives him considerable pain." As Preston's foot lay in my lap, I wondered if maybe I shouldn't give it a chance to begin discharging first? Let Preston be even more like Clark?

"Are you going to fix it or do I have to take on that responsibility as well?" he asked, shaking his foot impatiently. I drew out a needle from our sewing kit and commenced digging.

"Hey, that hurts!"

"Shut up." I yanked his foot.

"You have a truly horrible bedside manner, Dr. Carter. I'm going to tell everybody."

To my delight, I found that I rather enjoyed tearing open his sole. After I pulled the first one out, I went looking for more and eventually found another thorn that appeared to be buried beneath the skin. I yanked his foot around and twisted his leg to get a better view as the coyotes welcomed the settling dusk and the aspens rustled under an evening breeze.

The next day we walked to Salmon, Idaho. A third of the way there we connected with the main highway. Eighteen-wheelers and pickup after pickup blared by us. We did see two coyotes, one deer, a mouse, and a hedgehog. All roadkill. And Copenhagen was now the favored brand of chewing tobacco. Preston retrieved a Rams cap out of a ditch and wore it unwashed.

Salmon itself was fairly depressing. It was mostly a thruway for the highway. A few stores offered tourists' items: maps, scenic mementos, and Lewis and Clark statues. We visited the Lemhi County Museum and half of the display area was taken up by an exhibit of Chinese artifacts. A placard explained that the Ray Edwards family had donated the Chinese items. Ray had traveled to the Orient in 1920 and brought back many keepsakes, including twenty-nine bronze incense burners—all in the form of Chinese horses and their riders.

In comparison, there wasn't much on Lemhi County. The Lewis and Clark display's main feature were statues of Lewis, Clark, York (Clark's slave, whom he later freed), Sacagawea, and Toby, their guide who caused them to stray from the traditional and easier route across the mountains. These statues were actually bottles of Kentucky Straight whiskey. There was a real statue of Sacagawea, bronze and one-foot tall. There were many copies of it and they all sold for $1,000. The idea had been to sell these to raise money to build a life-size version out front. But there hadn't been enough interest or, judging by the dust on most of the displays, enough visitors.

We were forced to camp in a tent and trailer park that night within the town's limits. When a nighttime thunderstorm hit, we were thankful for the park's cabana. Our backpacks stayed dry.

The clouds hung around most of the following morning

and covered the mountains. The valley felt like a prison.

The road, and thus our hike, wound its way along the Salmon River, providing a more scenic walk than the day before. Cottonwoods with their fall colors dropped leaves at our feet, and pines of all kinds freshened the atmosphere. The trash alongside the road lessened some, except for the countless cigarette cartons. Skunks were the number one roadkill of the day.

We watched a black-billed magpie chase a red-tailed hawk for a couple of hundred yards. The hawk dove and rose, cutting through trees and swooping through open air, but the magpie stayed right on him. Luckily, the ill-advised extermination contests to wipe out magpies in the United States held up until the thirties had failed. Otherwise, what bird would be around to give the mighty hawk such a wonderful chase?

When we stopped for a snack, Preston approached me, stuck out his hand, and said, "Oh, good to see you. I haven't seen you in so long."

When we stopped laughing, he continued, "It's a good thing we do get along. And we have so many things in common. That's probably why. For instance, we both like to read the nutrition information on the back of food packages." He proceeded to read aloud the information on the back of our fifteen-ounce box of Western Family natural raisins. Copper was listed at 15 percent of the U.S. recommended daily allowance. "Boy, I'm sure glad we're getting so much copper. Where would we be without it?" When did they start listing copper as a necessary mineral?

We only had to cover nine miles for the day according to my calculations. Around two-thirty we arrived at a Bureau of Land Management camping site. It was ten yards from the road but slightly protected by a couple of ten-foot-tall boulders. The river was only yards away as well.

Not much farther along the river sat a trailer park. Our water filter was clogged, and after a fitful night's sleep, we determined it was necessary to procure clean water. In other words, I decided to beg for some from one of the mobile-home dwellers. Preston wasn't so sure this was the brightest idea considering our appearance. Also, it was eight in the morning.

Without a second thought, I knocked at a likely home; likely because it had a wooden stoop. All the others had barren fronts.

"Come on in," a deep voice said. I opened the door and a cloud of egg, bacon, toast, and coffee smell blew over me. Preston followed a few seconds later once he realized I hadn't been shot.

One man sat on a beat-up old couch, watching the morning news. He only asked us one thing: "How'd you get here?" He was stocky with blond hair and a beat-up face. The man who'd told us to come in stood behind the counter. He peppered us with friendly questions about our trip.

But as soon as I was finished filling our water bottles, the friendliness stopped. We weren't being asked to breakfast, that was for sure. We left.

"That guy on the couch was running from something," Preston said. "From a wife or the law, I don't know, but he gave me the creeps."

We were both a bit upset that they hadn't offered us any food. People just weren't like they were back on the Missouri—like the people who'd given us free pancakes, a tow from their boat, a fishing rod.

"But you know," Preston realized, "they have no reason to. We're just hobo scum now. Back then we had property— a Zodiac raft and a brand-new motor. We were propertied folk. We were one of them. Look at us now. For all they know, this is all we own in the world."

"But we've got . . ." I started to say we had nice backpacks, but both of ours were at least ten years old and badly beaten. Even our sleeping pads and tent were wrapped in trash bags, contributing to our air of dirtiness. "We do have a pair of binoculars and your camera."

"Yeah, but they just look like props. My camera is pretty trashed. But the main thing is our appearance. Look at us. Would you help us out? Your greasy, long hair is plastered to your head. Your nose is bright red—which some might think is from drinking. All of your clothes are stained, and if anyone gets close enough to smell them, they'd probably feel woozy. You stink as bad as some of this roadkill. It's pretty simple; we're degenerates in the eyes of everyone around us."

He was proven correct about an hour later. We were taking a break at a "Sportsman's Access" area (that's what the sign had said)—a parking lot beside the river, really, when a mobile home pulled in next to us. A short, stocky man climbed out, followed by a cat, a dog, and a woman. He didn't say anything to us until Preston gave him a hearty greeting. Then he started talking, but warily, as if he might run to the truck at any minute. He bragged about his '93 Ford pickup most of the time. And then out of the blue, he referred to his handgun. Was he warning us?

His wife, who'd disappeared for a while, poked her head out the trailer-home door and asked if he wanted a ham sandwich with his scrambled eggs. He did.

"Well, I've gotta go," he said, and went inside.

As if none of this were enough to confirm our newfound station in life, our next rest stop was even worse. We'd been walking beside the Salmon River for two days now, unable to cross to the other side. We wanted to cross because it was nicer on the other side. There was no road there and all the trees lining the banks were on that side. We'd finally come to a bridge.

It was an old railroad crossing that had been converted into a car and foot bridge with long wooden planks laid across it. It did have a gate and two or three no-trespassing signs, but we figured they were simply trying to keep off cars.

What did they care about foot traffic?

Also, there was a FOR SALE sign posted beside the KEEP OFF signs. Maybe we'd buy it.

And besides, it wasn't as if there were a private home on the other side.

At least, not one we could see.

We climbed the gate and ambled over to the closest bank. A soft, grassy meadow rose gently up the hill from the water. Preston wanted to catch some fish, so I set about gathering crickets for him. For some reason, it was my job.

So there I was, walking around in circles, pouncing on the ground every few seconds (my bug net had been broken and discarded weeks before), when Preston whispered, "There's a truck coming."

"Huh?" I asked, but he didn't repeat himself. I kept my head down, only looking at him. Preston casually slipped the fishing line and hooks back into his packs.

The truck arrived and a gruff voice asked, "What are you doing here?" It didn't sound as if this guy was expecting to hear an answer he'd like.

"Well, we were just going to . . . ," Preston began when suddenly the man's arm shot out from his body at the most menacing right angle imaginable, with his index finger pointing the way back across the bridge, "have some lunch."

His arm continued to hang in the air, demanding our departure. I only looked at him briefly, but his yellow-tinted shooting glasses made everything clear. We gathered our stuff quickly and slunk across the bridge. The man then drove his truck over to the bridge, backed it up, and stood with one leg propped on the bumper as we walked out of sight.

It was settled. We really were hobos. Certainly, Lewis and Clark didn't have to put up with this.

I thought it was fairly funny until Preston pointed out that the man could call the cops and make our life miserable: Preston still had that pot Wild Bill had picked for him. We ate our lunch beside the road a little farther down, watching for yellow-glasses the entire time.

That afternoon we came upon a campground/fishing/hunting lodge that hadn't opened for business yet. It looked like a floodplain with water-logged, withered trees interspersed with thick, lively ones. The owner of the camp said the Salmon River had flooded his property the winter before and had set back the opening. "You can stay here for a dollar. That'll pay for the hot water you use to take showers with," he offered.

Once he had the place cleaned up it would make an excellent campground. We pitched our tent just yards from the river beneath a canopy of cottonwoods and ponderosa pines. A blue heron—our old friend—fished in a slough just a dozen or so yards downstream from us. It looked as if he caught two or three minnows as we watched.

When I went back up to the lodge to give the man, Mr. Faulkner, his dollar, he told me his most recent life story—just the tragic parts. "My divorce was finalized today as of ten-thirty," he said as I signed his unused guest book. Even as hobos, we represented a sympathetic ear. I was having a hard time taking him seriously at first because he looked just like Ronald Reagan, but as he told his story, Mr. Faulkner became all too real. "As you might guess, this hasn't been a good year for me. My wife started spending all her time with her girlfriend and none with me. Now, a lot of people around here think I mean they were gay lovers or something. Well, I don't. You see, this woman's husband ran off with a younger woman and then she felt pretty low, which is understandable. My wife started to comfort her, and pretty soon they were spending all their time together. It got so I couldn't even get one meal a day at home. As a matter of fact, there were plenty of days when I couldn't. So anyway, we've gotten a divorce, and well, that's taken care of a lot of my money so I'm working pretty slow on this place."

He sighed. Could he handle all these changes? I wondered. He looked well into his sixties. "I never knew how bad a housekeeper I was until last night. I'll have to work on that," he summed up.

He didn't appear to want to talk much more after he let all that out and told me, as he started upstairs, that he'd set out some shampoo, soap, and towels for us.

Preston was sleeping when I went back to our tent and so I wandered along the shore of the river, looking for bugs. Although there'd been frost and ice on the ground in the morning, it'd warmed up considerably during the day. Grasshoppers were jumping all over the place. Between some reeds and the water I found a grasshoppers' haven. I watched two through my binoculars, which I could adjust to have a microscopic view of them. A small one sneaked up on a larger one for about five minutes, slowly inching closer and closer. When it was within pouncing range, it crawled up onto a rock (boulder to them) just far enough so it could see the larger one without being seen. Or so it thought. The larger hopper was on another rock, seemingly looking the other way. The little one prepared to leap, bunching its legs up. The larger one suddenly turned toward it, facing his attacker head-on. The little guy leaped anyway. They bashed heads, wiggled their legs, then disappeared simultaneously. A few seconds later the little one scurried off and the big hopper climbed back onto his rock. I think the little one was trying to mate.

The next two days held more of the same. We were moving at such a slow pace. The oddest thing we came across was that the Forest Service had clear-cut all the trees lining the roadway. The trees had been a good fifteen to twenty feet from the road, so there had been no chance of obstructing traffic. So why do it? Preston figured it was because they had nothing better to do, which made as much sense as anything.

We climbed 1,700 feet in elevation on the third day, following the switchbacking road to the top of Lost Trail Pass. Along the way I found a large onion on the shoulder that I kept for the night's dinner. It had probably fallen out of some car that had taken a sharp turn too quickly. We also came upon a trucker who was pulled over at a pin curve. He was standing outside his cab, looking down into the trees below; the sides of the mountains were covered with trees.

"What's up?" Preston asked.

"Well, I'm looking for a wreck. You see these trees—the way they're torn down—and these ruts in the turf right here?" He pointed to both. The ruts, which looked like car tracks, led twenty to thirty yards down the steep drop into the trees and ravine below. "They've been here the last couple of days. The other guys"—he was driving a logging truck of which we'd seen countless others since Gibbonsville—"and I keep seeing this dog around since two days ago. Right near here. It looks like one of those chows. I was thinking maybe someone's down there, but we don't have much time to check it out. I've walked down there as far as I could and still haven't seen anything."

We stood there looking with him. He had to go shortly but Preston and I were worried. Why would a chow be hanging out at nearly seven thousand feet?

"We should take a look," Preston said. "I'll go first for half an hour and then come up." He descended into dense woods.

He returned thirty minutes later with a skeleton. It wasn't human. It appeared to be the head and antlers of an elk. A little bit of hair remained intact. He strapped the skull to his pack, saying his sister would love it.

I went down for my look. I followed the tiny creek bed and kept a good watch on my compass so I'd know exactly how to return. Nevertheless, it was still frightening and exhilarating. The largest trees—dead and alive—were down there. The whitened, dead roots looked like the limbs of dead humans. There were many tracks, but only of elk and deer. There was no sign of a car or humans. Even though it looked as if a car had gone thirty feet down, all signs stopped after that. We gave up.

When we walked a little farther up the road, we ran into the brown chow. It wouldn't let us come near it, though. We tried hurrying toward it, but it always kept a good fifty yards between us. Out of the blue—or from around one of the S curves, really—a woman from a local humane society appeared in a jeep. "We get a couple of dogs up here every year. Either the dogs escape when no one is paying attention or people are simply getting rid of the poor things." She, too, tried to lure the dog in, but failed. She said she would contact someone from the ASPCA and have them set a trap.

We continued on our way.

As we reached Lost Trail Pass, it began to snow. A historical marker at the top was frank about Lewis and Clark: "The Lewis and Clark expedition lost the trail to the pass.

They camped three miles west of here the night of September 3, 1805." The mountains looked high and rugged where they'd strayed, and we wondered why they'd been led over there. A Native American trail existed over this pass even then, and it was certainly much lower and easier. The following day Lewis and Clark did cross Lost Trail Pass, but only after twenty-four hours of torture. Clark recorded, "The high mountains closed the Creek on each Side and obliged us to take on the Steep Sides of those Mountains, So Steep that the horses Could Scurly keep from Slippiong down, Several sliped & Injured themselves verry much . . . little to eate . . . our last Themometer broken . . . Snow about 2 inches deep when it began to rain which termonated in a Sleet."

Another sign read, "General Gibbons and Captain Howard pursued Chief Joseph and his Nezperce Indians over Gibbons Pass just prior to the historic battle of the Big Hole, August 9, 1877." It struck me as odd that they called it Gibbons Pass when nearly all other maps labeled it Chief Joseph's Pass.

In 1877, the U.S. government decided it was kicking the Nez Perce out of their homeland—the Wallowa Valley. (These are the same Nez Perce who saved the Lewis and Clark expedition from starvation, led them to the Clearwater River in Idaho, herded their horses during the winter of 1805–6, and protected some of the team's buried goods from spring floods.) Joseph had his people obey the orders, but on the march to their reservation some of his warriors killed eleven whites to avenge the loss of their homeland and some cattle that other whites had stolen. The first battle ensued soon thereafter, and Joseph routed the Army, although he and his warriors were outnumbered two to one. He then raced to the Clearwater River where another chief, Looking Glass, was waiting with more warriors.

Not far from there, he held council and he and his chiefs determined to flee to Canada. He had 450 noncombatants and 250 soldiers—no match for the Army.

But somehow they were. For 1,300 hundred miles Joseph

and his people eluded the entire Northwest Army. In attacks and counterattacks the U.S. Army killed more women and children than warriors. Finally, they had the Nez Perce surrounded—after five months of chasing and killing. Joseph surrendered but only after being promised that his people would be allowed to go to the reservation on their land. Eventually, they went—eight years later and when only 287 were still alive. Joseph, though, was never allowed to return home. Upon giving up his gun, Joseph spoke his now famous words: "Hear me, my chiefs! I am tired; my heart is sick and sad. From where the sun now stands I will fight no more forever."

While we ate lunch beneath the sign that robbed Chief Joseph of this pass's name, two gray jays attempted to rob us of any food that we inadvertently placed on the ground. They managed to make off with one prune.

Would it have the same effect on their bowels as on ours? I felt sorry for whoever might be sitting under them later.

A group of Californians in a Dodge Dart—"Now, that's a good car," Preston said—started talking to us. The driver, Gus, had been chasing after a woman he'd fallen in love with after meeting her at a party. Two sidekicks, Robert and Roxanne, accompanied him. Gus had sideburns similar to John Best's, but Preston liked him anyway because of the Dart.

"We didn't know where she was going," Roxanne explained, "but by checking Amtrak schedules we figured out she was headed for Montana." Somehow they'd even found her in Montana—none of it was very clear—and Gus had had a wonderful time. They were now driving back to California. Gus's wife had run off with her high school sweetheart earlier in the year.

"I couldn't really blame her. The guy'd just gotten outta the Navy," Gus said. Roxanne handed us some of their doughnuts. "Roxanne was married, too."

Robert, it seemed, hadn't been married. He was interested in all the new growth on the surrounding mountains.

"They must've had some kinda fire around here," he said more than once. You could see, though, that some of the new growth was simply from clear-cutting. The patches of growth were perfectly outlined—as if they'd been mapped.

For some reason, Gus started telling us about his grandfather. He'd been a country-and-western musician who'd written a lot of famous songs without receiving any credit. Gus had begun helping him get the credit he deserved, but his grandfather had died the previous month. Gus and his sister were now trying to do it alone. They were working on a court case and would be traveling through Tennessee to gather evidence.

Roxanne continued feeding us doughnuts and I found myself wishing she were coming along. But we went our opposite ways when the doughnuts were all gone.

As we descended the mountain, the light snow stopped completely and it felt slightly warmer. But finding a campsite was a problem. It would be another day's hike before we reached the valley, and there seemed to be no level ground on which to pitch our tent. The land dropped off in steep slides below the road and rose in the same manner above it. After ten miles for the day, though, I couldn't go much farther. We'd have to make do. We chose the most gradual drop-off. It was still steep enough, though, that it was imperative we not gather any speed while descending. More than once I found myself frantically grabbing for a branch.

After nearly twenty minutes of winding our way through a dense growth of trees, we came to an area that was level for ten or so yards. It was the best we'd seen. Bear grass padded the ground. (Although bears don't like to eat it, it must be called that for a reason.) According to some reports, there might be a few grizzlies in this area. Lodgepole pines and Engelmann spruces—according to Preston— towered above us. Deer and elk scats lay scattered about. Ahhh.

We only had one bottle of water left, but as luck would have it, a creek flowed not more than a hundred yards farther down.

The elk called out in their rut again that evening, and in the middle of the night a group of the horny beasts stumbled into our camp. Not only did we hear them but we found their fresh scats in the morning. Preston and I were ecstatic: since the elk—cautious creatures—had come so close to us, we must have lost a lot of our modern human scent. Either that or we were emitting some female-elk odor.

After walking for nearly three hours in the morning, completing our descent into the Bitterroot Valley, we plopped into the drainage ditch that ran parallel to the highway with only the shoulder to separate us from the now-countless logging trucks and passenger cars. (Ever since we'd crossed back into Montana the traffic had become unbearable. Automobiles passed nearly every minute.) After peeling off our packs, we sprawled out, our legs spread wide, our possessions scattered about, our greased-down hair unruffled by the constant breeze sweeping through the valley. We were lying on a combination of grass and litter. I started laughing.

"What are you laughing about?" Preston asked, sounding defensive or maybe worried that I'd lost it.

"Us!" I answered. "Look at where we are . . . we think it's the most natural thing."

He started laughing, too. "We're two bums, aren't we? As comfortable as can be."

Sula, Montana, was our goal for the day. We'd seen it on a map. A camping marker distinguished it from everything else and we lusted after it, figuring we'd get hot showers. So we pressed on, walking ten miles by lunch and reaching the tiny town. It was not what we expected. There was one store—the Sula Store—and the only camping was a trailer park behind it.

Preston went inside to find out about local camping. I took off my shoes—to air out my feet and dry them. A huge swarm of flies immediately landed on them. It felt bad to have them move in so quickly.

I escaped into the store. The owner had already explained to Preston that the real town was a few miles down a road perpendicular to us, but that was too far. We bought a couple of nasty new rations—canned chili and instant rice—and were about to be on our way when another traveler swept into the store.

We got to talking. She was a heavyset woman from Alabama, driving out to Los Angeles for a few months of work. "Hollywood stuff," she said as if nothing else need be said.

"Oh, have you read *Sacajawea* by Anna Lee Waldo? I've read it half a dozen times and I'm reading it again on this trip," she said. We admitted we hadn't. *Sacajawea* is a fictional account of the Shoshone woman's life. This was the first time anybody had ever recommended it.

"It is the best book on the subject," she continued. "You have to read it. The woman had such a life force. I have such a strong attachment to her. I've driven this way to California simply so I could go to her death site. I was there the day before yesterday, and the most amazing thing happened to me. It was such a spiritual place . . . I felt I was Sacagawea reincarnated. It was so strong I began crying. You've got to read it."

She looked around the store, commenting on the beauty of some Native American blankets made expressly for tourists. Then she was off in her station wagon. We followed on foot.

We slept along the highway again that night. A stand of head-high willows served as a barrier from the traffic. The Bitterroot River gurgled beside us.

FOURTEEN

Rain, Snow, Dogs, and Blood

The next week of hiking was pure torture. The terrain wasn't difficult. It was actually a flat stretch along the valley floor all the way to Lolo, Montana. And it wasn't that the landscape was ugly. The Bitterroot Mountains to our west were stunning. Every few miles a valley opened up into them, and in between, craggy, snow-covered peaks filled the sky.

The problem was growth and thus traffic. Too many Californians, we were told again and again. Ever since that last earthquake they've been moving into here like ants, was the common complaint. In everyone's mind, it was a great place until those Californians came. Graffiti in a truck stop summed it up for the locals: "NO MORE CALIFAGGOTS!" Every few miles, we walked past a log-home company, and we passed their handiwork—shiny new log homes made of varnished wood—even more often.

For us, the new popularity of the Bitterroot Valley meant an increased fear of being run over and decreased camping spots.

For Native Americans it meant the demise of a worshiping tree. An old ponderosa pine stood, sad and beaten, beside the highway. Its top was dead. A sign read, "Cultural resource of the Salish and Kootenai Tribes. Protected by Federal, State and Tribal Law. Any damage, destruction, alteration, or defacing of this site is prohibited, and is punishable by law." Feathers were stuck to its trunk and colorful streamers hung from its branches. Despite all the finery, it didn't look as if it would last another ten years.

Across the highway, as if it were keeping watch, a lone golden eagle sat in a pine tree. It was the first one we'd seen. A magpie flew near but didn't dare chase it as it would a hawk.

Preston avenged the stone-throwing-while-he-had-diarrhea episode when we rested in a supermarket parking lot in Darby, Montana. People were driving by slowly, giving us the thrice-over. It may have had something to do with the elk skeleton strapped to Preston's pack. Probably, it was the kind of look all vagrants receive. I felt uncomfortable.

Preston sensed this and immediately hiked up his shorts so they were straining against his crotch. He buckled at his knees, set a terrific grin on his face, and began singing at the top of his voice, "I love to go a wandering along the mountain track. And when I go, I love to sing—my knapsack on my back. Vala-ree! Vala-raa! Vala-ree! Vala-ha-ha-ha-ha-ha . . . my knapsack on my back!" He trilled and cooed at the appropriate parts, never hesitating, even as some fat-faced, bearded guys stared with disbelief. He shuffled and sidestepped across the lot.

We walked twelve miles all told that day, simply because we could find no place to camp. Our feet were killing us. The bottoms of mine had become bruised. Preston thought it was from having to walk on the highway pavement so much. His feet were scaly and bleeding between the toes, looking as bad as mine smelled.

When we'd had enough, we slipped through another barbed-wire fence into what we believed was a wooded, safe haven. No sooner had we started a fire than a dog commenced barking, not more than forty yards away. Sheep blared and human voices drifted our way. We crept toward all the noise. It was a home and we were on their property.

Our campfire blew directly toward the house, but we couldn't kill it. Our stove was broken and we needed to cook on the fire. The dog continued to bark all night, but thankfully it stayed tied up. We didn't speak much, reserving our energy for fear.

"All right, you hippie hobos, get your hands up," I kept expecting some checked-shirt Californian-turned-Montanan to blurt out. "This here is the Big Sky Country and we don't like your kind. Move it."

Then another would chip in, "Hey, didn't we see you at Smut's place? What did you do to those good people, huh?" He'd prod us with his telescopic rifle.

"I didn't do anything, mister. It was him. He made me do it!" I'd answer, pointing to Preston.

"Let's just shoot 'em both. No one will care. And I don't believe the long-haired one anyway." *Blam. Blam. Blam.*

Conditions worsened over the next couple of days. We couldn't even find land to sneak onto. At one place, dogs literally chased us away. On another day, a man ran us off his land the second we asked him if we could camp nearby; we ended up walking fourteen miles as a result. So we stayed in commercial trailer-home parks along the highway.

The weather worsened as well. It rained on us most of one day. Stayed well below freezing on the following day and snowed the next.

The Bitterroot Mountains to our west remained stunning, but all the land between was more and more populated. The highway was as busy as the New Jersey Turnpike. Nearly every store, bar, or restaurant we passed slung banners on the outside provided by either Budweiser or Miller. The Miller banner read WELCOME MONTANA HUNTERS and was accompanied by a drawing of mountains and elk. The

Bud one said THIS BUD'S FOR YOU with a wilderness scene as backdrop. Drinking and hunting seemed to go together in Montana.

We did hitch a ride into a canyon leading into the mountains one afternoon from a young boy on an all-terrain four-wheeler. His name was Joey and it was his grandfather's 350 Suzuki. He nearly hit us as he screeched to a halt at our feet.

"I can't shift the gears so well. I broke my leg." He was eight and slightly pudgy. "So you'll have to help me."

"How'd you do that?"

"Oh," he said as we jerked into gear and an all-too-fast pace, "I broke it wrecking my own four-wheeler. It's only an 80." We spun around a turn and half of me slid off the thing. As I frantically grabbed for some support (Preston sat laughing and not helping), the kid admitted, "I'm a little crazy on these things."

Preston gave him a buck when he dropped us off. I wasn't too sure if it was for the ride or for scaring the hell out of me. "He's not going to live to see nine," Preston said as the kid jumped over a dirt mound and drove out of sight.

Another night, at one of the trailer-home sites, an old man—weather-worn, torn jeans and a dirty old plaid shirt—hobbled over to me after slowly climbing out of his silver Airstream home.

"I thought you might need this," he said, handing me his Sterno stove. "I hate to see you out here without a stove." I hadn't seen or spoken to him before, but there he was, giving me something. I explained that we had a stove, and only after much persuasion would he take it back.

We got to talking and I asked if he wintered at the trailer park. "Heavens, no. I'll stay here this year, but I've got my own place on the east side of the highway—five acres. I'm letting my granddaughter stay there right now. She's had some troubles. I like this bachelor's life anyway. I don't need no mothering. It's just me and my dog over here." He wished me a good night and headed back to his mobile home. Just wanted to make sure we were comfortable.

The morning after that we had to hike through a snow-storm—a daunting prospect in the woods but a terrifying one along the highway. The snow stopped, though, by mid-morning and the temperature rose to forty degrees—warm enough for a melt-off. It was the second-to-last day of our hike. And we were both feeling giddy—we'd actually hiked 190 miles; the following day would make it 200.

Preston, to mark the occasion, asked himself as if he were an interviewer, "Preston, what are you going to do when you get to Lolo?"

He squinted his eyes and scrunched up his face. His voice thickened with countryness. A slimy grin topped it all off. "Why, I'm gonna go to the nursery school and hand out some candy. I likes da little boys." He shifted his eyes and leered at me.

When we stopped in Florence for the night's groceries, three young girls on bicycles rode up next to us in a super-market parking lot. They were laughing and giggling among themselves. We were innocently eating some bread and drinking grapefruit juice. When they spotted us, one of them turned to the other two and stage-whispered, "I better stay here and watch the bikes." She pointed us out with her eyes as she said it.

That evening we walked a mile off the highway to Chief Looking Glass Fishing Access and Camping Area, a quiet site along the Bitterroot River, dotted with ponderosa pines. We pitched our tent beside water and soon discov-ered we had a neighbor. A furry creature splashed just be-neath our feet and raced across the river. Once it was safely on the other bank, it alternately dried itself on a large log and took dives into a deep pool. Preston and I raced to our books—me to the tracking book and him to Audubon—to identify it. What with our running about, flipping pages, and loud exclamations, the creature had disappeared by the time we could give it a name. But it was a mink. The telltale sign had been its white mark beneath its chin.

As we hunted for firewood, we realized this wasn't only a good place for camping. Car after car of teenagers cruised through the camp's roadway—most of them were blasting music. Preston happened upon a disposable douche kit, making us think some young woman needed a little more sex education. I spotted two used condoms. We were camping in lovers' lane. Luckily, it was a school night, and after the dozen or so cruisers, things settled down at sunset.

We'd heard no coyotes since Lemhi Pass, and the night at Chief Looking Glass's place was no different. We'd run into a burly man earlier in the day who'd presented an explanation of sorts.

"Have you seen any coyotes?" he asked. We said no, not since Lemhi, but we'd heard plenty of them there.

"Aren't they beautiful?" I asked.

"Well, I like them myself, but my boss—I work at a ranch—has me kill them. They attack the cattle."

"Really?"

"Yep. All the ranchers hunt 'em." He changed the subject then and said we could get showers at the truck stop in Lolo. The funny thing was we hadn't asked him about showers, but we were glad we stank too much for this coyote-hunting man. It was a victory, we believed, for canines. And anyway, most coyote experts agree that they don't attack cattle.

It was freezing the following morning—the last day of our hike. We procrastinated, realizing it was the end of our complete independence. Everything we'd done over the past nineteen days was propelled by our own feet and our own choice. Soon we'd be riding horses, being led by someone else.

We spent nearly thirty minutes watching a female hairy woodpecker hunt for bugs in a nearby pine. She took her time, combing the entire circumference. Her feathers were ruffled, maybe because it was so cold out.

After a hearty meal of grits with fried mushrooms and tomatoes, we departed.

By noon, we reached Traveller's Rest on the outskirts of Lolo, Montana. The Lewis and Clark expedition had stopped here in September of 1805. The Indians who were accompanying the team at this time explained that it was possible to reach the Missouri in four days by a native road.

Neither Lewis or Clark recorded how he felt upon learning this, but since they'd just spent fifty-two days to reach this point, we thought they couldn't have been too happy. (On the return leg, Lewis used this route to return to the Missouri when he and Clark split up. Crossing what is now called Lewis and Clark Pass, he reached the Great Falls of the Missouri in less than eight days.)

"I can just see the proctologist. He stood here with his hands on his hips and said, 'You can feel them here. Ahhh," Preston joked as the traffic roared by. The proctologist? Now there was somebody I'd forgotten all about. I guess Preston thought of him because of the gross incongruity of the area. A large metal storage center stood behind the plaque marking this spot. Litter was tossed all about, along with broken and rusting fence parts. An upscale housing development was being raised across the highway—ugly, prefab houses that were too close together—called Bitterroot Meadows.

A half hour later we were in Lolo. It was mainly an intersection for Highways 93 and 12. The truck stop where we'd be meeting our outfitter, Harlan Opdahl, sat there along with a bar across the street. A small, dirty shopping center stood about a mile farther up 93, on the way to Missoula.

We were excited about completing the hike with only that one ride from John Best, but we couldn't really celebrate until we'd found somewhere to camp. Of course, there was no scenic camping area, so we settled for an RV park that had a large, grassy yard for tent campers. We almost couldn't hear the highway.

We did absolutely nothing for the rest of the day or that night, except take showers. It was time to rest. But we did make plans: Lolo Hot Springs the following day and a trip to Missoula on Sunday. Monday morning was our rendezvous with Harlan Opdahl.

I woke Saturday morning with a wet twig stuck to my cheek. I brushed it aside, opened my eyes for a moment, and noticed that the twig was moving. It was about two and a half inches long, black, with a yellow stripe down its back. There was a tail and four legs as well. And bulbous eyes that resembled teardrops in their liquidity. It was a long-toed salamander. I had time to look it up and still make all these observations because one of its back legs was broken. Had a big monster—me—crushed its leg? We watched each other for a while; then I freed it next to the trunk of the large willow we were camped beneath.

Over breakfast at a local diner an old curmudgeon struck up a conversation. He told us how awful people from New York and California were. When Preston said he was originally from New York, the man said, "Too bad."

He then proceeded to scoff at the attention given to Lewis and Clark. "Everywhere you go, they've got those damned signs, crisscrossing all over the place. I don't believe any of them."

I explained that they actually did some crisscrossing and that on the return they split up for a large amount of time—so they really had covered an incredible amount of territory. But he wasn't having any of it.

He then tore into coyotes and how they always attack sheep. "Coyotes are the worst pests we have to put up with." He'd never had any sheep himself.

"But don't sheep dogs take care of that?" Preston asked, and the old man admitted they did for all he knew.

That didn't stop him, though. He simply launched into an attack on wolves. "You've got your type from the city coming in here," he started, giving us a hard stare, "saying let the wolves be. They don't know what they're talking about. Those things are hunters."

Wolves do hunt. They will even attack cattle, although that is highly unusual. "I guess you're right, there," I said, "but I sure like the idea of wolves existing somewhere. And there certainly can't be that many around here. We haven't heard one yet." He agreed they shouldn't be exterminated but said there were plenty around.

"But they're vicious creatures, I know that," he went on. "Some friends of mine had a neighbor with a half-wolf as a pet. Their granddaughter went by the yard one day and that thing ripped right into her, taking her whole arm. It was awful. And some Californians who live up by me have a half-wolf that ate a neighbor's sheep. It kept doing it and doing it. The Californians wouldn't believe it was their wolf—until it was killed trying one time too many."

After breakfast we hitchhiked west about twenty miles to Lolo Hot Springs. Lewis—the expedition stopped at the springs on the return—enticingly described it: "These springs issue from the bottoms and through the interstices of a grey freestone rock . . . immediately above the springs on the creek there is a handsome little quamas [camas; flowery plant with edible bulb] plain of about ten acres. the prinsipal spring is about the temperature of the warmest baths used at the hot springs in Virginia. In this bath which had been prepared by the Indians by stoping the run with stone and gravel, I bathed and remained 19 minutes, it was with dificulty I could remain thus long and it caused a profuse sweat."

We expected the springs to be in the same condition, maybe a small amount of cement to hold the pool together. But what had been built was quite different. Where natural "grey freestone rock" once stood was now concrete and cement. It resembled an outdoor city pool, right down to the pale green paint. There was one large concrete pool that retained cooler water and a smaller indoor one that stayed a little over a hundred degrees. We had to pay to enter.

But as we soaked, switching from cool pool to hot, our complaints drifted away—along with the aching in our feet and backs. The only thing we couldn't do was run to the cold waters of the nearby creek because of the fence surrounding the pools. The Native Americans had done this in front of Lewis but he had chosen not to.

That night we ate a whole fried chicken each and eight jo-jos (fried battered quartered potatoes). The cook came from the kitchen to take a look at us when she heard it was only two guys. "I just served one order of this to my entire family and they didn't even finish it all. There were four of them. This has never been done," she said, smiling. We smiled back.

Sunday was equally relaxing. We hitched to Missoula to wander around the Southgate Mall. A brochure we'd picked up had whet our appetites: "Southgate Mall merchants welcome you to the largest enclosed shopping center in a 200-mile radius, with over 100 stores . . . the hub of western Montana's retail trade center . . . unlocks treasures for your pleasure . . . tax-free shopping."

More than an hour passed before a freckle-faced man pulled over for us. He was driving a covered pickup with a Billy Graham sticker on back. He introduced himself first; his name was John. He was the first person ever to introduce himself to us first while we were hitching. That got me to worrying. Then he asked us to ride in back, taking off the two locks on the door. I tried to send Preston eye signals that we shouldn't get in, but he didn't catch on. We climbed in. John set both the locks back on and closed them.

"Thank God, we finally got a ride," Preston said. "It's only because he's from out of state I bet." John's license plate said Oregon—home of Aryan sickos and mass murderers. Or was that Idaho?

"Preston, what are you talking about. I don't think we should be in here. He locked the door with two locks."

"What?" Preston tried to look out the back window then, but the angle was wrong to see the locks. He pushed at the door but of course it didn't open.

"I think he might be a mass murderer. Look around you. This truck bed is immaculate. He probably just cleaned all the blood out. And what are a broom and a shovel doing back here? I can understand the shovel, sort of. But a broom?" We were sitting on a couple of wooden chests, which were locked as well. He obviously had hacksaws and axes in the chests. He'd use those to cut us up; the shovel to bury us; and the broom to sweep away any evidence. Any fool could see that.

"I don't know, Hod. He seemed all right to me," Preston replied, but sounded a little worried.

"If he goes past the mall, I say we start banging the shit out of this thing with the shovel. Okay?"

Preston nodded his head, but a few minutes later John pulled to a stop in front of the mall. He'd probably decided we were too big for him. But if there had been only one of us . . .

Before we walked off, John asked, "Have you two heard of Bo Gritz?"

"Hey, we've been wondering about him," Preston said. "We've seen his signs running for president all over the place. We thought it was some kinda joke. Is he for real?"

"I think so. I'd seen the signs, too, and then when I heard he was speaking in town, I went to hear him. He makes a lot of sense. He wants to protect us from all those elements in government and business that are controlling things in Washington. There's a conspiracy out there against our democracy. It's pretty spooky, what's going on. . . . Here, I've got an extra pamphlet." He handed us a photocopied campaign brochure.

"Thanks," Preston said.

"No problem. And God bless you."

"Um, take care," I said, not knowing how to respond to John's blessing. Maybe I had overreacted with the mass-murderer thing—much as Lewis had done with the Black-feet—but John was spooky.

Bo Gritz's campaign pamphlet was weird. He was some kind of Rambo by the looks of it. He'd completed four "operations into Communist Asia to rescue U.S. POWs." He'd trained Afghan *mujahedeen* freedom fighters. His qualifications included a karate sixth-degree black belt, underwater-demolitions expertise, and a master's in communications from American University.

I sorta liked this guy. It was such fun imagining him going to meet some flabby-butt Congressmen and karate-chopping them into line. Maybe he was what we needed.

But then I read on. He was a member of the NRA and the Kiwanis. General Westmoreland thought Gritz was "the" American soldier. And Gritz stood for "Christian ethic and Constitutional government under the Declaration of Independence and Bill of Rights."

Our first stop in the mall was the International King's Table—a cafeteria-style restaurant that had an all-you-can-eat buffet. Preston and I loaded up, eating three full platefuls. The meat carver had never seen anyone eat so much and asked if we were having a competition. I told him no and that it would be a bad thing for the restaurant and us.

After thirty minutes inside the mall itself—strolling past the Portrait Express with its fuzzy photos, Hickory Farms with its rows of aluminum-wrapped cheeses and identical sausages, and the chemical pollutants wafting out of Claire's Boutique—we were running for the exits. It hadn't been as much of a lark as we thought it'd be. I did buy a copy of *Sacajawea* for some light reading, however, and Preston bought Steinbeck's *Travels with Charley*.

From there we walked three miles to Ft. Missoula—site of a government bastion for raping and pillaging the local Native American land. Ironically, a man named Dean Bear Claw presented a documentary film he'd made of his people. He had interwoven old footage of the Crows with film he'd taken a few years back at a tribal gathering. The film was eloquent and not sentimental. It merely showed the changes. Everyone in the audience—mostly college students—appeared teary eyed by the end.

PART 4

IT'S BETTER TO RIDE A HORSE THAN EAT ONE

FIFTEEN

Preston Breaks a Rib

When it came to horse bartering, Lewis told some mighty whoppers to Sacagawea's brother and the other chiefs accompanying them. "I told them . . . that after our finally returning to our homes toward the rising sun," he recorded on August 20, 1805, "whitemen would come to them with an abundance of guns and every other article necessary to their defence and comfort, and that they would be enabled to supply themselves with these articles on reasonable terms in exchange for the skins of the beaver Otter and Ermin." Those words plus Clark's "Fuzee" (fusee—a friction match that would burn in the wind), some trinkets, and at least one musket got them their initial twenty-nine horses—not enough for all the men and all their goods. Then, when they reached the Nez Perce Indians below Lost Trail Pass, they told the same stories and traded for the rest of the horses they needed.

Our horses were a different matter. After I learned no one would rent them for the entire overland leg of our journey, a former president of the Lewis and Clark Trail Heritage Foundation suggested we use the Opdahls as outfitters. They specialized in riding part of the Lewis and Clark Trail. It irked me only a little to have guides for this section since Lewis and Clark themselves had been guided over it by Native Americans.

"Harlan's a real cowboy-looking guy," Barb Opdahl, his wife, had told me over the phone. "You won't have any problems picking him out. And our truck will have the Triple O logo on the side. Just be at the truck stop at Highways Twelve and Ninety-three at eight on October nineteenth."

Right at eight we spotted this guy dressed in a checked shirt, faded jeans, a woven cowboy hat, and well-used brown cowboy boots. This was our man. It was the woven, beaten cowboy hat that did it. All the other "cowboys" in the joint had hats that were too slick—as if they'd never seen dirt.

After a quick breakfast, we headed west. The logistics of our horse ride hadn't been too clear before, but Harlan explained he would drive us across the Lolo Pass and then head off the highway to his base camp in the Clearwater National Forest. Whenever we passed a Lewis and Clark sign, Harlan would pull over for us to read it. And he talked about them as he drove: "From reading the journals so many times, I've about decided those boys were in the early stages of scurvy and vitamin depletion by the time they reached the Lochsa [a small river they hiked along to the Clearwater, which they took to the Snake, and that to Columbia]. They'd only been eating meat, and while there's some vitamins in that, it simply isn't enough. But those boys were tough. All their Western clothes had been worn away by then. They were only wearing their leather skins, and leather sure isn't warm when it gets wet and snowed on."

In the summers Harlan and his wife, Barb, led Smithsonian members on a Lewis and Clark tour, and so he was up on all the lore. "Most of what I tell you I've gleaned out of the journals and picked up along the way."

The truck ride lasted eight hours, allowing plenty of time to learn about Harlan. He'd been in Idaho (that's where we were again once we crossed Lolo Pass) since 1965, having come from Minnesota to work in a lumber mill. "The guy who ran the filling station in Pierce looked at my license and didn't even want to fill up my car until he found out I was leaving town. And that's still their attitude to outsiders. That's why they don't like the Californians." He worked driving trucks and loading logs for timber companies, until 1979. That was when he started outfitting.

Although he used to work lumbering, he was upset that there wasn't more of a buffer zone for the Lewis and Clark Trail. He pointed to the nearby checkerboard land and explained that the sections were divided up between the Forest Service and such companies as Burlington Northern. The deforestation was devastating at times. We'd look out the windows and see masses of clear-cut land. The hillsides looked like a skinned animal.

Around midmorning, we stopped at Colt Killed Creek—so named by Lewis and Clark because they were forced to kill one of their colts to feed the expedition. Then by two we were at Indian Post Office—a site along the old Nez Perce trail (Lolo Trail) that took Lewis and Clark two days to reach from Colt Killed Creek. It was the highest point on the trail—7,033 feet.

Local lore, Harlan explained, holds that the Native Americans used to leave messages for each other at Indian Post Office. A couple of rock cairns marked the spot, and it was certainly along the old Nez Perce trail. Since at least the turn of this past century, though, it had been used by whites as a place to leave messages. People still do it today.

"I always like to stop here and read them," Harlan said. "It's hard to say if this was here when Lewis and Clark passed by since they don't mention it in their journals." Once that was said, we all set to reading the old notes. They were tucked underneath one of the cairns inside old peanut-butter, mayonnaise, aspirin, and spice jars. One from 1984 reassured us, "If you ever need a friend remember Jesus loves you."

A more recent note read, "Hi there peoples! Just stopped here to read some letters and to tell whoever will listen that I'm totally bored! I've been hunting for 2 weeks for Elk, and I've seen about 20 head, but haven't made a kill yet. Well enough about hunting, if there's any girls out there 16 or older who likes a *MAN* that is 18, blue eyes, lifts weights, plays football, loves to hunt, fish and PARTY! Girl must be awesome looking. Write Sam McCutchen, P.O. Box 1171, Kamiah, ID 83536." Sam also included his telephone number in case the girls really needed him quickly.

"Some of these get pretty steamy," Harlan said, apparently blushing, and handed over another one. It turned out to be my favorite.

"This mountain makes the earth move for a woman," someone recorded without leaving her name or a date. "It is so powerful! I made love last night to Jay Michaelson and I had an orgasm such as I have never experienced!! All of one's senses are alert and responsive and love in unison is dynamic. I wish this ultimate in physical pleasure to anyone who comes here. We all deserve what this earth and each other have to offer."

And there I was, with Preston and Harlan. Preston wrote a note—probably equally as steamy—and then we returned to the road. By five we were at the Opdahls' base camp—a bit of land they leased from the Forest Service.

"Now this is camping as it ought to be. We're leading the easy life," Preston said as we walked around the camp. The canvas tents were large enough to stand and walk around in. Ours had a wood stove. The mess tent stretched forty feet by fifteen—big enough for a kitchen table seating at least a dozen people.

We went in for supper and met the entire crew. Barb was the cook. Her graying hair matched Harlan's, but she had a lot of energy. When Harlan said something about her bear hunt, she said, "That story again! It was just something I had to do. I tell you. I'm just so tired of all the damage the bears have done at our camp and how much money they've cost us. I didn't feel sorry for her at all. It did take a couple of trips down there and a lot of urging, but I finally crawled in there and shot her." She was talking about a female bear she'd shot two years earlier by crawling headfirst into the bear's den. She did it with a .357 pistol. All the while she was telling this, she was busy preparing sourdough biscuits, baked onions and potatoes, baked chicken and grouse, broccoli, and a lemon pie for dessert.

Harlan had brought the story up because he thought we might be eating the last of the bear for dinner. They'd eaten most of it, saving the last bit for Rob, one of their guides. He was from Ohio and had never eaten bear. "We were going to make sausage out of it—you know, like summer sausage. But it was so good, we didn't want to waste it like that," Barb said. They'd finished it all the night before while Harlan was gone.

Rob and Virgil sat around the table listening to Barb. Rob was thirty and was from near Cincinnati. A truck driver, he only came out for a few months each year to guide. Virgil was the other hand, an older man around Harlan's age. Virgil mostly kept quiet and watched.

When Preston was out of the tent for a few minutes, Virgil told me, "After Lewiston, that river is pure slackwater. You two are going to have it rough. They've taken the current right out of the Columbia with all those dams."

"That's certainly true," Harlan added. "You're going to wish you had your motor." I asked them not to repeat this to Preston, considering we'd have about five hundred miles to go from Lewiston to the ocean, but sometime during the night I heard Virgil telling him.

After dinner began, their final hand appeared. Barb had been worried about him, wondering if we should go out looking for him since it was dark. His name was Dave. "He's been mentally abused," she'd explained before he returned, "and has the mind of a fourteen-year-old boy although he's thirty. He's as nice as can be. We bring him up here to help him break free of all the mess at home."

Dave had killed the grouse we were eating and told us how: "I had two hatfuls of rocks and I hit it with the last one. First he was on the ground and then he flew up in the tree. I was talking to him the entire time. I knew if I climbed it, he'd just fly to another tree." During dinner, Virgil, who seemed to be very protective of Dave, chastised him for eating his dessert first. But Dave didn't seem to have any problems finishing off his allotment. His warm smile encouraged Preston and me to relax. Soon enough we did, drawing belly laughs out of the entire bunch as we talked about our fascination with animal scats. Or, more truthfully, as Preston told them how I liked to carry different shits in my pockets and bring them back to camp for him. Virgil simply shook his head, as if he'd never heard of such foolishness.

"Wake up there, son," I commanded Preston in a fatherly voice. "The wood stove has burned out. It needs some kindling. Hop to it!" I hadn't even bothered to wipe the sleep out of my eyes. The cots in our tent felt like the fluffiest down-filled mattresses. "Get a move on," I continued.

To my surprise, Preston, who'd been sleeping up until the moment I spoke, rose out of his cot without a complaint and started to light the stove. "I feel too good to argue with you," he said by way of explanation. "Also, I want to try out this pitch Harlan gave us last night."

The pitch was not the dark, tarry substance I'd seen before—the stuff used to seal ship seams together. This pitch was part of a conifer tree. It was resin soaked. When it dries out, the wood becomes a natural incinerator and burns with a high, strong flame—as if it were coated in kerosene. You simply shave off a sliver, stick it under some wood, and watch your fire burn. Preston would no longer have to pour gasoline on our fires to get them going.

But as I lay in my cot, watching him blow on the fledgling flames, I chose not to point this out. It would be best to wait until after the tent was toasty.

Eventually, I rose and we made our way over to the mess tent. Barb had a huge stack of pancakes waiting for us, as well as eggs, bacon, and hot coffee.

"You boys are the first Lewis and Clark riders we've seen who've woken up refreshed their first night out here. This is the easy life for you two, huh?" Barb asked.

This was how we yearned to be regarded—as rugged, outdoorsy types. Barb, I decided at that moment, was a great woman. But I did happen to notice that everyone else had been awake and had breakfasted long before we walked out of our tent.

No one was talking much except Barb, Preston, and me. The others were busy preparing the horses and receiving last-minute instructions from Harlan. He and Barb would be gone with us for the next couple of days, so the men had to get their assignments.

"You know," she said, "we are the only outfitters in Idaho to do historic-trail rides. Both the Lewis and Clark and the Nez Perce rides bring in a lot of people. And the Indians who come here to do the Nez Perce trail love it. We were even on the local PBS station in September because of this. . . . But even so, I'm awfully worried about doing this ride this time of year. Our last Lewis and Clark ride is usually in early September. I mean, a blizzard could hit here anytime now and then where'd we be?"

It was just below freezing when we woke up, but since then it had warmed considerably. Also, there wasn't a cloud in the sky. Barb, I thought, didn't know what she was talking about. Of course, I was ignoring my own Lewis and Clark journals in which Clark wrote on September 16, 1805, "Began to snow about 3 hours before Day and continued all day the Snow in the morning 4 inches deep on the old snow, and by night we found it from 6 to 8 inches deep. . . . I have been wet and as cold in every part as I ever was in my life."

I told Barb it looked nice out to me.

"Weather can change here so fast, you won't know what hit you. People are always getting stuck in snow up here this time of year."

A few minutes later, we were told to get going. Our horses were already saddled and waiting. We climbed up—both of us acting as nonchalant as possible—and within minutes Harlan was leading the way. We were off into the wilds—just like Lewis and Clark, with nothing but open country to cross and wild game to be caught and eaten.

Well, not exactly. As it turned out, Barb and Dwayne (Harlan's older brother, who'd been in town the night before) would meet us along the way. First they'd stop halfway with our lunch, arriving there by truck. And then they'd meet up with us for the night's rest, setting up camp before we arrived. That way, we—unlike the Lewis and Clark expedition members—wouldn't be eating any colts.

The Clearwater National Forest was interwoven with various trails—the Lewis and Clark Trail, the Nez Perce and the Bird-Truax trail—and dirt roads. Most times the trails were one and the same, and sometimes they converged with the forest roads. There was not one clear Lewis and Clark Trail that led through the mountains. But over the years Harlan and others had etched out the closest thing possible.

Harlan set the pace, a slow walk. That gave us plenty of time to take in the view, which was alternately stunning and depressing. The land and trees were pristine and lush when we were on the real, barely marked trails. Tamarack—a deciduous tree that looks much like a conifer until its leaves turn orange in the fall—pines, spruces, firs, and some aspens rose all around us. The air was piney and light. Then, when we plodded along the dirt roads and passed campsites used by fall hunters, the ride would turn depressing. Trash was inevitably scattered about—beer cans, cigarette butts, paper, plastic, and bottles. It made no sense. They'd had cars and trucks with them. It would've taken only minutes to pack it into the car and drive it out. Harlan had a trash bag with him and filled it with some of the more glaring debris.

At one point, Harlan stopped his horse along the trail and waited for us to approach. He was staring down at the ground. Was something wrong? Then, he suddenly looked up with a smile.

"That's a black-bear scat," he said, pointing to a dark, globby mass beside the trail. "And next to it is a coyote's, I think. Do you want a baggy for them? I've got one." He and Preston both had a good laugh over that one.

Like Lewis and Clark, we saw only grouse in this area. It was a ruffed grouse.

Barb and Dwayne were waiting for us on the road around one. She had turkey and cheese sandwiches, chips, and chocolate bars laid out. Dwayne, much heavier than Harlan but with a similar Minnesota twang, was busy cleaning an adjacent campground. He seemed particularly disturbed by all the cigarette butts.

Barb had us all check what letters were inside our Snickers wrappers because Dave was collecting them to win a trip to Disneyland. He had to send in the letters *K-O-O-B-I-E* and then his name would be entered in a drawing. We sat around repeating the same letters over and over.

"I've got a *K.*"

"Well, I've got a *K.*"

"Does he need a *K?*" Like that, until it was clear he had enough *K*s. The same went on for all the other letters, except for the *B*. No one ever got a *B*.

When we were back on the horses, Preston whispered to me, "Is this what you were expecting? I thought we'd be more out there, you know?"

Barb had said she'd meet up with us and provide food, but I'd thought it'd only be at the end of the day. I hadn't expected a midday rendezvous as well. We were being pampered. So I sulked for the afternoon ride, taking little interest in nature. When Harlan pointed out a lone bald eagle flying over a nearby escarpment, I barely bothered to look up. Preston remained gung ho, though, peppering Harlan with questions about the trees.

By the time we stopped before Greensward Camp—site of a Lewis and Clark camp on their return—my knees were stabbing me with pain due to the weird angle they'd been forced into all day. My groin muscles felt as if they were beginning to rip. And my butt was busily signaling it'd had more than enough.

However, when Harlan asked how we were doing and Preston immediately said fine, I echoed him.

At some point, Preston asked Harlan about the next day's ride. Harlan listed the different places we'd pass and mentioned a place called Chimney Butte.

"What's that?" Preston asked.

"It's a Nez Perce vision-quest site. It's a holy place and I usually lead a bunch of them to it in the summer."

"Can we go up there?" I asked, changing moods instantly. I told him about my interest.

"I don't go up there usually," he responded. "I haven't even cut a real trail to it because I don't want others finding it. But we'll see. . . . We ought to have time for it."

Ah, I thought, this is a wonderful experience. Harlan was great. My horse, Domingo, was a tough Appaloosa. And even old Preston wasn't so bad.

That night we camped just below a mountaintop called Sherman's Peak. We'd covered twenty-four miles and I was happy to see Barb, Dwayne, and all their creature comforts. They had a roaring fire going stoked with logs as big as my horse's hindquarters. A canopy stood over a collapsible card table for the night's meal, which was also ready and waiting.

After dinner, we sat before the fire, watching it as if it were a TV. "You know," Dwayne said while recalling his trip to town, "I had the hardest time finding that Epsom salt. And when I was in a drugstore, looking for it, I noticed they had one of those hearing machines set up—so you could check your hearing for free. So I stopped at it." He paused and then continued, "Well, that thing sure wasn't working."

He was a quietly funny man, making jokes at his own expense. A little later, he poked at a large log—more than a foot in diameter—he'd been trying to burn all night. He'd commented on its fire-retarding tendencies frequently, and we'd all taken turns teasing him about it.

"Hey," he called out, "that thing is finally burning."

"You mean that big one of yours?" I asked.

"Oh, heaven's no. Just one of those little ones I tucked under it."

By nine, we were in our tents. Barb and Harlan hadn't

brought the cots, and the wood stoves had stayed behind, too. But our tent still seemed like a palace to us since we could stand in it. Preston read *Travels with Charley*. I fell asleep immediately.

Our first stop the next morning was Sherman's Peak. The expedition had ridden to the top of this mountain to view their surroundings. Barb had said, "Going to Sherman's Peak is always a big thing for the Lewis and Clark fans. They get a real feel for the adventure. One lady was so overwhelmed up there she said, 'I know I stood on the very rock Clark looked out from!' "

Preston and I dismounted at the peak—a flat meadow, really—and surveyed the valleys and mountains around us. We said things like, "Yep, this sure is something," and we climbed onto a rock ledge so we could see if we felt anything. We didn't.

We rode out of there, heading southwest. It was our next stop that interested us—Chimney Butte, the Nez Perce vision-quest site. The only thing was, Harlan had decided not to take us to it. Maybe he felt it was too sacred.

Instead, we climbed an adjacent peak that was like a gigantic rock cairn. The entire mountaintop was covered with fist-sized rocks.

"From what I understand, this place was used by the Nez Perce for meditating, too. I've never been up here before."

Some of the rocks slid beneath our feet as we ascended (we'd left the horses down at the base of the peak), but within a quarter hour we'd reached the top.

Everything was entirely still. A number of rock cairns stood about, indicating that this was some sort of Native American site. There were no trees or boulders obstructing one's view. It felt as if we were at one of the world's vantage points.

"You can see why they'd come up here to get away from it all," Harlan said. We agreed that we felt a calmness. This seemed particularly telling, coming from Preston and Harlan. (I doubted my own senses because of the failed vision quest.)

We talked about the Nez Perce some—retelling each other how good they'd been to the expedition. When passing through this area, the team had been extremely low on food. They ran out of colts to kill and even resorted to eating portable soup—a gloopy concoction made by reducing stock to a paste.

The soup did no good. They continued to grow extremely weak and sick, until they came upon the Nez Perce down in the valley. The Nez Perce fed them roots and dried fish, and their chief provided Lewis with a gentle horse because he'd become so ill. All recovered.

After adding a rock to one of the larger cairns I clambered around a bit to get a feel for the area. Looking down, I spotted some mouse-sized scats on a couple of flat rocks. The scats led to a hole. Just outside this hole were some large cat-sized scats on top of pine needles and leaves. Where had these needles and leaves come from? There were no trees on this rocky peak. Then I looked farther into the hole and saw many more leaves and needles. It had been the home of some rodent.

The larger scats had hair and bone fibers in them. They stank like decaying meat and tapered off at the ends. I brought Preston and Harlan over. Together, we surmised that the cat—probably a bobcat or even a lynx, Harlan thought—tracked the little rodents to the hole and then sat there eating away—until he'd gotten to all of them. Some of the cat scats were much fresher than the others.

The mountain became even holier in my mind.

Descending on our horses to a lower trail, we rode through white and red firs. They were the most wonderfully pungent trees we'd yet encountered. Countless patches of bear grass, pearly everlasting, and inedible mushrooms blanketed the forest floor.

A herd of six elk cows allowed us to come within fifty feet of them. Harlan explained they thought we were just horses. "The minute we get off these things they'll take off," he said.

We did. They did.

Preston's day worsened considerably after that. It'd already been slightly off. The lever that advances the film in his camera had fallen off in the morning, requiring him to sift through his pockets for it whenever he wanted to take a picture. Then, when we were riding along one of the forest roads after seeing the elk, disaster struck. My horse had been farting on his horse for nearly half an hour. Preston was complaining and making faces the entire time. Eventually, he attempted to ride past me, but at each attempt I cut him off. Domingo continued to fart.

I rode up adjacent to Harlan to make it even more difficult for Preston to pass; the road was too narrow for three horses. We talked about Harlan's lumbering days. Before working for a lumbering company he'd taken a job at a plywood mill, and it had been the dullest, worst job he'd ever had. Then, Harlan's horse began to fart as well. Preston was right behind us, trying to figure out a way to break through and listen to our conversation

Preston rode up even closer to Harlan's horse's ass. Suddenly, out of the corner of my eye, I caught some frantic movement. Then, Harlan's and my horses jumped, rearing up slightly. At about the same moment, we heard this terrific *ka wump!* After calming our horses, we turned around and there was Preston on the ground. He'd been bucked off his horse and had landed on his shoulder. Apparently the wind had been knocked out of him because he wasn't breathing, just motioning as if he wanted some air. The next second, though, he was breathing normally.

"Anything broken?" Harlan asked. We tied up our horses.

"I don't think so, but my shoulder is pretty bad."

I went over and poked him all over. Apparently, I was doing it harder than necessary and he told me to lay off. I was laughing nervously. "Don't tell Harlan, but I think I've broken a couple of ribs," he whispered to me.

We climbed back onto our mounts. "That doesn't make sense, your horse doing that," Harlan said. "Never had a problem with it. Maybe a bee stung it."

"Yeah, that's probably it. This is a great horse. She's been super except for that."

I suggested it happened because Preston's horse was tired of getting farted on, but they both told me the horses were more than used to that.

Later, when we were mounting after an afternoon break, Preston dropped his hat in a freshly made pile of horse shit. His horse, Stormy, stepped on it. Preston dismounted, picked up the hat, and put it on his head after a cursory cleaning. I think he'd given up at that point.

Our campsite that evening was the trashiest yet. Many hunters had used the area, Dwayne told me, and there was ample evidence of this. Magazines, newspapers, plastic bags, battery packages, batteries, toilet paper, paper towels, cigarette butts, and metal utensils lay scattered on the ground. I couldn't even count all of the beer and soda cans.

Preston didn't speak much during dinner and I caught him holding on to his ribs a number of times. They were definitely cracked but he wanted to continue anyway. "A doctor couldn't do anything for them," he told me later in our tent.

The next day, our last day on the horses, was much calmer. Preston's horse gave him no trouble, and Harlan gathered different edible plants when he learned we were interested.

The first thing was a plant he called couse-couse. When growing, it looks a lot like water hemlock, which is deadly poisonous. But the root of the couse-couse is medicinal and celery scented; the water hemlock is not.

"The Indians use it in their sweat lodges. They put pieces of it in the water so its vapors fill the air. You can chew on a little bit and it helps with the sinuses," Harlan said. I happened to have a stuffed nose so I tried some. It was minty-celery flavored. My nose cleared up a little.

We hit our most beautiful scenery in the afternoon. After viewing a Lewis and Clark campsite that the Forest Service had named Full Stomach Camp (because the men had eaten a horse that Clark had come upon), we rode through an old stand of cedars, white firs, and ponderosa pines. The trail wound through these woods and it felt as if we wound back in time as well. Everything was quiet and appeared untouched—as if only Harlan knew of this trail. The old-growth trees looked as if they could last forever, and the dead ones—with diameters of at least five feet—lay calmly on the ground. This, I thought, is a safe place.

Harlan abruptly hopped off his horse and stepped over to a fallen tree. "Here's one of those mushrooms I was telling you about," he called to me as he bent over. The next thing I knew he held up this cauliflower-shaped mushroom. "It only grows on dead white-fir trees. That's how I know it's the right one. We'll fry it up in some butter when we get to camp." He didn't know the name for it.

We found more of them, but they were too old and woody.

Barb sautéed them when we arrived at our last camp and they tasted great—a lot like chanterelles. She also made us steaks to celebrate the final evening.

The horses were led into their trailer the next morning. Dwayne would drive us to Orofino, Idaho—site of the expedition's embarkation on the Clearwater River and soon to be ours. But first we stopped at a place called Musselshell Meadows, a traditional gathering grounds for the Nez Perce. The field was covered with gray-brown camas stalks.

We walked onto the field and Harlan dug up a bulb for us. As I began nibbling on the bulb he'd handed us, he said, "The white camas is poisonous. The only way you can tell the difference between the blue and white camas is by seeing the flowers in the spring." Since it was the fall, everything had dried up and withered away.

"What grows here?" I asked, attempting to spit out the bulb that was making its way down my throat.

"Blue." I continued swallowing. It tasted extremely starchy and would be good boiled or steamed. (Lewis, Clark, and their men ate a mess of it when they met up with the Nez Perce in this same area and became fairly sick the next couple of days.)

Barb and Harlan drove back to their camp soon afterward, and we headed off with Dwayne. We were in the Weippe Prairie then, and the mountains were finally behind us. From this point, Lewis wrote, "The pleasure I now felt in having triumphed over the rockey Mountains and descending once more to a level and fertile country where there was every rational hope of finding a comfortable subsistence for myself and party can be more readily conceived than expressed, nor was the flattering prospect of the final success of the expedition less pleasing." Ditto for Preston and me.

We waited for Temple and John at the Holzers'—Dwayne's daughter and son-in-law's house. The son-in-law was an inventor. One of his big sellers was a Telescoping Rolla Roaster. His flyer said it all: "A fun, handy tool for roasting hot dogs and marshmallows over campfires, backyard barbeques, and fireplaces. The stainless-steel fork telescopes from twelve inches long for backyard barbeques to forty-two inches long for campfire cooking. The wooden handle never overheats, and under your thumb you will find a knob that you move to turn the fork like a rotisserie. This tool comes in a vinyl pack for convenient storage."

They were kind enough to let us bathe and wash our clothes. Or else our smell was so overwhelming that they had no other recourse. Whatever the case, we were well taken care of until Temple and John arrived that evening with our boat and belongings. It was good to see them and *Sacky* again.

We camped at an access area—Temple and John in their Taj Mahal and Preston and I in our pup tent. Preston's ribs were still aching and stiff so I did most of the work.

Temple wasn't showing yet but John looked a little heavier. I told her about a petite friend of mine who'd gained fifty pounds during her pregnancy and Temple laughed heartily, saying it could never happen. (It eventually did.)

Camping beside the river was a joy. Preston pointed out various constellations and I simply listened to the rush of the water. The next day would begin the last leg, and thankfully, I thought, this would be just like Lewis and Clark's last leg—riding downriver with only the rapids and paddles to power us. The current looked strong and hard, giving the lie to Virgil's warning. There was no way a current like this could simply peter out.

PART 5

A RIVER DOESN'T RUN THROUGH IT

SIXTEEN
━ ━ ━ ━ ━
Dog, Anyone?

We said farewell to Temple and John around noon the next day, October 24, and started our descent to the Pacific Ocean. Roughly five hundred miles awaited, and if all went well, we'd arrive on November 7. It would be the same day the expedition thought they saw the ocean for the first time (it may have been only the bay).

The extent of our white-water rafting preparation consisted of seeing a brochure published by a white-water rafting company. It depicted a guide riding near the middle of the boat, oars in hands and facing the bow. So we decided to tackle the rapids in the same manner, except we chose to have the oarsman with his back to the bow. The other person sat in the stern, calling out orders. Unbelievably, this worked, and we rode through many sets of rapids that afternoon without flipping over or, even more important, without fighting.

The Clearwater River lived up to its name and we could see to the bottom, even in the deeper parts. There were plenty of fish—steelhead and other trout. The river formed a gorge, cutting through steep hills to the south and rolling prairies to the north. The hills usually had many conifers covering them, but the prairies were barren, except for low-lying sagebrush. And once again we were in the company of blue herons. We spotted five of them all told, and they were either hunting along the shores or flying fairly low over the water.

Between the rapids, in calmer water, we passed a total of thirty fishing boats. We asked them all—out of sheer orneriness, I guess—if they'd caught anything, and every last one of them answered, "Naw. But we seen 'em rollin'."

Pretty soon, Preston was asking them if they'd seen any rolling, just so they'd think we were in the know. But the way they stared at our engineless, badly patched raft, I got the feeling they were the ones who were truly in the know. "Now, what are those two boys up to?" each of their faces read.

Sometimes they'd even ask. One of us would yell back, "Goin' to the Pacific!" And then they'd start laughing, as if it were the funniest joke they'd ever heard.

"Good luck," would always follow, but offered sarcastically. They thought we were only joking.

We stopped around five-thirty on a large, tree-covered island. We'd rafted roughly twenty-five miles in five hours, right on schedule.

We set up the tent, ate pork chops and rice (we'd shopped in Orofino with Temple and John), built a roaring fire, and laid our clothes out next to it so they'd dry. A group of coyotes began howling as soon as the last bit of daylight had disappeared.

"I've got to hand it to you, Hod," Preston said as he spread out before the fire. "This rafting is four aces. I didn't believe it was going to be so easy . . . yep."

From near this point on, the Lewis and Clark expedition was in such dire straits as far as food was concerned that they resorted to eating dogs bought from the locals. Clark blithely recorded these purchases. Not until they are wintering on the Pacific coast and still eating dog do Lewis and Clark reveal their separate attitudes to eating man's best friend.

Lewis wrote, "Our party from necessaty having been obliged to subsist some length of time on dogs have now become extremely fond of their flesh; it is worthy of remark that while we lived principally on the flesh of this anamal we were much more healthy and strong and more fleshy than we had been since we left the Buffaloe country. for my own part I have become so perfectly reconciled to the dog that I think it an agreeable food and would prefer it vastly to lean Venison or Elk."

On the same day, Clark wrote, "As for my own part I have not become reconsiled to the taste of this animal as yet."

And later, when they were on the return leg, Lewis was still eating dog. A young warrior along the way took exception to men eating dogs. "While at dinner an indian fellow verry impertinently threw a poor half starved puppy nearly into my plait by the way of derision for our eating dogs and laughed very heartily at his own impertinence," Lewis recorded. "I was so provoked at his insolence that I caught the puppy and threw it with great violence at him and struck him in the breast and face, seized my tomahawk and shewed him by signs if he repeated his insolence I would tommahawk him, the fellow withdrew apparently mortifyed and I continued my repast on dog without further molestation."

If our choices had been eating dog or having the following day unfold, I would have chosen the former. The first couple of hours were the same as the previous day—plenty of current and rapids. By midmorning, however, we started running into patches of still water. There were mile-long stretches of no current, and even paddling as hard as we could, we were only making two miles an hour. I sort of wished I hadn't shipped the boat motor home.

Preston suggested we take turns walking along the shore. A railroad track ran adjacent to the shoreline and it

would be an easy hike. The lightened load would make rowing that much easier. He hiked first and luckily I ran into
two sets of rapids. I was waiting for him when my hour was
up.

Then it was my turn to walk. We were on the outskirts of
Lewiston, Idaho, having traveled forty-odd miles since
Orofino. I followed the tracks just as Preston had. It was a
pleasant change. I scared up dozens of quail and realized
why aristocrats had always hunted them: they were an easy
target. I also spotted a red-bellied hawk and heard its pierc-
ing, haunting call. It was beautiful. But then I came upon a
huge, never-ending paper mill. It stood between me and
the river. I tried cutting through it but a guard kicked me
out. I'd have to go around.

Of course, I started panicking. I could no longer see
Preston so neither of us knew who was ahead. We were supposed to meet at two. Would he stop at two, thinking I was
behind him while I was actually ahead? Or would I do the
same? Or some reverse situation that was equally dreadful?
I didn't have my wallet or food. All of my belongings were
in the boat.

I did have Preston's wallet in the pack on my back, as
well as both of our boots. But he had no money nor credit
cards in it. Why had we done such a stupid thing?

I started running, racing past long-forgotten railroad
cars and mounds of trash. It looked like a railroad burial
ground. With a little luck, I made it back to the river right
at two.

But where was Preston? What would I do without him?

Wait, I thought, did I just think that? Were we that close
now?

I scanned the river for him and *Sacky*. I asked fishermen
standing along the concrete levee—I was beneath a highway bridge—if they'd seen an odd, beat-up raft come by
with one dirty man in it.

None of them had. Good, I was ahead. I sat down and
waited, trying not to worry. After half an hour, I gave up
and just let myself fret.

But about then, with my binoculars I caught sight of him

upstream. Only, there was obviously no stream—no current. He was rowing hard the entire time.

When he finally arrived twenty minutes later, he was exhausted. "The water went dead five minutes after you started walking," he explained after we'd tied *Sacky* to a rock on the levee. "I had to row hard the entire time, but the left oar is falling apart. There's no way it's going to make it to the Pacific."

"I got really worried once that paper mill popped up," I told him, ignoring the part about the oar. What could we do about that?

"I know," he said, smiling. "I could feel you worrying."

We gave up on separating as he hadn't been able to row any faster without my weight in *Sacky* and because neither of us felt comfortable without the other now. We rowed for a couple more hours, passing hundreds of anchored fishing boats as we neared the confluence of the Clearwater and Snake rivers. None of the fishermen looked too pleased as we slowly paddled near them, but when we kept on going—past their lifeless lines—they usually gave us a smile. One of them even caught a steelhead—a large fish more than three feet in length. It would've fed us for a few days.

The river was more than two miles wide at the confluence. The Snake approached from the south. (On its western bank stood the town of Clarkston, Washington, and on its eastern was Lewiston. They were named after the two explorers, and Clarkston was the poorer of the two.) But there was no current at all. Two wide, large rivers were joining each other and there was no current. We felt like screaming—not only because of our predicament but also because of the sheer unnaturalness of it all. After descending hundreds of miles out of the mountains, the Clearwater was ending quite unceremoniously. These mighty Western rivers had been turned into weak reservoirs for the surrounding towns, farms, and ranches. There had to be a better way.

We camped on what looked to be a man-made peninsula of rocks directly across from both towns. In the morning we would follow the Snake, not south but northwest into the state of Washington, where it, too, would empty into another river—the Columbia. Would there be no current there as well?

It turned dark by five-thirty that night. We'd set our watches back in the morning along with the rest of the nation. The twin cities' lights flashed and glowed, dancing along the water until they reached our shore. The green and red neons were the prettiest. And as I imagined that they would one day break or burn out, I acquired some comfort in realizing that the same would happen to all the dams we'd built along these rivers. It might take a few decades or even a couple of hundred years, but it would happen. Things do fall apart.

SEVENTEEN

"Build a Fire! Get High!"

We were up early the next morning thanks to the unset-
tling time change. The fishermen weren't even out yet. After grits and coffee, we set out for Clarkston. We needed
gas for our stove and drinking water (we weren't about to
filter the Snake). It took more than an hour and a half of
constant rowing to reach the town's marina.

Of course, the marina wasn't open so early. Another
boater was there and directed us to a gas station a few miles
down the road. He also told us that the Snake, as we now
figured, had no current, and neither did the Columbia.

We walked to the gas station, bought gas and a few jugs
of water, and returned to *Sacky*. Along the way, we figured
out how long it would now take to reach Astoria, Oregon—
the town where the Columbia meets the Pacific. The fastest
we could hope to travel was two miles an hour. If we did
that for six to eight hours a day—unlikely considering the

effort it took to row that fast—we'd make roughly fifteen miles a day. We wouldn't finish until sometime well into December—an impossibility since we weren't prepared for winter boating.

"But that only works if we don't get any headwinds. Otherwise, it could take until February or March," Preston pointed out as I rowed. We were back on the water. "Right now, we're lucky. There's a slight wind at our backs. What happens when the wind stops? Do we only make one mile an hour? And when it's blowing in our faces, do we go backward?"

I didn't have a response and so I simply continued rowing.

"I think we have to try and hitch a tow," Preston continued.

"All the way there?"

"Whatever. There are plenty of boats around here. We'll just stick out our thumb and then latch on. They'll be happy to help us out."

We rowed for three hours without seeing any boats except for some kind of cruise ship and a number of docked barges. And then we heard a speedboat fast approaching.

Preston stood up and stuck out his thumb, gesturing with his other hand as well. To my surprise, the boat headed across the water for us. It was a tinny, flat-bottomed boat that was jet powered, like many we'd seen around Clarkston. It'd be perfect for towing us.

Preston immediately explained what had happened, making us sound pretty desperate, which we were. I helped out by explaining I'd expected the rivers to be the same as when Lewis and Clark were here. That at least procured a good laugh from the two men in the boat.

"Well, we're out fishing so I don't know about towing," the big-faced, mustached captain of the boat answered. His name was Glen. "It would slow us up too much." Then he stopped talking. The other fellow, a dark-haired man who was even bigger, didn't say anything either. Glen, though, looked as if he were thinking. We waited, smiling. "I do have an extra engine," Glen continued. "It ain't much. Really old. But it'll get you to the Pacific—I can guarantee that. And much faster than you'll ever paddle that thing." He saw our skepticism. "You've been lucky today. Usually, the wind picks up the waves pretty badly around here. The swells get a couple feet high. You wouldn't be able to go anywhere."

Preston and I stood there, holding on to his boat. Preston didn't even bother to look at me. He knew I'd never buy another engine, having sent our perfectly good one back just a month earlier.

"How much?" I asked.

"Three hundred. I was asking more before, but I'll sell it to you with a gas tank and gas for three hundred. I'll tow you back there and you can take a look at it for yourself before you decide."

"Let's do it," I said. There wasn't much debate going on in my head. This had to be done if we were going to finish this trip. It was a lot like Lewis and Clark's decision to start buying dogs from the locals. We might be derided by Temple and other friends, but it had to be done. We lashed *Sacky* to Glen's boat and sped back to Clarkston.

The engine was stored at a boat repair shop across the street from the marina. We walked over. It was hitched to the back of a truck. Glen, Bill, and Jack (the owner of the repair shop) let us inspect it alone.

The engine was a beat-up eighteen-horsepower Evinrude. It was thirty years old.

"Let's try and look like we know what we're doing," Preston whispered as we stood before it. So we fiddled with the outer workings, nodding our heads knowingly. Put our hands on our hips and pretended to be discussing it, but in truth, just mouthing words. Put our hands on top of it, secretly looking and feeling for the latch so we could take the covering off, not wanting them to know that we didn't know where the damned latch was supposed to be. Lifted the latch and lid eventually. Fiddled with the inner workings—pushing and tugging on things until they were slightly moved and then moving them exactly back into place. I knew where the spark plugs were so I pulled off their rubber casings and inspected them for corrosion (none).

We walked back to the men, who were standing around laughing, which didn't seem like a good sign.

"We'd like to see it started," Preston sort of demanded.

"But if it starts up fine, we'll take it," I added, blowing our cover. I hadn't even bargained with him. What a sucker I was.

While Jack, Bill, and Preston took the motor down to our boat to start it up, Glen and I drove to the bank to get a cash advance off my VISA. It was then that I learned from Glen that Clarkston is poorer than Lewiston. Glen also told me that he's part Indian and that some local Nez Perce were going to make him a full Indian outfit and headdress made with thirty-eight eagle feathers that he'd collected. "You see," he confided, "I'm allowed to collect the eagle feathers since I'm part Indian." It is against federal law for all nonnatives to collect eagle feathers, and it seemed to me the only reason Glen claimed he was Indian was because he wanted to keep the feathers. But then, maybe I was still pissed over not having bargained better. A fellow feels like a fool when he hasn't talked somebody down in a deal—let alone not even attempted to talk him down.

When we returned to the boat and our new old motor, Preston took me aside to say it started fairly easily. So I handed over the money.

About then, Bill, who had been mostly silent during the proceedings, told a joke—"I don't see anything wrong with blacks," he croaked, "I think everybody ought to own one." He and Glen laughed fairly hard over that one. Jack, I was interested to see, didn't.

"Yeah, well, I guess we better get going," I said, fighting back the impulse to push fat, old Bill into the water. Being the chicken that I am, though, I said what I said, and we left.

"That Bill is some kinda guy, huh?" Preston said. The engine was terribly loud and even at full power quite slow. It seemed as if we were going about 6 mph. "You would've been real proud of me back there while you were gone," he continued. "I just stood there real silent and not smiling while Jack got the engine going. I didn't even make any small talk. I think we coulda gotten the engine for less."

I didn't need him to say that, especially since I wished more than anything that I'd bargained, considering what kind of people they were.

But we were going three times as fast as before. When we'd gone about ten miles, I knew we'd done the right thing. The lake—I refused to call it a river—had become choppy and the swells were a few feet high. We would've been pushed backward if we'd been rowing.

After another five miles, though, we realized there was one major problem. The engine was devouring the gas and the tank was nearly empty.

Well, really, there was more than one major problem. The rubber fuel line was falling apart before our very eyes. All the vibrating from the engine's being pushed too hard had caused it to split. Twice, we'd been forced to pull it off, cut off the split, corroded section, and then jam it back on. At that rate, the fuel line would only last another four days. We did seem to have cut off most of the bad parts by the second time, though.

Each time we stopped, the engine had been more difficult to restart.

When we were down to a fifth of a tank, we pulled over to a boat landing on our starboard side. A ground crew was working at the campsite and a boat sat at the dock. We begged two gallons of gas off of them and learned the dam was about another fifteen miles away. We just might make it.

Before attempting to restart the engine, we fixed the fuel line again. Then, we pulled on the starter cord for nearly an hour—Preston couldn't pull on it much because of his ribs—until my arm was exhausted.

We checked the plugs and they were blacker than hell. We cleaned them off, but the engine still wouldn't start. It sounded as if it was flooded.

We were obviously camping where we were. Maybe it would start in the morning.

After we'd unloaded our gear from the boat and were standing over it, Preston intoned in a reverent voice, "We christen thee Charbono, in honor of that heroic member of the Lewis and Clark expedition." He then bowed before our fussy engine.

It was more than fitting. Just like his namesake, our Charbono was belligerent, unreliable, and required an inordinate amount of pampering. Charbono (correctly spelled Charbonneau) was the interpreter hired on at Fort Mandan. His main contribution to the expedition was his wife, Sacagawea. Other than that, he was a nuisance. He didn't ever want to work. One day, he nearly overturned a canoe that was carrying the expedition's most important items: their notes, medicine, and presents for the Indians. On another, Charbono actually succeeded in turning the canoe on its side. "Charbono still crying to his god for mercy, had not yet recollected the rudder," Lewis recorded, "nor could the repeated orders of the Bowsman, Cruzat, bring him to his recollection untill he threatened to shoot him instantly if he did not take hold of the rudder and do his duty."

We entered the tent early, before seven-thirty even, and a pack of coyotes quickly serenaded us to sleep. It had been a long day.

At eight-thirty that same night an unrelenting disturbance rousted me from my rest. Rumbling tires, blaring music, lights flashing all around illuminating our tent. My heart immediately began racing, along with my mind. Satan worshipers. This was, after all, the state of Washington. People were always being tortured and chased by Satan worshipers out here.

I woke Preston.

Then I realized they were playing reggae music. At least they weren't satanist: Bob Marley and the devil just didn't fit.

"Shit," Preston said as he, too, heard the commotion. He slowly unzipped our back flap, which was directly facing the noise.

There was a truck. It was backing up to a fire pit not more than a hundred yards away.

Then we heard screaming. "*Yeah!* We'll have the entire KKK here tonight, man!"

"A big fire!"

"Hey, do you think they're in the tent?"

Great, they were talking about us.

"There's no car."

"We're gonna get fucked *up!*"

All the while, they were pulling heavy things out of the bed of the truck and piling the objects up. It sounded like wooden chairs but heavier. We couldn't see anything because they'd killed the truck lights.

Needless to say, I was scared shitless. "What are they doing?" I asked Preston. He whispered he didn't know.

Did they have guns? All we had were two pocket knives. Our oars, fairly decent weapons, were in the boat—too far away.

Liquid was poured onto something and the next thing we saw was a ten-foot-high flame. Three human figures were silhouetted. They started screaming again and piling more of the wooden objects onto the fire. The wood, we could finally tell, was pallets.

"Do you think we ought to sneak out of here—put everything into the boat and float away?" I asked.

"Why?" Preston responded. "We'll stay here."

Good, I thought, he wants to hide as well. But then I noticed him putting on his clothes, rustling around all too loudly.

"What are you doing?" I asked

"I'm gonna go tell them to keep it down," Preston said matter-of-factly.

What? my mind screamed. That's crazy. There are three lunatics running around with gallons of gas, yelling about the Klan, and maybe loaded to the hilt with guns, and he wants to go talk to them? I calmed myself long enough to suggest we lie low, not show our faces until we've figured out what they're up to. Preston agreed but continued to dress.

For the next thirty minutes we watched them. They played with the fire, pouring gasoline on it, in big circles, onto nearby trees, and onto the picnic bench. Eventually, we realized they were probably seniors in high school. They drank a lot of beers and kept talking about getting fucked up. One of them, a fatter fellow, kept running back to the truck to put on different tapes: Metallica, Led Zeppelin, and more Bob Marley. They put Marley on when they lit up a joint.

We realized that the music guy was uncoordinated as well as fat. "We can take him no problem," Preston explained.

Then, they started arguing politics.

One of them was a Ross Perot fan. "He'll cut spending here. He'll take some from there," were his exact words.

They had two dogs that approached our tent. Preston growled, low and hard. The animals ran off with their tails between their legs.

After about an hour, their fire died down. "Oh, good, they'll leave soon," I said. But then we heard this breaking of wood, loud cracks, and the fire soared once more. They'd broken up the picnic bench.

It was then that we decided to do something about them. I'd been scared up to then and now I was mad. I guess it was the vandalism.

Preston coached me on what to do.

"If we approach them and they want to fight, there's no holding back. We have to beat them mercilessly when we take them," he explained. "Once your guy is down, beat him again and again. Go for the face and the stomach. Contrary to the old saying, the best thing is kicking him when he's down."

"So," I added, "we'll tell the chubby guy, while we're beating his friends, to stay out of it—that we don't want to beat him up, too."

"No, no. You never say you don't want to do it. Say, 'I'll be glad to beat the hell out of you, too, anytime,' " Preston reprimanded me.

Just as I finished getting dressed, though, they decided to leave. The chubbster did doughnuts in the parking lot a few times with the truck. One of them—the pyro of the three—climbed in with him. The last one started our way. When he was within fifteen feet, we popped out of the tent. Preston was first.

"How ya doing?" were Preston's opening words, but it sounded more like, "You're about to get the living shit beat out of you, you dumb fuck."

Even more startling were my next moves. Without hesitating, I advanced face-to-face with the guy. How dare he come near our tent, is all I was thinking.

"Whoa, you're in your tent, dudes?" he sputtered, and then I realized I was a good six inches taller than he. He was long-haired and skinny. I stood a little straighter.

"We been fishin'," I grunted. It was the first thing that'd popped into my head. What could I have meant? Fishing?

For some reason this scared him senseless. He started backing up and muttered, "So, you guys all right? Do you need anything? A beer?"

His friends were calling to him from the truck. Their headlights were focused in a different direction so they had no way of knowing what had occurred. He ran back to the truck.

As he climbed in, we could hear him say, "Hey, those guys were there. They're hard-core, man. They hopped out of the tent the second I came up. . . . They're just like we were that time. They've been dropped off here. They're hard-core!"

He slammed the door, and as they peeled out of the parking lot, he screamed, feeling a little braver, "Build a *fire! Get high!*" again and again.

Later, as we doused the remainder of their fire, we were only sorry we hadn't come out earlier. Preston had been right at first and we probably could've stopped them from destroying the picnic bench.

Although Charbono had the whole night for the gas to dry in the flooded carburetor, it still wouldn't start in the morning. We pulled and pulled on it for ninety minutes. Every few pulls we'd check the workings and once again the carburetor would be flooded. We weren't even giving it gas.

Obviously, this wasn't going to work. I'd been ripped off.

Two men, a father and son, arrived with their huge

powerboat in tow. They saw the black grease and frustration covering our faces and asked if we needed some help. We explained our predicament.

The father, Ray Heglar, offered to take us back to Clarkston. "And you might as well throw your engine into the back of the truck so you don't have to go back and forth," he added.

We gushed with gratitude, and Paul, the son, said, "If I was in your predicament, I sure hope someone would do the same for me. I mean, you're up the creek without a paddle so to speak." He then helped us load Charbono into the truck. We rode in the boat because Ray said it would be more comfortable.

Jack Whorl, the owner of the boat repair shop, didn't seem very surprised to see us. He let us use his phone to call Glen, the man who'd sold me the engine (I left a message for Glen at his shop, but he never showed up). While we waited, Jack fixed the engine.

A lever that regulated the amount of gas in the carburetor was causing it to flood, so Jack simply took it off. After that, the engine started on the first pull.

The day before we'd thought Jack might be an ex-convict or something. He'd been quiet and stern the entire time we'd been around him, Glen, and the racist. But now he was laughing with us and explaining about the river and our engine. He drove us around town so we could buy an extra gas can, a wrench, and a screwdriver—that's all we needed to use on the engine, he said. As we made each stop, he talked more and more, and finally we found out a little about him.

He used to be in the Air Force—in intelligence—and was now running the boat shop with his dad. Jack was lean and dark haired and he did look a little tired under the eyes, giving him that ex-con look. But he turned out to be one of the nicest people we'd met on the entire trip.

After we'd done all our errands and given up on Glen, Jack drove us back to our campsite. He helped put the motor back on the transom and then fired her up for us, fiddling with the lean and rich valves on the engine as he did so. "Is the engine running okay, otherwise?" he asked.

"Oh, yeah, fine," I quickly answered. I didn't want him to know how slowly it was running—some sort of misplaced pride.

"Then just leave these valves like they are," he finished. "Make sure you keep cleaning those plugs, too." As we said good-bye, we tried offering him some money, but he wouldn't take it. "You're the ones trying to make it to the Pacific Ocean," he explained, chuckling. "You need it more than me."

We headed up the river/lake at full speed—a whopping six miles an hour. The scenery didn't change much—barren cliffs intermixed with barren hills.

At one-thirty, we arrived at our first dam. There was a mighty difference from the ones on the Missouri. All the dams on the Columbia River system (which includes the Snake) have locks. Since we were an engine-powered craft, they were required to let us use them. We'd never have to portage—another good reason for having bought the motor.

Two sour-faced fellows in a fishing boat were trolling the waters in front of the lock.

"Hey," I called as we narrowly missed their lines, "when do they open these gates?" Huge metal doors closed off the entrance to the lock.

"Huh?" the captain answered.

"Two o'clock," the other filled in. "They open it up every hour on the hour."

So we tied up to a metal ladder that climbed up one of the concrete walls of the dam and followed it to the top. A railing separated us from the lock, but we could see down into it anyway. The lock was empty—meaning it was at the lower level we wanted to descend to. It looked to be a hundred feet down and made me wonder if the hydraulics—they controlled the doors—ever simply stopped working without any warning.

We returned to the boat a few minutes before two. The

time arrived and nothing happened. We pulled on a rope that was accompanied by a sign suggesting we pull it for attention. No response. 2:05. 2:15. 2:30.

Preston climbed the ladder again to search for the lockkeeper. Maybe he couldn't see us since our boat was so small.

He returned in a half hour. "The guy was watching an espionage movie down at their base. He didn't hear us pulling on the rope—it rings a bell in his office."

"Espionage movie? Not spy or killer movie?"

"Espionage. That's what he said. I think he was a fanatic of some sort. Anyway, he said that fisherman was bullshit. They only open the locks when someone pulls on the rope or radios in that they're coming. And he said this thing will release enough water when we're going down to power a single-family home for eight months."

Riding down the lock felt creepy and exciting. The chamber—at least a hundred yards long—echoed and clanged as we descended, tied to a metal hook that descended with the water. I felt as if we were in the hull of a sunken ship. Various boaters had scribbled graffiti on the upper walls, but nothing beyond: *J.B. was here.*

It took ten minutes for all the water to drain out. Then they opened the lock doors and we rode valiantly out of the whale's mouth. Only seven more to go.

It was past three-thirty by then so we only traveled for another hour, putting in at a public campground that was closed for the season—meaning there was no charge. The place had a small marina as well, and the fellow who ran it happened to be around. We filled our gas can and tank.

Planted on the grounds were many deciduous trees that seemed wholly out of place, including maples and oaks. There was also the requisite Lewis and Clark sign. It indicated that the expedition camped out a mile downstream at the mouth of the Almota Creek on October 11, 1805. They bought three dogs to eat that night. We were sixteen days behind them and hoped that Charbono would help us make up the difference over the next ten days. Even at its top speed of 6 mph we could do it with eight-hour days—if it didn't keep breaking down.

But making it on some kind of schedule didn't really seem to matter anymore. We were obviously going to make it one way or another.

As the Snake turned lavender from the setting sun, I cooked Kenya's national dish—maize (what we call hominy corn) and beans. Now that we had the boat again we were able to carry more supplies. First I sautéed a few cloves of chopped garlic and one onion in a couple tablespoons of olive oil. When they were tender, I emptied two cans of kidney beans and one can of hominy into the pot. I strained and rinsed them in the campground sink first to get off the gloop that inevitably covers canned beans. After allowing those to cook with the garlic and onions for a few minutes, I tossed in a handful of strong curry powder, stirring constantly. Then I poured in about two cups of water and slipped in a chicken bouillon cube, simmered the entire mess for about fifteen minutes, letting it thicken slightly, and finally poured it over a mound of rice.

To be fair to the original Charbono, he did have one redeeming quality. He could cook a mean boudin blanc, exciting Lewis to record the making in his journal: "About 6 feet of the lower extremity of the large gut of the Buffaloe is the first morsel that the cook makes love to, this he holds fast at one end with the right hand, while the forefinger and thumb of the left he gently compresses it, and discharges what he says *is not good to eat,* but of which in the sequel we get a moderate portion; the mustle lying underneath the shoulder blade next to the back, and fillets are next saught, these are needed up very fine with a good portion of kidney suit [suet]; to this composition is then added a just portion of pepper and salt and a small quantity of flour." Lewis continued the description, explaining how the sausage was stuffed and tied off. And he summed up, "It is then baptised in the Missouri with two dips and a flirt, and bobbed into the kettle; from whence, after it be well boiled it is taken and fryed with bears oil untill it becomes brown, when it is ready to esswage the pangs of a keen appetite or such as travelers in the wilderness are seldom at a loss for."

We were standing over our stove the next morning, drinking our coffee. Although it was in the high forties and cloudy, it felt cozy—a delicious fall morning that allowed us to feel lazy and comfortable. Preston was telling me about one of his dreams involving Marina when I suddenly remembered one of my own.

"Wait, wait," I interrupted. "I had a dream about Lewis and Clark last night."

"This sounds good."

"We'd met up with them during our trip. They were still on theirs as well. All four of us sat in a huge, soft meadow— four adventurers comparing notes—but it was only a brief encounter. We all had to be on our way. I talked to Lewis and you talked with Clark."

"That makes sense."

"Lewis was thin and had black hair. He was upset with his nails because they were dirty. I told him I was having the same problem and that it probably didn't matter. Clark couldn't believe it was only taking us two and a half months to finish the trail. He just kept shaking his head and chuckling. Other men were in the background, loading canoes. . . . The odd thing was that Lewis seemed settled finally—like everything was okay."

As I finished telling Preston this, my eyes started to well up and I had to look away. But I was happy for Lewis.

He was no longer the stick figure of my childhood or even the two-dimensional one of three months earlier. Preston and I had long since quit calling each other "Lewis" in jest. The joke had worn out not only over time but also over a hard-wrought respect. Yes, Lewis ate dog with relish, lost his head with the Blackfeet, and died under suspicious circumstances. But if Preston or I had been faced with the same circumstances, how would we have fared? Would we have been able to lead a troop of men through the rivers, prairies, mountains, and rain forests of North America and have all but one return?

No.

It rained on us all morning and it felt as if it were getting colder and colder. My feet stayed numb the entire time. And the next dam turned out to be forty miles away. That was fine except there was nowhere to stop for gas and we only had enough to make it thirty miles.

At thirty-one miles, Charbono started coughing and sputtering, and then suddenly it was running better than ever, at least three times faster. This lasted roughly one minute and then it quit completely. It was out of gas. At first we were both amazed at the speed it'd briefly attained.

"It must have something to do with the fuel/air ratio," Preston said. "We ought to be able to make it go that fast the entire time—if we can just figure it out."

But right then, we had more pressing problems. A head wind was blowing us backward.

We started rowing and paddling simultaneously, but all that did was keep the boat still. We couldn't go forward.

We weren't far from the northeast shore and we paddled to it. A farmhouse stood on a prairie hill on the other side of two fences and a railroad track. If no one was there, we'd have to walk along the railroad tracks for nine miles to the next dam and then buy or beg a few gallons off of someone.

After tying *Sacky* to a tree, we climbed through the barbed-wire fences and crossed the tracks to the house, calling out greetings the entire time so no one would shoot. We reached the barn with no answer. It had hay—no car, tractor, or cans of gas. We walked to the house. The backdoor was unlocked and we opened it—calling out first. No answer. We went in—breaking and entering.

"Hello, hello."

"We'd like to buy some gas."

There was still no answer. I walked from room to room. Maybe they had a gas can stored somewhere. We'd leave some money for it. There was none. I walked back into the kitchen, expecting some farmer to have a gun to Preston's head, and instead found him with his hand in the cookie jar. He pulled it out, along with a handful of hard rock candy.

"All right. So we'll go back to the boat, get some money and the gas can, then walk to the dam. And I'm not going to say anything about you stealing that candy if you give me a piece." He did.

As we were crossing the tracks, a train came by. We tried to flag the engineer to a stop, but he merely pulled on his whistle. But a white pickup truck, outfitted to ride the tracks, was right behind the train.

It stopped. And they—the driver and his passenger— had some spare gas. They gave us two gallons and wouldn't accept any money. "It's compliments of Camas Railways," the driver said. They were in charge of putting out any fires caused by the train, so they took off as soon as we'd taken the gift.

We made it to the dam. While Preston took the boat through the lock, I went looking for more gas. The closest gas station, a dam employee told me, was thirty miles away. And no, she couldn't give me a lift.

Down at the bottom of the dam, a slew of RVs were parked by the information center. All of their drivers appeared to be fishing, and I went up to each fisherman and asked to buy some gas. No one had any to spare, except for a fellow who said I could siphon it out of his tanks.

I got a hose we used to pump the raft and returned to the man's truck. Pretending as if I'd done this plenty of times before, I stuck the hose as far down as it would go. I breathed in, again and again. The next thing I knew, I was on my butt and everything was spinning. All I'd gotten was fumes, and belatedly I realized I wasn't supposed to breathe in—just suck. Another guy who'd been watching me said his tanks were full and that I should try his truck. Either they were now getting a good laugh at my expense or he truly felt sorry for me.

I stuck the hose down his tank and sucked. The gas gushed up the hose and filled my mouth. I accidentally swallowed half of it. I sucked again, got another mouthful, didn't swallow, and crammed the hose into my can.

The owner of the truck I'd been sucking on said, "So you're following the Lewis and Clark Trail? I've never wanted to follow those boys, but I've a mind to do the Oregon Trail someday. You see, my grandfather came across it when he was just a little boy. He was only seven years old. He used to talk about it all the time."

I nodded my head as he continued to talk. I felt woozy.

I had a full five gallons a few minutes later.

It was five by the time I made it back to Preston. Darkness was settling in and the closest campsite was four miles downriver.

I sat on the bow of the boat, flashing the water ahead with my headlamp, and Preston dodged real and imaginary debris. We pulled into the campground an hour later in complete darkness without a single mishap.

I began burping gas fumes then and continued to do so until the following morning. Luckily, I remembered from *Where There Is No Doctor* that I shouldn't attempt throwing up gasoline. I simply had to wait it out. Preston made me drink nearly a gallon of water, which seemed to dilute the burps somewhat. He said it would help pass it through me. He also fixed dinner—canned chili. That probably helped work the gas out of my system, too.

A huge gasoline belch woke me the next morning and I instantly thought of Charbono—not the French Canadian guide but our engine. Having gasoline problems in common with Charbono was probably what focused my attention. Maybe, I thought, the problem with the air-to-gas ratio could be solved by getting a new gas line. We had been forced to cut off more than a foot of it. The gas could be flooding through because of the shortened line. I woke Preston to tell him, but he quickly discounted it, pointing out that the air line had been reduced in length as well.

"But there's got to be some way," he said, "to increase the air and decrease the gas."

We set off after a leisurely breakfast of grits with hot sauce and two cups of hot chocolate each. Since things were so slow, I guess Preston had a chance to do some thinking, because soon enough he spoke up.

"Hod, you know that theory you had . . ."

"You mean, about the gas line being too short?"

"Huh?" he asked, and then continued, "No, no, I already told you it made no sense. I'm talking about back with Harlan and Barb. Remember how you thought my horse bucked because of all that farting your horse was subjecting it to?"

"Yeah?"

"Well, I have to tell you," he said, sounding truly anguished, "it just ain't so."

"Huh?"

"I was getting mighty tired of being farted on and so was the horse. That much is correct. All I wanted to do was get you back, but I got worried my horse wouldn't fart. I had to do something so I thought I'd lift his tail as I rode by. You know, expose his ass.

"Well, I leaned back to give it a trial pull, so to speak, just to see if I could reach back that far, and I guess the horse didn't care much for that."

After we both calmed down a bit, he said the only thing he really regretted was that Stormy might be blamed.

We chugged along for about an hour until we came across a marina. Luckily, it was still operating. After we'd filled up, I told the attendant about our engine troubles.

"That's easy. Your engine is running rich. Just fiddle with the rich and lean valves until its running leaner." We gave it a try, first turning the valves so that the engine sputtered and conked out. That was too rich. So we turned them the opposite way. It sounded better. We pushed away from the dock and all of a sudden Charbono was acting twenty years younger. It flattened *Sacky* out and we appeared to be going 20 mph. We'd been choking it to death the entire time.

Thanks to that improvement, we made forty-six miles for the day and used three times less gas than we would've before changing the mixture. It felt good to sort of figure out the mechanical problem ourselves. I mean, we had known it was an air-to-gas-ratio problem.

Most of the hills surrounding the lake/river were barren, just like the ones in South and North Dakota. There was very little brush and no trees, except where an occasional apple orchard had been planted. And most of those were planted too far away, until we reached a deserted campground that had an apple orchard adjacent to it. All we had to do was cross through three barbed-wire fences and those sweet things were ours.

The apples had already been harvested, but the pickers had missed a good many. Some of them were purple, they were so overripe, but most of the ones we picked were perfect. Sweet, juicy, and crisp. We ate half a dozen even before we made it back to *Sacky*.

Near the end of the day, we came around a bend in the river that had a rock mass rising straight up from its southwestern bank. A terrific commotion caught our attention as we were only a few feet from the rock. Four river otters had been startled by our appearance and were scrambling to escape, running along narrow pathways on the rock. They couldn't figure out what to do since we were on the water. They were about five feet up.

"Poor fellas," Preston said, and steered the boat in the opposite direction. They then realized the water was their safest bet and plopped into it, one right after the other. One of them, in characteristic otter fashion, raised its head high out of the water for a few moments to watch our progress. I wished we hadn't scared them because then we might've heard them chuckling with each other. They do that when they're being affectionate, a guidebook explained. Luckily, the river otter, as a species, seems to be adapting to all the toxic pollutants that had been wiping them out earlier in this century and they are supposedly on the rebound.

We found a fitting campsite that night—a Corps of Engineers recreational area called Charbono Park.

We set up our tent and paid the park manager. While we didn't like paying, there was a bathroom with hot showers—one more night of not sticking to my sleeping bag. It began raining as the sun set.

The rain continued throughout the night.

We ran into the bathroom the next morning with our food bag and cook kit. While I prepared our breakfast on the sink counter, Preston dried our socks and wool hats with the hot hand-dryers. We weren't in any rush now that we had Charbono working. So first we each drank a few cups of hot chocolate and coffee. Then we had some oatmeal, and to top it all off, a few cups of spicy grits.

Most campers who came into the bathroom seemed awfully disturbed by our presence. It was as if they weren't used to having two disgusting-looking, weather-beaten men cooking breakfast next to where they were going to shit and piss. As a matter of fact, a good number of them took one look at us and quickly left, without relieving themselves or even washing their hands.

At least two hours passed this way. After the socks and hats, we dried our boots and then applied Sno-Seal. It is best to heat the leather so the beeswax melts in. I only had to put it on a few strips of leather since my boots were mostly made of synthetic material.

"We're real degenerates now," Preston said as one old man hightailed it out of there. "Hanging out in public rest rooms."

"I kinda like it."

"Me, too."

The rain stopped around 10:30 A.M. We left the bathroom, packed up our equipment, and headed down to the boat.

An elderly couple came down to the water to see us off. The man had come into the bathroom earlier and had been brave enough to strike up a conversation with us, talking mostly about the weather. He had said it'd rain on us all the way to Astoria—the end of our trip. His wife wanted to know what we were doing and so we told them our story.

When we finished, as if this were the go-ahead signal, the husband told us about their grandson. "That boy would love to be doing this with you, but he can't right now. They've got him in that institution—all on account of his no-good daddy.

"The boy was sexually molested by his father and all sorts of other stuff. They even got him to believe he killed a baby. You see, they had him in some satanic cult, and one night they made him stab something while he was blind-folded. There was blood all over the place afterwards and the boy is convinced he stabbed a baby. He's such a good boy and that father of his . . . That man even stabbed and killed the boy's dog. It's sad."

Preston and I continued to pack our boat. We were com-pletely dumbfounded. Why did this almost always happen? Was it because we were drifters and these people could confess to us, knowing they'd never see us again?

"They've diagnosed him as schizophrenic. He has multi-ple personalities," he continued. His wife simply smiled quietly at us and him. "And his voice actually changes for each personality. You'll be sitting there and suddenly he'll become this little boy. It's the weirdest thing. He's big as you boys—six foot three inches."

We mumbled our condolences, not knowing what to say or do really. Then the woman hurried back to their camper to get her camera. While she was gone, the man offered us some money. "It would really tickle me to think I'd helped you out," he said. I guess we'd laid it on pretty thickly—about how everybody had been helping us. But we didn't take it.

We went through another dam shortly thereafter and then boated for about forty miles, stopping at a black-sand beach for the evening. The Snake had opened into the Co-lumbia a few miles after the last dam, but it was not a mo-mentous occasion. Back in New York and even when we were on the Missouri, I'd dreamed about the day we'd reach the Columbia. We'd ride the tough rapids, portage the impossible ones, and mostly scare ourselves to death. Clark, after all, had written of an area we were near: "The whole of the Current of this great river must at all Stages pass thro' this narrow chanel of 45 yards wide . . . accord-ingly I determined to pass through this place notwithstand-ing the horrid appearance of this agitated gut swelling, boiling & whorling in every direction, which from the top of the rock did not appear as bad as when I was in it; however we passed Safe to the astonishment of all the Inds. of the last Lodges who viewed us from the top of the rock."

The reality was a bitter pill. There was, of course, no current—no wonderful gut swelling, boiling, or whorling.

Although it was near the end of our trip, we were still bickering, or maybe it was because we were near the end. Or maybe it was because of the dead water.

Whatever the case, Preston didn't wash the dishes at the end of the meal that night. This had happened the last few days and I'd had to wash them in the morning before cooking breakfast.

Should I say something? I wondered. Wouldn't he resent it and say I was nagging him?

But we must retain discipline. The trip wasn't over yet.

Why couldn't I just lighten up?

"Preston, are you going to do the dishes?"

"Pardon?" he said as if I might be talking to somebody else. The only problem was that no one else was around.

"Are you going to do the dishes?" Admittedly, I could have put it more diplomatically.

He didn't answer. He dug in his pack, looking for something. I was thinking about exploding into a fight when he silently picked up the dishes and washed them down by the water.

When he was finished, he came back and started talking about the stars as if nothing had happened. I felt like a total asshole. Obviously, I had taken out my resentment over the Columbia on him. And then he asked, "Wouldn't it be great if we just decided not to stop in Astoria? We could take the boat out into the Pacific and follow the coast down to Los Angeles."

"But you'd have to put up with me and my nagging for a couple more weeks that way," I pointed out, surprised.

"I can handle it."

The next day, when we stopped for gas in the morning, we found out that we'd been boating through the driest parts of Washington and Oregon. And that after we reached The Dalles—a day away—it'd be very wet. Of course, it was raining when we found this out.

By then we'd become quite sympathetic to Clark's lament: "The rain . . . which has continued without a longer intermission than 2 hours at a time for ten days past has destroyd. the robes and rotted nearly one half of the fiew clothes the party has." Our rain gear leaked incessantly and we were constantly soaked through. Even the tent was finally giving in. The floor leaked in innumerable spots and two of the zippers no longer held the material together. And something was happening to my feet. Not only were they numb all day long but my little toes had turned red and were beginning to swell.

It rained most of that day and we camped on the edge of Arlington—a small highway town that was the birthplace of Doc Severinsen. The gas station attendant told us Severinsen held a concert in the town park every summer. The attendant also explained that Arlington made all its money by being a landfill for Portland. But in our minds, the town stood out because it had a public bathroom with a hot hand-dryer. We spent most of the evening drying our clothes and boots.

As I stood beneath the dryer, I noticed a strong stench of urine. Of course, I thought, I'm in a bathroom after all.

The smell, though was coming from me. The hot air blew beneath my rain pants, drying out the long underwear underneath. That was where the smell originated.

Then I realized what had happened. I'd worn the underwear every day since leaving Orofino. Every time a guy takes a piss he shakes off the drippage. Inevitably, he doesn't get everything off. A week's worth of dribble, I now realized, added up to a hefty amount of urine. I ran to tell Preston, who was drying himself in the women's bathroom, my discovery.

He seemed fairly impressed.

We stayed at our campsite—a peninsula sticking a hundred yards out into the river—until three the next afternoon, not because of the wonderful four-lane highway above our heads or the busy railroad tracks equally as close or even because we were waiting for Doc Severinsen, but because Charbono stopped working. It wouldn't go into gear. At first I ordered Preston to fix it since he was supposed to be in charge of boat repair. But when he pointed out that I had sent back our perfectly good, new motor, I realized I had to help out as well. We took the engine apart and eventually figured out that the shear pin had been ripped to shreds. When the propeller hits something, the shear pin, which holds the boat in gear, snaps, and the propeller is spared. The pin is then replaced.

We had no shear pins because our first motor didn't have one. The propeller on that one was made of weak aluminum. The idea was to make you buy a new propeller, instead of just a shear pin.

The gas station attendant allowed us to cut some old nails he had lying around to use as shear pins. Once we'd done that and then fit one into place, we were feeling pretty resourceful. I think we even patted each other on the back. We fired Charbono up and started on our way. The engine quit after about a minute.

Preston squeezed the gas bulb to feed the motor and said, "It's not holding pressure. There's got to be something wrong with the air valves leading to the carburetor."

Sure enough, that was the problem. A rubber hose within the engine casing had completely rotted. Damned thing. We took it off. Cussed a bit. Cut out the bad part. Cussed some more. Then worked it back into place, cussing the full hour it took to do so. By then, it was well after one and the river had swollen to four-foot-high swells.

At three, the swells were still fairly high but we went ahead anyway. We couldn't just sit still with the end so near. Also, anywhere was better than Arlington.

Preston drove the boat and I was instantly back in the Dakotas—where the waves had been so bad. "Only a fool could make the boat bounce so hard," I thought. "Why doesn't he slow down for this one? Now . . . now this one is obvious. If he'd only face the boat this way just a little . . . any fool . . . I'm gonna get him when it's my turn."

On and on until we sent a flock of snow geese flying off the water. Then I noticed that the barren, dead hills we'd been passing for the past few days actually had some trees on them. And by the time we reached another public campground—at the mouth of the John Day River (no current)—my moodiness had disappeared. The weather, though, hadn't.

It continued to rain and the wind simply kept on increasing. We cooked and ate dinner beneath a cabana-type structure and pitched the tent behind it to protect us from the wind and rain. The wind shifted during the night. By the next morning it was ripping through the campground and threatening to lift the tent and us off the ground with every gust. It was actually howling.

We were up by six but couldn't leave until the wind died down some—after ten. Another shear pin broke immediately upon setting out. We replaced it and the second one promptly broke. We then sprayed some Liquid Wrench into the inner gears, figuring the parts were rusty. For some reason that worked.

The John Day Dam was only three miles away, so the waves and wind, coming from the west, weren't that bad. We were merely soaked, not beaten to death. After the dam, though, we faced the worst water yet. The spray thoroughly drenched us through within a quarter hour. The swells rose five feet and rolled directly at us. They weren't thick but sharp and narrow. We crashed to the surface after each one passed. We were completely airborne a number of times, and the only other boaters out on the water were some insane windsurfers. As we chugged along, they'd cut across our bow or barely miss our stern, whipping by at an easy 40 mph. They appeared to be happy.

After about two hours we gave up and landed on the northeastern shore of a large island. It was barely past noon. A couple of high hills blocked the wind so we were able to dry off and warm up some. The rain had stopped and we took off our wet clothes except our long underwear.

"Damn, my dick is shriveled and cold," Preston said. It was dangling out in the cold air through a hole in the crotch of his underwear. He was grateful when I pointed this out.

Deer pellets were everywhere, and while we were lying on the ground, allowing the sun to do its duty, five mule deer ran directly in front of us. We chased them, still in our long underwear, going opposite ways around a rock they'd gone around. Suddenly, they charged past me again, within fifty feet, skipping and hopping along. They were beautiful.

The great thing was that I saw what their tracks looked like when fresh. The sand displaced by the hoof lay in grainy mounds beside the print, as if it had trickled out of someone's hand. By the next morning that evidence would have disappeared.

Around four, we set out again, thinking the swells had died down enough for us to make more progress. We were wrong. We only made it to the other end of the island, about two miles. We beached *Sacky* in a tiny cove.

This end of the island received the full force of the winds, and we were hard pressed to find a protected spot for the tent. The second we set something on the ground the wind would carry it away; it even pulled the tent out of our hands. Also, there were no trees or any other signs of life, except for some scraggly brush.

I made dinner by five. Eating it ended the evening's entertainment. The sun had set and with it went the wind. Now it was cold, too cold to simply sit, and the clouds blocked the stars. There was nothing to do. We were in the tent by six-thirty. Preston finished *Travels with Charley* and I looked at pictures of scats. I'd given up on Anna Lee Waldo's *Sacajawea*. It was too ridiculous. For example, this is Lewis thinking about Sacagawea: "Why that little savage loves Bill Clark. She loves him as deeply as any white girl could. And I do believe that Bill enjoys her attentions. Good Lord! I hope that man of hers does not find out! Lewis hunched his back against a tree and stared at the sky. He thought he could understand the relationship between Sacajawea and Bill Clark, the man who was his equal in rank and authority and whom he respected as men of great intellect respect one another. His silence was without strain. The day lost itself, and he slept."

Before I fell asleep Preston told me he thought I was suffering from MSG poisoning since my little toes had nearly doubled in size and hurt to the touch. The noodle-and-rice mixes we ate most evenings all had MSG in them.

"Who knows?" he hypothesized. "Maybe we'll have to chop 'em off."

EIGHTEEN
Astoria

Somebody decided we'd been toyed with long enough, and the Columbia River Gorge worked in our favor the following day. The winds, gusting well above 30 mph, stayed behind us the entire time. Although the scenery changed dramatically—deciduous trees and evergreens covered the land—we hardly had time to notice. We traveled nearly one hundred miles and cleared the last two dams.

We had passed the Cascade mountain range, and apparently that caused the climatic change. All the moist, warm air was usually kept west of them. Oddly, though, it didn't rain the entire day.

By the middle of the afternoon we arrived at Government Island—a large, well-treed island off the shores of Portland. It was November 3. Lewis and Clark arrived at this island on the very same day 187 years earlier. We'd finally caught them.

"Proceeded on to the center of a large Island in the middle of the river which we call Diamond Island from its appearance," recorded Clark. "Capt. L walked out with his gun on the Island, sent out hunters & fowlers, the country is low rich and thickly timbered . . . river wide and emence numbers of fowls flying in every direction, Such as Swan, geese, Brants, Cranes, Stalks, white guls, comerants & plevers & c. also great numbers of sea otter in the river."

Cottonwoods and birches rose above us. We saw all the same birds and even a bald eagle. It soared overhead twice and then quickly disappeared.

The only thing we didn't see were the stalks (storks) and sea otter. Clark had mistakenly labeled the harbor seals as sea otter, and the company had first seen them nearly two weeks earlier. Apparently, the harbor seals no longer swam this far up, probably because of the pollution and dangerous humans. Maybe they would be down by Astoria.

Preston walked around the island for both of us. My little toes were much worse. They were nearly the size of my big toes and they hurt whenever I touched them or walked.

"Well, things have changed here somewhat since Lewis and Clark's day. Besides the two portable outhouses," he said, displaying a new role of toilet paper he'd pilfered, "there are cattle all over this thing. I guess they were brought over by a barge."

It rained all night and throughout the next morning. We had to cook, eat, and break camp in the downpour—an unpleasant experience. A thin fog hung over the island.

As soon as we'd broken camp, though, the rain stopped. The mist dispersed and the clouds began to break up.

Or at least we thought they had. No sooner were we out on the water than a huge dark mass of clouds loomed on the horizon ahead of us.

"I can't believe this damned weather," Preston cried. "One front right after another."

We moved closer and closer to those ugly clouds, cursing them all along, until we realized they weren't rain clouds at all. They were clouds of pollution put out by a city-sized factory. This was much worse than rain. We came upon more than a dozen of these pollution clouds. Some of them were clear or white—a sign that they were meeting EPA standards—but others were gray or dingy yellow. Real polluters.

We passed a massive nuclear power plant, and a number of boats were fishing in the waters right beneath it.

The river became a parking lot for ocean-going ships. They lined the deep channel of the river, arriving from all over the world. We felt like water bugs in comparison to those three-hundred-to-four-hundred-foot-long ships. But every once in a while Preston would call out a challenge to them.

"Try following our trail, you behemoths!"

"Too bad you're all going to rust one day!"

"I bet you can't do this!" And he made a complete circle with the boat at full speed. Earlier in the morning, he'd tied a warbonnet onto *Sacky*'s tiny flag mast that he'd worked on for nearly a week. It had Steller's-jay feathers, sage-grouse feathers, a couple of unidentified ones, and an assortment of colorful bandannas. I guess it'd gone to his head.

"We're going out on the ocean, too!"

We stopped for gas in a scenic river town called St. Helens around noon. It was built on a hill overlooking the river, and a number of old brick buildings still stood their ground.

Truthfully, we didn't really stop so much as get towed there. We ran out of gas about three miles before the town. We tried rowing, but an hour later it looked as if we'd only made half a mile. Two fishermen eventually pulled us to the town's marina.

The marina didn't have any gas because the building inspectors were making them relocate their storage tanks. The marina owner drove us to a gas station, though, and when he brought us back, he and his mom gave us some shear pins, candy, and a fishing lure for free—simply because we were following the Lewis and Clark Trail. The owner also gave us an old navigational chart of the river, pointing out an island that would be good for camping.

"You need a place that will protect you from the wake of those ocean ships," he explained. "Gull Island will do it if you swing into this tiny bay on the northern side. And be careful of the tides there. They'll change by six feet."

Good thing we'd run out of gas.

"And the only time you'll have any problems," he continued, "is when you reach the bay. You have to watch the channel markers closely down there or you'll end up on the ground. Good luck."

From there, we had about eighty miles to Astoria, and we made forty of them that afternoon. We'd learned from the St. Helens guy that the tide was going out, so we had an easy time of it.

Although the land was lush along the river's shores and well beyond, its beauty continued to be offset by the factories and paper mills. One minute we'd be commenting on the rich green of the land, and then the next minute we'd have to hold our noses until we passed an offending polluter.

The Columbia had turned north for the stretch from Portland through St. Helens and continued northward until we passed the town of Rainier. There, the pollution began to thin out. We camped a few miles northwest of Rainier on Gull Island.

Most of the island was impregnable with overgrown vines and bramble except for one isolated sandy peninsula that formed a tiny cove. We paddled *Sacky* in—the water was too low to motor through—and beached her on the cove side of the peninsula. It was an open spot and the sand was easy to run the tent stakes through, but it was not ideal. The highest point of the peninsula was only a few feet above the high-tide mark. If any ocean vessels passed during high tide (around midnight), our camp could be swamped.

Why the island was called Gull Island was a mystery. Plenty of birds were around, but they were all Canada geese and blue heron—hundreds of the former and dozens of the latter. And to stress the point that it was their island, flocks of the geese periodically flew within twenty feet of our heads, bombarding us with guano.

Oddly, my toes were now feeling better. They had simply turned dark purple and so I was able to help Preston gather firewood. I mistakenly crushed a stinkbug in my left hand as I gathered wood. Although it stank badly and I'd killed it, I was happy to be around bugs again. We'd hardly seen any for the past month. And there were plenty of animal tracks on the island, too: raccoon, muskrat, and countless bird. The raccoon had come out of the woods after the last high-tide, walked below the high-tide mark along the shore, circled the area where our tent now stood, then rushed back to the woods. Had he found something to eat or had it only been reconnaissance?

Preston built a tremendous fire, but it wasn't huge enough to keep at bay the encroaching dew. The minute the sun set it began to accumulate, and by eight our equipment and bodies were as soaked as if it'd rained. Since we couldn't zip the tent completely closed anymore, our sleeping bags were drenched, too.

None of this much mattered. It was probably our last night out and we soaked up the warmth of the fire and the glow of the stars. A few ships passed by and we happily watched their wakes die against our beach. We even believed we heard coyotes, thinking their company fitting for our last night, but more likely the howling rose from some dogs across the river.

We completed chores that had become routine. We sharpened our knives, wrapped our packs in plastic bags, dried our boots by the fire, checked the boat's air pressure: everything we needed to do to carry on.

I guess if we'd known anything about coastal weather or if we'd taken the incessant horn-blowing from the passing ships as a warning, we would've been prepared for the next morning. But I guess we were so worried about being flooded that we didn't have time to think or worry about the amount of moisture. Anyway, we awoke to the densest fog imaginable. *Sacky* was tied up not more than ten yards away and we couldn't even see her.

After about an hour, the fog began to clear some and we set out on the river. Other boats were out and they were all blowing their foghorns. Preston yelled a lot, hoping it would have the same effect. Twice we thought the fog was going to lift completely, but it never did.

It became worse and soon we were in the middle of the river, unable to see either bank, which meant we couldn't see the all-important channel markers. We couldn't see more than twenty yards in front of us, and the nearby ships' foghorns no longer seemed so amusing. The river had started to widen into a fifteen-mile-wide bay, so it was not a great place to play in the fog. We slowly worked our way to the shore and tied *Sacky* to some rocks. Fogged in.

But what a place to be stuck. The ground was covered with ferns and moss. Strongly scented evergreens stood above us. We squeezed the needles between our fingers, and a lovely, lemony scent filled the air. Preston looked the tree up in a guidebook and determined it was a Sitka spruce.

"It's supposed to have a hairless twig," Preston explained.

"What is a 'hairless twig'?"

"I don't know, but that is how we can positively identify it." Since the twigs had no hair on them, we were confident we'd found the Sitka. It is only one of the most common trees on the West Coast. The other is the red alder. We liked it because it not only had needles and cones like all pines but also catkins. The red alder, Preston read aloud, is the most lumbered hardwood in the Pacific Northwest.

We waited the fog out, studying the trees and eating some soup I'd heated up. Neither of us minded the wait. We wanted to stretch out our final day. But as soon as the fog lifted a few hours later, we were out there, driven by a three-month habit of always jumping at the slightest opportunity.

We sped beneath the rising fog, cutting across the bay, barely following the channel markers, and within an hour we could see Astoria.

The ocean roared on the horizon.

"Great joy in camp we are in view of the Ocian this great Pacific Octean which we been so long anxious to See," Clark recorded on November 7.

Preston tasted the water and pronounced our arrival. It was salty. We'd made it.

Our engine broke down the very next minute. It was still running, but it wouldn't go faster than a snail's pace. When we revved the engine to go faster, it instantly slipped into neutral.

"Oh, that's easy," I announced, "its shear pin is broken." We tilted the engine out of the water to dismantle the propeller, but the propeller wouldn't come off. It was stuck.

"I guess we'll just have to putter in," Preston said.

I nodded my head.

A harbor seal popped up a few yards away, curious as to why we'd stopped. It was the first one we'd seen. Then, as we slowly made our way to the Astoria West Basin marina, we saw a dozen more. So luck was on our side. If our engine hadn't broken down, we would probably have zoomed right by them all. As it was, they provided a noble escort.

When we pulled into the marina, Preston and I shook hands. A few minutes later, we hugged. But then we busied ourselves with fixing the engine. We still wanted to take *Sacky* up to Fort Clatsop by the Lewis and Clark River.

"Don't you think we ought to take the engine off the boat?" Preston suggested.

"Why should we do that?" I snapped. "We know what's wrong. We'll fix it like it is."

Everything went fine at first. We banged the propeller off and replaced the shear pin. But when I was screwing on the cap that held the propeller in place, it slipped through my fingers and sank to the bottom of the bay.

Preston kindly did not laugh. As it turned out, replacing the shear pin did not fix the engine, and while we were circling the harbor, the engine completely quit running. The air hose was split from beginning to end.

Over the past two weeks, the boat had been taking in a lot of water whenever she was at a standstill, but we'd always been able to run the motor fast enough to drain the water out. The accumulated holes hadn't mattered much. Now they did. *Sacky* began to sink.

We discovered that if one of us continually pumped the rubber bulb that forced gas into the engine from the gas tank, the motor would run. We were just able to make it back to the marina, but it wasn't fast enough to drain her. The water kept coming in.

Before she could sink to the harbor bottom, we tied *Sacky* to the dock, unloaded all our possessions, and deflated her for the final time.

Was this an ignoble ending?

Yes.

But it was also fitting. "We have nothing to eate but a little Pounded fish which we purchased at the Great falls," wrote Clark upon arriving near the fort's future site. "This is our present situation! truly disagreeable. added to this the robes of our selves and men are all rotten from being continually wet, and we cannot precure others, or blankets in these places."

Beaten and tattered, they had reached the Pacific Ocean. They had opened up the West. The expedition went on to make do that winter, as always, building the log stockade fort and trading with locals for food and skins.

Later that day, Preston and I took a $10 taxi ride to Fort Clatsop. We'd made do, too. Our voyage was over.

Epilogue
■ ■ ■ ■

The Lewis and Clark expedition returned to St. Louis within ten months by retracing their outward route. They encountered the same hardships: lack of food, snow, rain, and much more. Lewis had his skirmish with the Blackfeet in what is now Montana, and one of his men accidentally shot him in the butt while hunting elk a few months later.

Our return was much simpler. Preston and I rented another car and drove to his place in California. Then I flew home.

We went our separate ways—just as Lewis and Clark eventually did—but apparently there was more in store.

On July 5, while out riding my bike in Maine, I flipped over my handlebars, flew through the air, and landed head-first in a ditch. I broke my neck and back.

The very next day, Preston crashed a motorcycle in Los Angeles, flew through the air, and hit a concrete lamppost.

He punctured a lung and broke nine bones in nineteen places, including numerous ribs.

We have both recovered one hundred percent.

I don't know if this coincidence means anything mystical or not, but I do know one thing. We were two lucky fools for those three months on the trail of Lewis and Clark, and we thank them for watching over us for as long as they did. We couldn't have done it without them.